PEACE FOR OUR TIME

A Reflection on War and Peace and a
Third World War

First published by O-Books, 2018
O-Books is an imprint of John Hunt Publishing Ltd., Laurel House, Station Approach,
Alresford, Hants, SO24 9JH, UK
office1@jhpbooks.net
www.johnhuntpublishing.com

For distributor details and how to order please visit the 'Ordering' section on our website.

ISBN: 978 1 78535 706 0
978 1 78535 707 7 (ebook)
Library of Congress Control Number: 2017934769

A CIP catalogue record for this book is available from the British Library.

Design: Stuart Davies

Printed and bound by CPI Group (UK) Ltd, Croydon, CR0 4YY, UK

We operate a distinctive and ethical publishing philosophy in all areas of
our business, from our global network of authors to production and
worldwide distribution.

PEACE FOR OUR TIME

A Reflection on War and Peace and a
Third World War

Nicholas Hagger

BOOKS

Winchester, UK
Washington, USA

Also by Nicholas Hagger

The Fire and the Stones
Selected Poems
The Universe and the Light
A White Radiance
A Mystic Way
Awakening to the Light
A Spade Fresh with Mud
The Warlords
Overlord
A Smell of Leaves and Summer
The Tragedy of Prince Tudor
The One and the Many
Wheeling Bats and a Harvest Moon
The Warm Glow of the Monastery Courtyard
The Syndicate
The Secret History of the West
The Light of Civilization
Classical Odes
Overlord, one-volume edition
Collected Poems 1958–2005
Collected Verse Plays
Collected Stories
The Secret Founding of America
The Last Tourist in Iran
The Rise and Fall of Civilizations
The New Philosophy of Universalism
The Libyan Revolution
Armageddon
The World Government
The Secret American Dream
A New Philosophy of Literature
A View of Epping Forest
My Double Life 1: This Dark Wood
My Double Life 2: A Rainbow over the Hills

Selected Stories: Follies and Vices of the Modern Elizabethan Age
Selected Poems: Quest for the One
The Dream of Europa
Life Cycle and Other New Poems 2006–2016
The First Dazzling Chill of Winter
The Secret American Destiny

"I believe it is peace for our time."

Neville Chamberlain, 30 September 1938

"Blessed are the peacemakers: for they shall be called the children of God."

St Matthew 5.9, sermon on the mount

"Unless we establish some form of world government, it will not be possible for us to avert a World War III in the future."

Winston Churchill, 1945

"There is no salvation for civilisation, or even the human race, other than the creation of a world government."

Albert Einstein, 1945

To John Hunt, who has a shrewd understanding of the modern world; to Igor Kondrashin, in supranational amity; to the memory of Gillon Aitken, who though terminally ill suggested I should write an account of the themes that preoccupied me before I received the Gusi Peace Prize for Literature in November 2016; to Ambassador Barry Gusi and my fellow Peace Laureates in Manila, including Michael Nobel; to my wife Ann and my son Tony who accompanied me to Manila (with thanks to Tony for his extensive filming); to my PA Ingrid Kirk who helped me complete this record with impressive speed; and to the delegates of the UN General Assembly, who I hope will have the opportunity to hear me present my new thinking regarding a new world structure.

CONTENTS

Sketch for a portrait of Nicholas Hagger by Stuart Davies

Prologue

Now after a writing career of nearly sixty years that has included two poetic epics on war, one on the Second World War and one on the War on Terror, I sit above a calm sea and reflect on war and peace in my lifetime and how best to bequeath peace to my grandchildren. I have lived an active as well as a contemplative life and through extraordinary circumstances found myself involved in humanity's best hope of establishing world peace. To my amazement I found myself a participator in the West's efforts to prevent a Third World War. I cannot but recount the strange events that led to this pass. But I am also drawn back to my own wartime childhood, and, seeking to understand it, my mind goes back to Munich in July 1994.

Munich and war

My wife and I had taken our two nearly-adult boys on a coach tour through seven countries in Europe, and the coach party were served beer in Munich's Hofbräuhaus, a beer 'cellar' that could seat 3,000 on the ground floor where Adolf Hitler made an impassioned speech on 8 November 1923.

"We will be here at least half an hour," our guide said.

I said to my wife, "Come on, we're going for a drive in Munich." We slipped out, leaving our two boys with enormous glasses of German dark beer under our guide's watchful eye, and found a nearby taxi rank.

The driver of the first car spoke English and I said, "All the Hitler places in half an hour." He talked in German to his controller and plotted a route and set off.

We found Hitler's nine-room second-floor apartment in Prinzregentenplatz which Neville Chamberlain visited during the morning of 30 September 1938 following the 2am signing of the four-power Munich Agreement (backdated to 29 September). Chamberlain took from his pocket a typed sheet of paper, the Anglo-German Declaration, and read three paragraphs, one of which stated that the British and German nations considered the 1938 Munich Agreement and the 1935 Anglo-German Naval Agreement "symbolic of the desire of our two peoples never to go to war with one another again".

According to Chamberlain, Hitler exclaimed *"Ja, ja"* ("Yes, yes").

Later that day, the German Foreign Minister Joachim von Ribbentrop remonstrated with Hitler for signing the Declaration.

The Führer replied, "Don't take it so seriously. That piece of paper is of no further significance whatever."

Hitler renounced the Anglo-German Naval Agreement on 28 April 1939. The apartment now houses the headquarters of Munich's regional police.

We saw the Odeonsplatz, where Hitler was caught on film at a rally to celebrate the declaration of war in 1914. We saw the arches of the Feldherrnhalle where Hitler's 1923 putsch was stopped by Bavarian police. We went on to the public building near the Gate of Victory in which Heinrich Hoffman had a photographic shop, where Hitler met Eva Braun. We passed three buildings in Königsplatz that housed the Nazi Party and were associated with Hitler. Hitler spoke from the Greek-looking columns of the Propylaea (German Propyläen). We went on to the site of the Bürgerbräu beer hall from which Hitler launched his 1923 putsch. I was doing local research for my epic poem on the Second World War, *Overlord*.

We re-entered the Hofbräuhaus half an hour after leaving it. Our party were still sitting over their beer, but I had seen the apartment where Neville Chamberlain produced his Anglo-German Declaration that Hitler signed at the end of his visit to Munich on 30 September 1938, the day German troops entered the Sudetenland.

Peace for our time

After his meetings with Hitler in Munich and the surrender of the Sudetenland Chamberlain flew back to Heston aerodrome and waved the Anglo-German Declaration "which bears his name upon it as well as mine". This paper Chamberlain and Hitler had signed on 30 September 1938, that said that the 1938 Munich Agreement and the 1935 Anglo-German Naval Agreement were "symbolic of the desire of our two peoples never to go to war with one another again", was in fact a declaration of appeasement. It handed Hitler the Sudetenland despite Czech opposition.

Later in the day Chamberlain stood outside 10 Downing Street and announced: "For the second time in our history a British Prime Minister has returned from Germany bringing peace with honour. I believe it is peace for our time."[1]

Neville Chamberlain, British Prime Minister, waves the Anglo-German Declaration at Heston aerodrome on 30 September 1938

The first Prime Minister in British history to return from Germany with a promise of peace was Benjamin Disraeli. Back from the Congress of Berlin in 1878 Disraeli stated, "I have returned from Germany with peace for our time." The British had just balanced their interests with Russia's and Austria-Hungary's, and the Congress had been a success. Chamberlain was echoing Disraeli's phrase.

There is a line in the *Book of Common Prayer*, "Give peace in our time, O Lord", which I often heard in Chigwell School's chapel in my boyhood and which may have been based on a 7th-century hymn: "*Da pacem, Domine, in diebus nostris.*" In a popular reinterpretation (probably influenced by the *Book of Common Prayer*) Chamberlain's "peace *for* our time" became 'peace *in* our time', a misquotation that passed into Noel Coward's 1947 play, *Peace in our Time.*

Looking at the rippling waves I now reflect that Chamberlain's "peace for our time" proved illusory, for the reality turned out to be impending war with Germany. I am haunted by the possibly illusory 'peace for our time' I have sought, for perhaps that will turn out to be impending war with Russia, and perhaps a proxy Third World War has already begun. I have wanted to work for a universal peace my grandchildren will know so they do not have to live through war from the air as I did as a small boy.

V-1s and V-2s

I was conceived around 29 August 1938. As far back as in 1934 Hitler told his military leaders that 1942 was the target date for going to war in the east.[2] As Goebbels' *Diaries* make clear, Hitler was already planning the Second World War – war against Britain and eastward expansion following an invasion of Czechoslovakia on 1 October – from early 1938.

In March 1938 Hitler had successfully invaded Austria and turned his attention to the Sudetenland. On 20 May he presented his Generals with a draft plan to attack Czechoslovakia codenamed Operation Green. On 28 May he ordered an acceleration in the construction of U-boats and in the building of two new battleships. Ten days later he signed a directive for war against Czechoslovakia to begin not later than 1 October 1938.[3]

Hitler was already planning the Second World War in May, and certainly in early August 1938, well before the signing of the Munich Agreement on 30 September 1938. Hitler invaded Poland on 1 September 1939 and Chamberlain's declaration of war in his radio broadcast followed on 3 September 1939.

I was born into war. We lived in Norbury and Caterham, suburbs of south-west London, and after Caterham was bombed on a Sunday in May 1940 we moved to East Grinstead in Sussex to live with my maternal grandmother out of harm's way. In November 1942 my father began a new job in Loughton, Essex as chief accountant in the treasurer's department of the Chigwell Urban District Council. He lived in digs until March 1943, when my mother, my infant younger brother and I, not yet four, moved to a rented semi-detached house near his work.

We were in Churchill's constituency and therefore had to endure nightly air attacks. In March 1944, when I was four, a string of German bombs blew out our windows. I was leaving our house with my father one late afternoon when it was nearly dark to walk to the Post Office, and had reached the end of our garden path. I can still see the early night sky light up in a flash as bright as day.

In June 1944 a first V-1 (Vengeance-1) pilotless doodle-bug rocket landed in our part of the UK. I was just five. Between June and the following March over 9,500 V-1 rockets were fired at south-east Britain and from September to the following March these were supplemented by over 1,400 silent V-2 (Vengeance-2) rockets which also targeted south-east Britain.

For nine months I lay in bed each night and listened to the doodle-bugs cut out. When the drone of their engines stopped they fell to earth and exploded ten seconds later. Lying in bed I would count to ten and when I heard a distant bang I sighed with

Nicholas Hagger (left) and his brother under blown-out windows of garage following a string of German bombs in March 1944

relief, for we were still safe, the rocket had fallen elsewhere. We had no warning of the silent V-2s. There was a sudden bang. Lying in bed I was aware that any second there could be a sudden deafening bang that would wipe us all out. During those nine months, lying in bed at night I longed for peace.

Having lived with the imminent prospect of attacks from the air in 1944–1945 we faced sudden extinction from Soviet missiles all through the Cold War. I recall the imminent prospect of sudden extinction from the Soviet Union during the Cuban missile crisis of 16–28 October 1962. And a hostile Russia has again pointed nuclear missiles at European capitals from its exclave in Kaliningrad. We now face admittedly less-imminent sudden extinction from jihadist terrorism. I have lived with the prospect of sudden extinction in varying degrees of imminence all my life, and long for a true 'peace for our time' that will remove this dread from the lives of future generations.

World State and peace
For more than seventy years after the end of the war European peace has been safeguarded by the EEC, EC and EU, which have locked France and Germany into the same institutions so both sides settle their differences by talking rather than by going to war; and by NATO, which watches over the former Soviet states of Eastern Europe that have broken away from Russia and preserve a fragile democratic independence.

Now we live in a time when Islamic terrorists are targeting France, Belgium, Germany and the UK. I lectured at the University of Baghdad from October 1961 to June 1962, and a pupil there three decades later founded the IS (Islamic State), who are reported to have seized enough radioactive material from government facilities to have the capacity to build a large and devastating 'dirty bomb', according to Australian intelligence reports.[4] IS are reported to be developing a radioactive dirty bomb they can let off in a Western capital, perhaps borne by a drone.[5]

I observe the intensifying war in the Middle East, centred round a war in Syria that has lasted more than five years, longer than the First and Second World Wars. It has the feel of a Third World War. And I observe the fragility of peace in Asia and see nation-state at loggerheads with nation-state. Since the war the UN has failed to stop 162 local wars.[6] The UN is 'inter-national', 'between nation-states'. It has no supranational authority over nation-states, and conflicts between nation-states are still settled by war. During the last seventy years I have seen collisions between nation-states lead to 162 wars, and I have seen terrorist war seek to undermine nation-states.

Over the decades I have developed the new philosophy of Universalism, which sees the universe as one and studies the activities of the whole of humankind. My Universalism, as set out in *The New Philosophy of Universalism*, includes political Universalism: a plan for the government of the whole of humankind that sees the 7.33 billion of the world's population as a potentially unified electorate.

Over the decades I have come to the view that the best guarantee of world peace in future generations is a World State: a democratic world government that reins in all oligarchs and *élite*s who have sought to enrich their families by seizing the world's gas and oil.

I believe that a World State should be created as soon as possible. Partly federal, it will have enough authority to control all radioactive material, end terrorism and abolish war. In my view this is the most effective way of achieving 'peace for our time'. In the 20th century such a World State was advocated by Winston Churchill, President Truman, Albert Einstein, President Eisenhower, Bertrand Russell, Mahatma Gandhi, President John F. Kennedy and President Mikhail Gorbachev. I believe that following my book *The World Government* I am the only Western literary author continuing this tradition.

Over the decades amid the desolated landscapes of what looks like a Third World War I have seen beyond nation-statehood a partly-supranational World State that can bring in a universal peace. I see a contrast between nation-statehood that leads to war and a partly-supranational World State that brings peace. This is the essence of my reflection on war and peace.

I gaze at the sea. It is so calm and peaceful now, yet how quickly it is whipped up by stormy wind so waves boil through rocks and crash onto the beach. The same is true of the international landscape. It has both calm and turmoil at different times and in different places at the same time. I see the conflicting tides and currents of world history in this serene sea. And though I know the universe enfolds opposites – day and night, life and death, time and eternity – it is this serenity I would like to prevail.

In the East I was told by the then elderly distinguished Japanese poet, Junzaburo Nishiwaki, "+A + –A = 0", that all opposites are reconciled in a unity. I did not know that I would come to found a World State and be asked to lead an international peace initiative. Now I have a deep conviction that I would like to see war and peace, the shattered streets of Syrian towns and the tranquillity of the English countryside, reconciled in an enduring World State in which violent passions and gentleness are unified as exquisitely as the wind-rustled calm of the sea beneath my window now.

PART ONE

1
A Russian Writes

My concern for the preservation of peace came out of my writing. Over the years, besides creating four schools that employ 320 staff and allow a rural family life I have toiled at my study desk and accumulated literary, historical and philosophical works, and have delved into current affairs and international politics and statecraft. I am the author of more than 40 books, and my Universalist approach has led me to write within seven disciplines. Within the social stability of an English institutional life I have made daily forays into solitude and, like a stag that roams the woods with seven-branched antlers that are always with him, I take my books with me wherever I am asked to go.

Conscious TV
Soon after *My Double Life 1: This Dark Wood* and *My Double Life 2: A Rainbow over the Hills* came out I was interviewed on *Conscious TV* at Battersea Studios in South London.[1] On 20 March 2015 I sat on a plum couch against a black background in the ramshackle studio and for an hour talked before three cameras about my life and my writing, how my works and Universalism came out of my life as I described in *My Double Life 1* and *2*.

My interviewer, Iain McNay, was especially interested in my mystical experiences: how I first glimpsed the Light in Japan and then, despite being routinely followed by surveillance squads on the London streets when I was doing my secret work, how I had a full experience of illumination at 13 Egerton Gardens, SW3. He asked me to read a poem about the experience. I read 'Visions: Golden Flower, Celestial Curtain', which sees the Light as "a gold-white flower" that "changed into a celestial curtain".

Chart and civilizations
I passed on to my philosophy of history and held up the seven-foot-long chart that accompanied *The Fire and the Stones* (1991).

The chart summarises my view of history. It shows 25 civilizations each going through 61 parallel stages (see rainbow chart in Appendix 2). Prepared in 1989, it shows the European civilization passing into a union (later the European Union), a United States of Europe, in stage 43; and the Soviet Union (stage 43) passing into a federation (later the Russian Federation) in stage 46.

On my wall in Essex is a framed copy of the chart behind glass. It used to be on a first-floor landing wall in Otley Hall in Suffolk, a Tudor Hall with guides that I ran for seven years. We had 40,000 people round, many of whom came on coach tours and on Open Days, and there was always a small crowd round the chart. I often stood before it, both in company and alone, and contemplated the sweep of civilizations.

Each civilization rises through a metaphysical vision and declines when the metaphysical vision turns secular. The European civilization rose through a vision of the 'divine' Light shown as a halo in art, the illumination of Christ's transfiguration which passed into the *New Testament* and into the European civilization's stage 1. The European civilization has turned secular within the EU conglomerate and is in decline.

The Arab civilization rose through Mohammed's metaphysical vision of the 'divine' Fire in the cave of Hira near Mecca c.610 – in his first vision Mohammed saw the opening passage of the *Koran* in letters of fire written on cloth – and its political unification (stage 11) began with Mohammed's founding of the *ummah*, the Muslim community, in 622. The Arab civilization has turned secular but a faction has reached stage 45 when there is a yearning for a lost past and a revival of cultural purity – the Muslim revival of fundamentalist Islamic values under Islamic State (IS).

The Arab civilization's fundamentalist strain, which is expressed in a number of groups including IS, has retained its metaphysical vision. But it is a further stage in the process of the Arab civilization's decline.

When a civilization ends in stage 61 it passes into another

civilization just as the Egyptian civilization passed into the Arab civilization in 642 when its gods, such as Ra, were absorbed within the new Allah-worshipping Arab civilization.

My chart shows each civilization's progress as it passes through 61 stages. The most recent civilization, the North-American civilization, began with the metaphysical vision brought by Catholics, Anglicans and Puritans and was consolidated by the establishment of the Jamestown Settlement of 1607, which was the basis of the 400th anniversary of America's founding that was celebrated in 2007. The Jamestown Settlement is thought to have been planned in the Great Hall at Otley Hall, where I often sat.[2] The North-American civilization has reached stage 15 and is in the same stage that the Roman civilization was in when the Roman Empire was being established in the 3rd century BC at the time of the two Punic Wars which facilitated the Roman civilization's expanding influence just as the European civilization's First and Second World Wars facilitated the North-American civilization's expanding influence.

My chart shows that most living civilizations are now in stage 43 (union) or stage 46 (federalism). The chart does not show a World State because there has never been one, although there have been several attempts from the time of Alexander the Great to the time of Adolf Hitler, our time, to found one by conquest.

The chart shows that stage 15 of all civilizations, the imperial stage of the Roman civilization which included the Roman Empire, covers a large part of the known world and effectively introduces a World State by force. According to the pattern of history in my chart some sort of a World State will be created by the North-American civilization in the course of its stage 15.

World State by consent
I have come to wonder if a World State can be created by consent rather than conquest, by all the civilizations coming together and creating a partly-supranational state into which their stages 43 and 46 can flow for a while before eventually resuming their progress towards their final, terminal, stage 61. It is not impos-

sible that the North-American civilization could act as a philanthropic midwife to assist the birth of such a World State. Such
a development would break the mould of my pattern of history
(or 'law of history', as Ted Hughes[3] called it), which shows civilizations' empires as being conducted on the basis of their self-
interest rather than philanthropy.

I have said (see p.xvii) that I believe I am the only Western
literary author continuing the tradition of those who in the 20th
century dreamt of, and advocated, a democratic World State
and world government with the power to abolish war: Winston
Churchill, President Truman, Albert Einstein, President Eisenhower, Bertrand Russell, Mahatma Gandhi, President John F.
Kennedy and President Mikhail Gorbachev. I long for a solution
to the world's intransigent problems and yearn for a universal
government that can resolve all issues and benefit humankind.
As we have just seen, in recent years I have seen beyond the pattern on my chart of rising and falling civilizations. I have taken
account of globalism, air and digital communications and the
internet, and, having foreseen a democratic World State, I knew
I should do something to help bring it in.

Visit to Asa Briggs
Soon after my interview on *Conscious TV*, on 24 April 2015, I
visited Lord Asa Briggs in Lewes, Sussex. He was Provost of
Worcester College, Oxford, after I was there, and he spoke at the
launch of my book *The Fire and the Stones* – and of the chart – in
the Museum of London in April 1991. At a gaudy (reunion) at
my College in 1978 he had had a long discussion with me in the
Buttery and urged me to write down my experiences as a British
intelligence agent in Libya and then in London. He followed up
this discussion with a letter that again urged me to write my experiences down. (It took me thirty-five years to do it as I knew it
would be prudent to wait until Gaddafi was dead.) Without his
encouragement I might not have written *My Double Life 1* and *2*,
and I sent him signed copies.

I arrived at his large house, The Caprons, in Lewes and was

admitted by his carer and shown through to the kitchen. I sat opposite him at the large kitchen table. He was ninety-three and looked as if he had put a sweater over his pyjamas. He sat with his back to bookshelves and said, "I'm completely immobile, by land, sea and air." He said, "I've been reading your book, *My Double Life 1*. You've had such a range of experience and met so many varied people." I thanked him for urging me to write it.

I had brought his *Secret Days*, which came out when he was ninety, about his involvement in Bletchley Park from 1943 to 1945, when he worked with Alan Turing. We discussed what he did in Hut 6 and his decoding. He talked about his predecessor at Worcester College, the Provost when I was there, Sir John Masterman, who had chaired the Twenty Committee (XX or Double-Cross Committee) that misinformed the Germans as to where the D-Day landings would be – the man who had spotted me as a potential intelligence agent. Briggs told me, "He was the only person I've ever been able to discuss my intelligence work with, apart from you now." He inscribed my copy of *Se-cret Days*, "For Nicholas Hagger, on a very special visit to Lewes, 24/4/15."

Nicholas Hagger with Asa Briggs (then 93) in Lewes on 24 April 2015, with copies of *My Double Life 1* and *Secret Days* on the table

Before I left I told him I would now be starting the third book in my "Secret American" trilogy. *The Secret Founding of America* and *The Secret American Dream* had already appeared, and I now had *The Secret American Destiny* in mind. I told him it would be about the reunification of world culture in seven disciplines as a preparation for an impending World State and universal peace. I started the book the next day.

Baltic cruise
On my wife Ann's prompting in late March I had booked a cruise

to the Baltic from 25 May. There would be a couple of days' visiting St Petersburg, and there would be a security expert aboard. Ann reckoned that I would be safe under his care even though my intelligence background could be accessed on the internet.

Igor Kondrashin and the World Philosophical Forum
A week before we were due to leave, on 19 May, I received an email out of the blue from a Russian, Igor Kondrashin, President of the World Philosophical Forum. He said that he was a Universalist (or Transuniversalist), and that as I am a Universalist I might consider attending a conference of philosophers to set up a World State in Athens in early October. He attached a draft Constitution for a World State, 'the Universal State of the Earth', which he had just finished, and a paper on Transuniversalism that was written in 2014.

I Googled the World Philosophical Forum and discovered it is like the World Economic Forum that has met at Davos since 1971. The World Philosophical Forum was founded six years previously, in 2009, and had met in Athens for six years.

I love Greece and realised we would be meeting within a mile or two of Plato's Academy, and with Plato's *Republic* in mind I thought I might indeed consider founding a new World State in Athens, an ideal state that would be a latter-day equivalent of Plato's *Republic*. I printed off the two attachments and packed them to read during the cruise.

I was wary, for why had he sent the draft Constitution to me when he had only just finished it, and why had it landed a week before I was going to St Petersburg? Was he just a Russian philosopher who had found my books *The World Government* and *The New Philosophy of Universalism* online and was understandably exploring if there was common ground? Or could this be an approach by pro-Putin Russians who had seen *My Double Life 1*? Though I was wary I was interested.

Nigel West
During the afternoon of my birthday, on 22 May 2015, I was

rung by an expert writer on intelligence, Nigel West (pen-name for Rupert Allason MP). He had been asked to review *My Double Life 1* for the online *International Journal of Intelligence and CounterIntelligence*. He spoke with me for half an hour. He said, "You were a case officer's nightmare, you've got all the times of all the meetings. Did they know you were keeping a diary? You were 'a diarist spy'."

I said I used to write an ongoing diary for them but kept a skeleton of dates and times for my own reference.

He said, "*My Double Life 1* is unique. There are books by case officers, intelligence officers, but no agent has written such an account, not since the Second World War, not since the First World War, not ever."

He asked me a number of questions and said at the end, "You might like to know the CIA asked me to write my review. They spotted your book and asked me to check whether the book is a fake, whether I found it genuine. I told them, 'It's genuine.' Some of the things you say are very recognisable. You come across as transparently honest."

He emailed me a draft of his review, which he titled 'The Diarist Spy', and told me it would appear in the *Journal* "within a few months". It appeared more than a year later, on 16 June 2016.[4]

My work in the Cold War: Philby, the Tehran Agreement
In the two days before I left for the cruise, aware of my impending visit to St Petersburg I reflected on my work in the Cold War for MI6. It began in Libya and I saw myself as a literary spy in the footsteps of Daniel Defoe, T.E. Lawrence, Somerset Maugham and Graham Greene. In London I was told that I had been appointed an 'unofficial Ambassador' for the African liberation movements to Prime Minister Edward Heath. I wrote articles on Africa for *The Times*, interviewed many freedom-fighters and visited Tanzania in 1972, where I saw the Chinese building the Tanzam Railway. I spent a night in a mud hut in the Chinese camp near Mlimba.

I reflected that my case officer told me that the Soviet spy Kim Philby knew of my secret work and was expected to name me as a British agent in a newspaper interview during the following weekend in 1971. In interviews in *Pravda* and *Izvestia* on 1 and 2 October 1971 Philby named a few British agents, and in the Estonian *Kodumaa* on 13 October 1971 he named 21 British agents, but for some reason I was not one of them. Nevertheless, I was told, the Russians knew what I was doing. For the last two years I operated openly, at (I was told) considerable personal risk.

I came to the Russians' attention again in 1986. As a sideline I had become a small publisher to promulgate books on Western political themes at the height of the Cold War. I brought out a book about the Hungarian Revolution, *Budapest Betrayed*, the 'betrayal' being of the 45 Western intelligence agents Philby named who were later executed by the pro-Russian Hungarian regime.

My author Paul Gorka had been a political prisoner in a Hungarian prison from 1950 to 1956, having been recruited into the British intelligence service in 1950 to report on the Russian occupying forces in Hungary. He had been betrayed by the Soviet spy, Kim Philby.[5] One of the 45 betrayed Western intelligence agents, Béla Bajomi, the leader of his resistance group, occupied a nearby cell and was hanged in the execution yard outside Paul's cell on 24 April 1951. Paul clambered on top of the bunkbed, pressed an ear to a ventilation hole and heard the prosecutor read a statement from the President refusing Bajomi's appeal. Paul heard Bajomi say firmly, calm and composed, "I die for my country. Christ help me." Paul heard a squeaking noise and then silence.[6]

I held a launch for the book in the Palace of Westminster on 4 November 1986. There were several dozen present in the Jubilee Room, including several MPs. There were two bearded Afghans who were fighting the occupying Soviet Russians. I shook their hands and wished them well in their quest to obtain arms. One of them looked like the young Osama bin Laden who was a character in my poetic epic *Armaged-don*. In fact Osama bin Laden and his half-brother Salem had visited London in mid-1986 to buy anti-aircraft missiles, and stayed at the Dorchester Hotel.[7]

In my speech I called for the Eastern-European states to leave the USSR. I called for FREE, Freedom for the Republics of Eastern Europe. My speech was made in the presence of several MPs and was broadcast live behind the Iron Curtain by the BBC World Service.

Nicholas Hagger speaking in favour of FREE, broadcast live into the Soviet Union by the BBC World Service, 4 November 1986, with Sir John Biggs-Davison, MP, listening

When the speeches were concluded the Prime Minister of the Polish Government-in-Exile, Kazimierz Sabbat, came and said: "You are to be congratulated. You have just challenged the entire British foreign policy since the war, which has been wrong. You have just breached the 1943 Tehran Agreement. I want to shake your hand."

He explained that at Tehran the world leaders including Churchill agreed the Great Powers' spheres of influence. He said that Eastern Europe was designated as being within the Soviet sphere of influence, and so the Soviet invasions of Hungary in 1956 and of Czechoslovakia in 1968 had been tolerated by the West.

Paul Gorka's Hungarian wife said to me outside, "You will now be on a [Soviet] blacklist, you will be the first to be hanged when the Russians come to London."

I reflected that I would be visiting St Petersburg as the challenger and breacher of the Tehran Agreement.

Moscow and the World State
As my wife Ann and I boarded the ship, *The Voyager*, at Harwich

on 25 May and made our way to cabin 4245, I was very aware that what I had been doing in the Cold War was online and that chunks of *My Double Life 1* and *2* were available at the click of a mouse. I was not sure whether I would even be allowed to land in St Petersburg.

But there was an appropriateness about the voyage. For I had first had a vision of a World State among the icons in Moscow's Cathedral of the Archangel, near the second icon from the left of the Archangel Michael, and now that I was speaking out for a World State I was returning to the country that had first given me the vision in 1966, nearly fifty years previously. I had returned from Japan to the UK on vacation, and had broken my journey in Moscow.

I put my vision in my poem on Communism, 'Archangel':

As I stared at the murals' centre
In this Cathedral-tomb,
The Archangel became a Shadow
With a sword and wings outstretched,
And I saw in the second icon
The future of the West,
From the Atlantic to the Urals:
Into the People's Square,
From the Cathedral gates,
File in the morning rush-hour
An *élite* of self-made Saints
Each still on the last hour's quest....
Decades of contemplation
Show in their white-haired peace
As, trusting to perfect feelings,
They value each equal they greet;
Until, whispering on silence,
They glide to the Leaders' Hall,
Their hearts, with a World-Lord's wholeness,
At the centre of life, of all,
Their hearts where all past and future meet.[8]

I had seen the 'World-Lord' ruling the world as a *primus inter pares* ('first among equals'), a wise collective leadership of gentle people who had spiritual depth and valued each other, and lived by universal – indeed, Universalist – values in a re-unified Europe in which the Cold War, indeed all wars, had ended.

Now I was aware that I was making the voyage at a time when there was talk that a proxy war in the Middle East could spread to the Baltic states, and that because Putin wanted to reverse Gorbachev's changes and restore Russian influence in Eastern Europe the world was going through an exceptionally dangerous phase which could end in the outbreak of a fully developed Third World War.

2
St Petersburg

Since the days of Henry VIII there has always been a foreign threat to England. In the Protestant Tudor time it was Catholic Spain, and the threat materialised in the Spanish Armada. After that it was the Dutch, whose ships had to be fought off until William of Orange came to England as the monarch William III in 1688. The Dutch were still a threat nearly a hundred years later. Then it was the French under Napoleon. Then it was Germany, which sent the *Blitz* under Hitler. Then our wartime ally the Soviet Union pointed nuclear weapons at the UK during the Cold War, which ended with the tearing-down of the Berlin Wall. But the fascination with the KGB's role in creating the Soviet Union's foreign threat persisted, and the subject was considered normal and appropriate for a Western cruise in the Baltic in 2015.

Cruise to St Petersburg
On the way to St Petersburg we had a day at sea, at the end of which there was a captain's dinner. The next day we passed the Renaissance Kronborg Castle at Helsingor (Elsinore in *Hamlet*, a green-turreted palace on the rocky shore) on the Danish island

of Zealand, which commanded an outlet of the Baltic (a sound between Denmark and Sweden).

We stopped at Copenhagen and took in the city and walked in the old Viking fishing village of Dragor. We went on to Stockholm and explored the city and the waterways. We sailed past many islands to Helsinki.

Keith Muras

We had had lectures while at sea. One of the lecturers was the security expert, Keith Muras, who had spent twenty-three years in the British Diplomatic Service focusing on the security and intelligence aspects of international political issues. He had moved to Moscow in 1981 and spent until 1984 working in the British Embassy when the Cold War was at its height. He was a balding man with an engaging conversational manner, smartly dressed in a suit.

His first talk ran through all the Soviet leaders during the 70 years of the Soviet Empire. He quoted Putin as having said, "Anyone who does not regret the passing of the Soviet Union has no heart. Anyone who wants it restored has no brains."

The KGB: the SVR and FSB

His second talk was about the KGB. He described how Gorbachev had shut down the KGB in 1991 and how it had been replaced by two organisations, the FSB (the Russian MI5) and the SVR (the Russian MI6).

He spoke of the KGB's First Chief Directorate (Foreign Operations) for foreign espionage, which had many successes including the recruiting of Philby, Burgess and Maclean. This had become the Foreign Intelligence Service or SVR, which worked in conjunction with the GRU (the main intelligence agency of the General Staff of the Armed Forces of the Russian Federation).

He spoke of the KGB's Second Chief Directorate for counterintelligence, internal political control and security, which had departments: the 1st for the US, the 2nd for the British Commonwealth, the 9th for foreign students and the 10th, the Foreign

Ministries Directorate, for servicing the Diplomatic Corps, the UPDK. This 10th department 'supported' the Diplomatic Corps and foreign residents with electricians, plumbers and the like. (When the fuses were turned off in the British Council not all the lights went out, and these could only be switched off in the UPDK.)

The Second Chief Directorate and other branches of the KGB had become the secret police agency, the Federal Security Service of the Russian Federation, the FSB.

He spoke of the KGB's Eighth Directorate for border troops, national, foreign and overseas communications and cipher services involving cryptographic equipment, research and development.

He spoke of the KGB's Ninth Directorate, the KGB Protection Service, the 40,000 uniformed bodyguards for the leaders of the Communist Party of the Soviet Union and government installations, including nuclear weapons. President Boris Yeltsin transformed this Ninth Directorate into the Federal Protection Service, the FPS.

Keith Muras ended by saying, "When you visit St Petersburg, I want you to take note of the Russians you come into contact with. In my next lecture I will ask you how many of them were in the FSB or the SVR."

Later I struck up conversation with him when I encountered him on one of the ship's decks.

Immigration
We berthed at St Petersburg on 31 May 2015 after an early lunch. We disembarked in fine weather, walked a couple of hundred yards to the Terminal building and queued at Immigration Control. We had to wait our turn to stand before a kiosk and have our passports examined. Keith Muras had escorted us, wearing an open-necked white shirt. He stood six feet from my right elbow when it was my turn to stand before the immigration officer, who was in a short-sleeved white shirt and tie. I presented my passport.

There followed a long, silent interview. The officer looked through my passport, stared at me and compared my face to the face in the passport photo. He scanned his screen and made a phone call. Had he found chunks of *My Double Life 1* online, details of my Cold War activities? He leafed through my passport, returned to his screen and made another phone call.

No other passenger was subjected to such a long, silent interview, and as I glanced at Keith Muras while I waited I saw that he was watching me intently.

Eventually the officer finished his telephone conversation, stamped my passport and gave me a white card.

I later found out that the previous day it had been announced on the BBC News that 89 EU politicians and military personnel including Nick Clegg, the British Deputy Prime Minister, had been banned from entering Russia.[1]

Gorbachev

We toured St Petersburg in a coach. I walked by the Neva opposite the distant green and white Hermitage and looked up at Minerva on the Academy of Art. We visited the Peter and Paul Fortress and were then taken to a large souvenir shop, which was staffed by young women and men. We stopped at St Isaac's Cathedral. I fell into conversation with our guide.

I said, "We passed a statue of Ivan the Terrible. There's no statue to Gorbachev. What do you think of Gorbachev, did he bring freedom and democracy?"

She said, "He was too liberal. He gave Eastern Europe away. We do not respect him. It is hard for us, we did so much for Poland, and now Poland does not appreciate the freedom Russia gave it."

I said, "We British had an Empire and trained our colonies up so they could be free. And the Soviet Union called us 'imperialists' and criticised us. Now Russia is called 'imperialist'. You are experiencing the same post-imperial criticism you inflicted on us."

Concert in the Winter Palace

We returned to the ship, passing through Immigration Control, and had an early supper. Then we again queued at Immigration Control for our evening visit to the Hermitage. Our coach arrived at the Hermitage by the Neva. It had been specially opened for a concert at 7pm.

Catherine the Great began the tradition of opening the Winter Palace's Tsarist residence for musical receptions during the 18th century. She called the rooms she opened her 'hermitage' as she made a show of forgetting State affairs and showing her paintings over coffee as if she was enjoying the private life of a hermit rather than the public life of a Tsarina.

Our group wore radio transmitters looped round our necks so we could hear our guide's explanation as we walked through rooms filled with Roman and Greek sculptures. We climbed the Ambassadors' marble staircase, admired the decorative gold leaf and walked through the Field Marshals' Room, the small Throne Room with a picture of Peter the Great alongside Minerva, and a suite of State rooms: the 1812 Gallery, the Big Throne Room with a large double-headed eagle, and the gallery to Catherine the Great's rooms. We reached the Small Hermitage and passed paintings by Leonardo, Raphael and Rembrandt.

In a hall with a large Italian skylight within the New Hermitage an audience was sitting on chairs. We sat near Mazzuoli's statue of the death of Adonis, gored by a boar, near a large malachite green urn and two candelabras. Almost immediately the State Symphony Orchestra of St Petersburg entered and the concert began.

I sat in the splendour of the Winter Palace, and to the music of Mozart, Rossini, Borodin, Tchaikovsky and Strauss I recalled film of the proletariat running across the square outside to storm this Winter Palace in 1905, and entered the mind-set of the Tsar's family cowering within at this revolutionary time. I reflected on when this room belonged to the Tsars and how the last Tsar was gored by the proletariat boar.

After the concert we returned to the Greek and Roman statues for a glass of champagne near the Ambassadors' staircase, and before we returned to the ship I pondered Communism's failed attempt to create a tyrannical, non-democratic World State.

Catherine's Palace

The next day we set off just after 7. Our coach took us to Catherine the Great's palace at Tsarskoe Seloe near the town of Pushkin. It had been burned during the war by retreating Russians carrying out a scorched-earth policy to impede the advancing Nazis, and had then been rebuilt. We saw five of Catherine's rooms and the Amber Room, which was reconstructed from plans after the Nazis looted most of the amber. We returned to St Isaac's Cathedral.

Tsars' tombs and prison

The coach took us to Peter and Paul's Fortress, and to the Peter and Paul Cathedral which faces a cobbled square and holds the tombs of the Romanovs. The family of the last Tsar, Nicholas II, are represented by one tomb as there were few remains after they were murdered in the Ekaterinburg cellar and their bodies set on fire. I wandered among the Romanovs' stone tombs and again reflected on the Tsars among their tombs, on the fall of an imperial regime and the rise of Communism.

We were given half an hour's free time. With our guide's help I bought a ticket in the cobbled square and, leaving Ann to sit in the sunshine, walked at a brisk pace to the Trubetskoy Bastion prison. I was hoping to find the cell Dostoevsky had occupied, but discovered that the prison of his day had been pulled down and rebuilt. This stone prison held all the 1860s Nihilists and the early Communists, including Lenin.

I walked along a stone corridor and peered into thirty stone cells. Each cell had a high-barred window and a truckle-bed. I passed as many cells on the first floor. I then went down and out to the exercise yard, which had uneven cobbles. Here prisoners were executed by firing-squad.

I lingered at the scene of Tsarist tyranny and imagined the

suffering of the early Nihilists and Communists, and then returned to the cobbled square where Ann was waiting for me, and to the ship.

Spilled Blood

The next day we took a boat along the Neva. We sat downstairs as the bridges are low. Those on the top deck had to duck. We disembarked and walked in Palace Square, where crowds rushed the Winter Palace in 1905 in the old film I had recalled.

We went on to the Cathedral of the Spilled Blood and I stood before the spot where Alexander II was blown up by a second bomb. He was taken to the Winter Palace, where he died.

Outside we had to be wary of pickpockets. Wallets and cameras had to be in zipped pockets.

Kronstadt naval base

The Voyager left Russia later. We dined on the veranda deck: butternut squash soup and baked salmon. Just after I had served myself with pudding (fruit and ice-cream) we passed Kotlin Island, which holds the Kronstadt naval base, the main naval base for the Russian Baltic fleet 30 kilometres west of St Petersburg.[2]

On the starboard side I saw tower blocks of flats that housed 43,000 workers and a small town with shops. A dam created a lake, and a tunnel beneath it had two six-lane motorways servicing the base, indicating its size. We passed three shipbuilding yards where tens of thousands of Russians were building ships for North Korea, Vietnam and Iran. We passed the *Aurora*, the ship which fired the momentous shot that began the Russian Revolution of 1917. It had three funnels and was still a sturdy warship.

We passed old wrecks and many Russian ships. I took photos of the Russian fleet, and was so long away from my deck table, with Ann beside me, that a waiter took my pudding, thinking I had left, and I had to queue for some more. We watched the Gulf of Finland recede while we finished eating on deck.

The KGB and Solzhenitsyn

The next time Keith Muras gave a lecture he asked us what Russians we had had contact with and who we thought was in the FSB and SVR. The audience called out: immigration officers, guides, coach drivers, gift-shop assistants. He went through each in turn. He had made his own study of who we encountered, and practically everyone we met was in one or other of these two organisations.

I came across him on one of the ship's decks. I told him how during our visit to St Petersburg, Moscow and Yalta in October 1995 Ann and I flew back from Yalta to Moscow and how at Moscow's Vnukovo airport two ladies in army uniform and peaked caps entered the plane at the front, shouted instructions and lined all the passengers up in the aisle: Ann and me in one line, the rest of the passengers in another line. They confiscated my passport and then Ann's, and left the plane without any explanation.

I said we had wandered about for an hour with our hand luggage trying to locate our passports, hearing my name being repeatedly broadcast over the public address system in Russian that nobody could translate, and had eventually, in desperation, gone up to the first floor. I said Ann had spotted toilets and had gone into a cubicle. I said a lady in army uniform and a peaked cap rushed across and banged on the door and shouted in English, "KGB toilet, not for you." I asked why in 1995 she had shouted "KGB toilet", not "FSB toilet" or "SVR toilet".

Keith said that 'KGB' was still used as a blanket term. The ladies in army uniform would have known the KGB had morphed into the FSB and SVR.

I said that when our guide asked in our Intourist Hotel following the passport incident, "Is there anywhere you would like to go?" and I said, "The KGB buildings," she took us to Ljubljana Square and pointed out some ten high-rise buildings in a compound, and referred to them as "the KGB", not the "FSB" or "SVR".

I did not tell Keith that Solzhenitsyn's secretary Mrs. Bankoul had rung soon after our arrival in room 1326 at the Intourist Hotel that same morning, 27 October 1995, and had given me the address of Solzhenitsyn's apartment. By prior arrangement I was to deliver four of my books for Solzhenitsyn to read, which I had brought with me: *The Fire and the Stones*, *The Universe and the Light*, *The Warlords* and *Overlord* books 1 and 2. I did not know if 'the KGB' had confiscated our passports because they had prior knowledge of my delivery to a Russian author they had perse-cuted, or whether they were retaliating for things I had done in the past. We delivered the books to his apartment at 1 Tru-zhenikov Pereulda 17, 64 apt. Solzhenitsyn was away and the books were taken in for him.

I pondered Russian expansionism. First Georgia, then the Crimea, then Eastern Ukraine. Would Estonia be next?

3
Tallinn, Estonia

The Russian threat had revived under Putin, a former career of-ficer in the KGB who wished to recover the territories Gorbachev gave away at the end of the Cold War. Under Putin the Cold War had begun to return, and the countries bordering Russia had as-sumed new importance as potential invadees. At another time Estonia might have been a European backwater. Now it was on the European front line, and in direct line to be invaded if Russia began an offensive to restore its East-European empire.

Threat of Russian invasion
We arrived in Tallinn at 8.30am on 3 June 2015. We disembarked and were driven by coach to the Upper Town, whose walls go back to the time of the Hanseatic League. We passed Fat Mar-garet and reached the Maiden's Tower, and from the Kiek in de Kök Bastion we peered down on the roofs and kitchens of the Lower Town. I spoke to our guide, an elderly lady whose hus-band (she told us) had been imprisoned by the Russians.

"Do you feel threatened by Russia?" I asked her.

"Oh yes. They are overflying us all the time. NATO was here last week, giving advice to head off an invasion. The Russians do not respect our air space. They contemptuously violate Estonian air space. They may arrive suddenly by land, sea and air, or after a two-week crisis."

I said, "I've heard that the Russian-speaking minority of 300,000 Estonians out of the 1.3 million Estonian population has appealed to Moscow as they don't want their children to learn Estonian compulsorily at school. I can see 300,000 Russian-speaking Estonians, a quarter of your population, complaining to Moscow, 'The Estonians are making us learn Estonian rather than Russian, please invade us to save our Russian language.'"

"Exactly," she said. "That is what we fear will happen. Russia will invade to answer the call of the Russian-speaking Estonians."

"Are there militias among the Russian-speaking Estonians?"

"No. But the Russians can send in troops as militias claiming to be Estonians. We hope NATO will protect us."

We resumed our tour of Tallinn and I mused on Putin's intentions. Would Putin, who invaded Georgia and Crimea just as Hitler invaded the Sudetenland and the rest of Czechoslovakia, go on to invade Estonia? And would Estonia, Lithuania and Latvia be NATO's red line just as Poland was Britain's red line in 1939?

We went to the 'Song Festival' grounds where 300,000 Estonians sang patriotic songs demanding independence in their 1988 'Singing Revolution'. As I walked on the site of Estonia's struggle for independence against the Soviet Union I again raised the prospect of a Russian invasion with the guide.

She said: "We will fight. They didn't fight in my parents' generation. They were invaded by the Russians, the Germans and then the Russians again. My father was imprisoned by the Russians. My mother used to say, 'Germans and Russians, which were worse? Which would you prefer to have, bubonic plague or smallpox?'"

We went on to a manor house for coffee and cake. Two girls in national costume played kannels, a kannel being a two-thousand-year-old Estonian string instrument which evolved into a zither. Originally it had five strings and the most sophisticated kannels now have sixty strings. The two kannels being played each had fifty strings.

The coach took us to the ruins of the 15th-century St Bridget's convent. It rained. I sat and looked across water at our distant ship. Soon afterwards we passed the ex-Russian submarine base, and in my mind's eye I foresaw the arrival of invading Russian ships launched from the Kronstadt base on Kotlin Island, off St Petersburg.

Is Russia expansionist?
The day after we left Tallinn I encountered Keith Muras sitting in a lounge. I sat beside him.

I asked him, "Could Gorbachev have been a British agent in the mid-1980s, before he closed down the USSR and the KGB and liberated Eastern Europe?"

He said, "I feel he wasn't."

I asked him, "Do you feel the Russians are now expansionist?"

He said, "No. What use would they have for Estonia?"

I said, "As a second front, to distract attention from Ukraine. And to connect up with their exclave in Kaliningrad on their way to recovering the Soviet territories Gorbachev surrendered."

From what he said next I gathered that the British Foreign Office did not want to think about possible future Russian invasions as their priority was to deliver cuts. I gathered that the climate was like that of the 1930s when Britain was reluctant to re-arm, despite Churchill's warnings.

Later, while queuing to shake hands with the captain at the captain's reception, I was handed a glass of champagne and found myself standing beside one of the other lecturers, who had shown slides of St Petersburg. I said that Keith Muras did not believe that Russia is expansionist.

He said to me, "I disagree, I believe Russia *is* expansionist."

We were now shaking hands with the captain, a Ukrainian.

Holding my glass of champagne, I included the captain in the conversation: "We were just wondering, is Putin expansionist? Will he take Estonia?"

The captain, in uniform white shirt and tie with navy epaulettes, looked at me as if I had hit him. He said: "All I can say is that two thousand Ukrainian soldiers have died. My brother is a West-Ukrainian soldier fighting the occupation of half our country by the Russians, and two thousand West-Ukrainian soldiers have died. I have no opinion on Estonia, but that is my opinion on Ukraine."

He meant that he thought Putin *was* expansionist.

Berlin
The next morning we docked at Warnemünde, the cruise port for Berlin, and were driven by coach to Berlin, which we toured. Starting at Charlottenburg, we drove from one end of Berlin to the other. We lunched near Gendarmenmarkt Square and took a boat trip along the Spree. We passed several domes and the Reichstag. We rejoined the coach and stopped at Checkpoint Charlie and a surviving section of the Berlin Wall.

European civilization as a tree
We walked in Unter den Linden and the Kurfürstendamm, where in a bookshop I found an image of European civilization as a tree. The main nation-states in the EU were written in German on branches, and the leaves (in German words) headlined events in their history. The image perfectly described how the UK, France, Germany, Holland, Italy and the other European nation-states stemmed from one Christian trunk.[1] The same image could have illustrated a World State: 193 countries shown as branches, all stemming from one trunk.

Two days later we were driven round Amsterdam. By now we had more or less traversed the Baltic, both ways.

Russian military manoeuvres in the Baltic
I only later discovered that earlier, on 12 June 2014, Russia held

a military exercise in its exclave between Lithuania and Poland, Kaliningrad, in response to NATO,[2] and that in March 2015 the Russians held a huge military exercise in the Baltic involving 33,000 troops to rehearse the capture of part of North Norway to protect Russian interests in the Arctic, and of Bornholm island from Denmark, Gotland island from Sweden and the Aland Islands from Finland.[3] The capture of these islands would allow Russia to seal the Baltic and isolate Estonia, Latvia and Lithuania as a link with its retained exclave of Kaliningrad.

Later still I discovered that fifteen days after my visit to Estonia, on 18 June 2015, Russia was in the process of transporting strategic and nuclear weapons on a warship, presumably from the Kronstadt base on Kotlin Island, to its retained exclave of Kaliningrad between Poland and Lithuania.

Inadvertently I had cruised through contested waters that might be an area of conflict if a Russian attempt at expansion was blocked by NATO.

4
War and Peace

Our time has been an unsettled time. Since 1945 – during my lifetime – the UN has failed to prevent 162 wars, mainly because it is 'inter-national', 'between nation-states' and on the level of nation-states, and is subject to the veto of nation-states in the Security Council. It lacks authority to prevent war. England has been involved in wars with European powers for a thousand years – there were European wars at regular intervals, in 1870, 1914 and 1939 – but thanks to NATO and the EU there have been no wars for seventy years after 1945, except on the fringes, for example in former Yugoslavia. I considered where the next major wars would be fought.

Back in Essex, writing *The Secret American Destiny* on the edge of Epping Forest, parakeets clustering round the bird feeders and enormous carp by the water-lilies in the main pool, I reflected on war and peace.

Russian expansionism

The main expansionist threat to peace was Putin's Hitler-like expansionism in Georgia and the Crimea, with Estonia, Latvia and Lithuania as a possible sticking-point, like Poland in 1939. Putin's manoeuvrings in the Baltic were presented as reactions to NATO but were arguably provocations.

I reflected that the Byzantine-Russian civilization was in the federation stage on my chart, stage 46, in which there is "an attempt at counterthrust... to restore [the] past". The Russian counterthrust to restore its pre-Gorbachev world standing was in full swing.

European civilization

The European civilization was in stage 43 (union), and the Byzantine-Russian civilization in stage 46 (federation). The evidence on my history chart is that in a conflict between two civilizations, the younger always triumphs over the older. This evidence is of course pre-nuclear, it preceded the Nuclear Age, and it is theoretically possible for an older civilization to drop nuclear bombs and triumph over a younger civilization, but this has never happened. I had no doubt that the evidence on my chart would assert that the North-American civilization (stage 15) and the European civilization of the EU (stage 43), together with NATO, would triumph over the Byzantine-Russian civilization (stage 46).

Syria

The threat to world peace was the war against Assad. Rebel groups had taken pockets of land in Syria and his regime had fought back and turned streets into bombed-out ruins, broken walls in which the inhabitants camped despite air raids. There had been many refugees. Assad was not expansionist, he just would not leave the country and therefore the rebels perpetuated the instability.

Islamic State and mustard gas
Within the *mêlée* of Syrian groups was Islamic State (IS). Saddam's Sunni military leadership had re-emerged within al-Qaeda in Iraq, and after the death of al-Zarqawi in 2006 the military Sunnis had re-emerged as IS under an al-Qaeda in Iraq officer, Abu Bakr al-Baghdadi, who had only appeared once, wearing 7th-century garb while giving a sermon in a Mosul mosque.

IS's re-creation of the 7th-century 'caliphate' signalled its aim of reviving the traditional Arab cultural purity and its yearning for the lost past of the Arab civilization (stage 45). That is what I would have explained to Al-Baghdadi had I been teaching at the University of Baghdad in the 1990s when he was there, after the appearance of my chart. Based in Raqqa, Syria, IS had spread to Mosul and had advanced to the outskirts of Baghdad before being driven back.

Although I had no doubt that the US (stage 15) and EU states (stage 43) would triumph over IS (stage 45) as again I would have explained to al-Baghdadi had I been teaching at the University of Baghdad in the 1990s, the danger was that IS would possess and use weapons of mass destruction before they were finally defeated.

IS had used mustard gas four times in Marea, 25 kms north of Aleppo, Syria in and after April 2015.[1] Where did IS obtain this mustard gas? Saddam Hussein had used mustard gas to kill 3,200–5,000 Kurds in Halabja, Kurdistan in 1988. Quantities of mustard gas were destroyed under UNSCOM (the United Nations Special Commission) supervision in 1991.

Hans Blix, 1st Executive Chairman of UNMOVIC (the United Nations Monitoring, Verification and Inspection Commission) between 1 March 2000 and 13 June 2003, reported to the UN Security Council on 14 February 2003: "We have now commenced the process of destroying approximately 50 litres of mustard gas declared by Iraq that was being kept under UNMOVIC seal at the Muthanna site. One-third of the quantity has already been destroyed."[2] According to the British Parliament's Select Committee on Foreign Affairs the weapons inspectors were still looking in July 2003 for 80 tonnes of mustard gas unaccounted for by Iraq.[3]

The UN's weapons inspectors had searched for Saddam's weapons of mass destruction, including mustard gas, after the 2003 Iraq war, but without success. The UN weapons inspector Dr David Kelly had not been able to find the hidden stock of mustard gas before his controversial death in Oxfordshire on 17 July 2003.

The Chilcot Report states that 500 mustard-filled shells and up to 450 mustard-filled aerial bombs have been unaccounted for since 1998. It is not clear if some of these shells and bombs were mistaken estimates within Iraq's accounting system.[4]

Had Saddam's stock of mustard gas passed via his henchmen to the also-Sunni IS? The Chilcot Report blamed intelligence failings for the Iraq War, and reported that the West was misled into believing that Saddam had weapons of mass destruction. Was the existence of a stock of mustard gas which Western intelligence failed to locate one of these intelligence failings?

My two poetic epics on war

I have seen wars loom on the fringes of Europe and in the Middle East, and have been grateful that for seventy years peace has held in Western Europe, thanks to the EU and NATO. So many take this peace for granted.

I have never taken peace for granted as I have been steeped in war. Having lived under the V-1s and V-2s as a boy of five (see p.xiv), I became a war poet in my two poetic epics of war. In *Overlord* (1994–1996, 41,000 lines of blank verse) I wrote about the Second World War from D-Day to the fall of Berlin and the dropping of the atomic bomb. Book 5 was on Auschwitz. My hero was Eisenhower, who pursued Hitler and on the way allowed Stalin to take Berlin and create the Soviet Eastern-European empire that would be protected by the 1943 Tehran Agreement. In my earlier verse play *The Warlords* I covered the same ground with Montgomery as my hero. In *Armageddon* (2008–2009, 25,000 lines of blank verse) I wrote on the War on Terror from 9/11 to

Obama's inauguration. I described the wars in Afghanistan and Iraq, and the activities of al-Qaeda in Iraq and the surge.

I have been glutted with war in these works. But beneath them is an underlying longing for peace: for a World State that can bring universal peace. The summary of book 12 of *Armageddon* states: "Christ's vision of coming world government. Dream of world state."[5]

I have said that I see war and peace as a +A + −A that can be reconciled in an enduring World State (see p.xvii). That is the underlying vision of my two poetic epics. (The vision included a reconciliation of war and peace at a metaphysical level, in terms of the One that unifies the universe.)

The World Government *and a World State*
I reflected on my book *The World Government*. It is subtitled *A Blueprint for a Universal World State*. It sets out the structure of a partly federal and supranationalist World State with 850 elected lower-house Representatives of all nation-states, 92 World Senators and 27 World Commissioners. (See Appendix 3.) It lists all the constituencies throughout the world that would return Representatives and Senators, and the regions from which the 27 Commissioners would be drawn.

I see the UN General Assembly being turned into a World Parliamentary Assembly (or UN Parliamentary Assembly), the lower house of 850 Representatives. There would have to be a presentation to the delegates of the UN General Assembly to begin the process of reform that would turn it into a democratic lower house for a world government.

The Secret American Destiny *and a World State*
During the summer of 2015 I wrote *The Secret American Destiny*, setting out Universalism in seven disciplines: mysticism, literature, philosophy and the sciences, history, comparative religion, international politics and statecraft and world culture. In all these seven disciplines there is a conflict between a traditional, metaphysical approach and a modern secular approach, and

in each discipline Universalism effects a reconciliation. In this book I see America as bringing the World State to birth, acting as a midwife rather than imposing a world empire. I completed the book on 21 October 2015.

Russia intervenes in Syria and swells refugees
On 30 September 2015 Russia intervened in the Syrian Civil War claiming to want to eradicate IS but in fact attacking the rebels against Assad, bombing their hide-outs among civilians from October onwards. Russian air attacks speeded up the flow of refugees to Europe, and it looked as if Putin was trying to split the unity of the European Union by forcing its nation-states, members of the Schengen Area, to build walls to keep out growing columns of refugees. The Russian role in Syria was viewed with deep suspicion.

By bombing Syrian cities on behalf of Assad Russia had restored its Cold-War imperialist influence in the Middle East.

5

Athens and World State

In the 1960s I thought deeply about the universe and the globe, whose unity could now be seen from space, and I arrived at the outlook that in the late 1980s I began describing as Universalism: the view that the universe and all humankind are one and should be treated as a unity in philosophy, history, literature, politics, religion and other disciplines. *The Fire and the Stones* (1991) begins with an introduction titled 'Introduction to the New Universalism'.

This appeared about the time that Soviet Communism collapsed, and I can now see that die-hard Communists, used to singing 'The Internationale' and to seeing the world swept by egalitarian Communism, might be attracted to a materialistic branch of my Universalism. Their Communism could morph into a 'neo-Communist' Universalism.

As can be seen in my work *The New Philosophy of Universal-*

ism my Universalism includes every known concept and therefore includes metaphysical tiers, which ex-Communists might conveniently ignore, dwelling on a world in which ideally all are equal but under firm central control as they are in modern Communist China. My political Universalism was founded on a democratic World State which ex-Communists might conveniently ignore, dwelling on a world in which the Greek *'demos'* ('people') was considered stupid and pointing out that democracy often throws up a miserable choice between wretched candidates. In short, my Universalism may have been a magnet for some Russians who may have seen secular Universalism as a gateway to a world domination that would serve Russian interests.

Now I come to a deepening in my direct involvement with Russia. Keith Muras had described a system in which practically all Russians who are in contact with foreigners have links with the State. Was he exaggerating, or was he right? And can Russians freely pursue principled beliefs in the same way that Westerners can? Do considerations of war and peace and Russia's national interests govern all political activity by Russian nationals?

I did not know. I, a supranational Universalist, was merely reacting to an approach through the internet, and as with all approaches involving a complete stranger there were two sides that needed to be weighed.

Athens and classical Greece
I had dipped into Igor Kondrashin's Constitution and his paper on Transuniversalism. His approach was humanistic, secular and materialistic whereas my Universalism included all the 7.33 billion of humankind in July 2015, including the 4.6 billion who regard themselves as religious and have a metaphysical perspective. Like a politician, I had decided to focus on our similarities rather than our differences, and I had chosen to make common cause with Igor and the international philosophers.

On Sunday 4 October 2015 I flew to Athens with Ann to attend the sixth annual conference of the World Philosophical Forum (WPF), at the invitation of Igor Kondrashin. The previous day I had attended a reunion at Worcester College, Oxford. I talked with Jonathan Bate, a world authority on Shakespeare, and left dinner at the end of his speech at 10.20. I drove back to Essex and arrived before midnight. I was up at 4.30am to catch the 9am flight from Stansted.

On the plane I recalled that at the previous year's reunion at Worcester College, on 6 September 2014, an elderly Scottish gentleman wearing a tam-o'-shanter and tartan trews and sporting many medals, approached me at the packed reception and said, "Here's someone who looks as if he's been in British intelligence." I found myself having a long talk with Brian Stewart, then 92, a D-Day veteran who blew up Panzers in Normandy and in 1968 became the secretary of the Joint Intelligence Committee, an MI6 director who nearly became 'C' when Sir Maurice Oldfield retired. He invited me to sit with him. We sat together for twenty minutes while he told me his intelligence career, and made it clear that he knew of my career in intelligence from 1969 to 1973. He turned out to be the father of Rory Stewart MP, and had recently died in August 2015, aged 93.

In heat we took a taxi from Athens airport to a hotel Igor had

Phaleron Bay, where the Persian fleet appeared in September 480BC, from
Nicholas Hagger's hotel balcony

recommended in Phaleron Bay, Paleo Faliro: the Poseidon Hotel. It overlooked the sea, and from our first-floor window I looked out over the beach from which Theseus set sail for Crete and to the horizon where the Persian fleet appeared in September 480BC. The hotel was between Themistocles' walls which once made a safe corridor from the bay to the centre of Athens.

I loved Greece. Having read Greek history and literature for 'A' level at school and having visited the Greek ruins several times over the years, first in 1958 when I was nineteen, I am a Philhellene. For me the 5th century BC was a magical time: the Greeks' heroic defeat of the Persians though outnumbered, thanks to the ingenuity of their leaders; the rise of the Athenian Empire and its treasury on Delos, silver talents collected to defend the Greek islands and city-states from future Persian attacks; the rise of democracy and of Pericles; the two destructive Peloponnesian Wars between Athens (and her allies) and Sparta (and her allies); and the philosophy of Socrates and Plato's Academy.

I got into Oxford on my Latin and Greek, and relished the comparison between the Greek Empire and the British Empire, and between two Peloponnesian Wars – the First Peloponnesian War of 460–446/5BC and the Second Peloponnesian War of 431–404BC – and two European World Wars. Those parallels were the perspective when I studied ancient history from 1954 to 1956, a time when the British Empire was still intact and when (until 1955) Churchill, our Pericles, was still Prime Minister.

Conference registration
We took a taxi to the City of Athens Cultural and Youth Centre, 50 Akadimias Street, to register before 5pm. On the first floor there was a large room filled with people in warm-weather attire, and on a small platform at a table sat Igor, a benevolent man in his sixties in a suit and tie, and his smiling blonde wife Lidia. He rose and greeted me with a bear-hug and after completing the paperwork and paying a small conference fee I was introduced to "your assistant for the conference", a young Chi-

nese female lawyer who lived in Greece, Junyan Hé. He introduced me to some of the international philosophers in the room, one of whom, Julian Korab-Karpowicz, had been a Presidential candidate in Poland. Junyan took Ann and me for a walk to look at the classical statues round the Academy.

Georgian Centre: I am Chairman of the Constitutional Convention
At Igor's request we took a taxi to the Georgian Centre, a cultural centre for Greek-Georgian friendship which was up stairs and on a first floor in a side street. Georgia had been invaded by Russia and Russianised in 2008.

Thirty or forty Georgians, Russians and international philosophers stood holding drinks and almost immediately there were speeches. Then a girl in Georgian national dress sang two Georgian national songs for us while food was served, including baklava.

I talked with Igor, who told me, "Please speak tomorrow for five minutes as a greeting and for twenty minutes the next day after me, about anything you want."

He had emailed, telling me that I was now the WPF's Special Envoy to the UN, and I had proposed leading a delegation to Ban Ki-moon. I had already submitted a paper on my Universalism (see Appendix 1), which had immediately been uploaded on the WPF's website. I knew I would talk about my Universalism and the proposed visit to Ban Ki-moon.

Then Igor said, "You will be Chairman of the Constitutional Convention that will approve the Constitution of the Universal State of the Earth."

I was surprised. I had been led to understand I was attending the conference, not running it. My appointment had been decided before I had arrived in Athens.

Conference: day 1
The next morning I arrived at the City of Athens Cultural and Youth Centre early, wearing a suit, white shirt and gold tie. I had brought some of my books – including *The New Philosophy*

of Universalism and *The World Government* – and I found the long conference room where we would be meeting and laid them on a display table. Then I joined two men sitting in a small room near the stairs: Raoul Weiler, the Belgian founding president of the EU-Chapter of The Club of Rome and an expert on the relationship between technology and society, who was writing a comprehensive study of global warming drawing on archived EU data; and Timi Ecimovic, a Slovenian who claimed to have been recommended four times for a Nobel Prize in basic physics for his work on Nature. He told me he worked on the unity between man and Nature, a theme close to my heart.

Igor Kondrashin shaking hands with Nicholas Hagger (above) and sitting between him and Junyan Hé (below) on 5 October 2015

We went through to the conference room. There were chairs either side of an aisle and a lectern at the front, from which there were greetings from some fifty delegates, mostly professors of philosophy from different countries, in English and sometimes Greek, all translated into Russian.

Aristotle was held up as the model to follow, and Socrates, who said: "I am a citizen not of Athens or of Greece, but of the world." He should have said: "I am a citizen of Athens *and* of Greece *and* of the world." The WPF's view was made clear that all 7.33 million humans are world *citizens*.

A Greek actor and director, Paris Katsivelos, showed a video of himself chanting in Greek to the goddess Mnemosyne in a ceremony based on an ancient Greek ritual in the ruins of Plato's Academy, and he powerfully overchanted so the words we heard from the screen were superimposed by his live words to us. Later he told me he was addressing the "universal spiritual Light". The Greek Minister of Culture was expected but sent a video instead.

Eventually I spoke on how I came to be a Universalist, on my seven disciplines and on my plan to lead a delegation to Ban Ki-moon and the UN General Assembly.

My speech was as follows:

> Greetings from the United Kingdom. I am very pleased to have been invited and to be here. In the past I was a professor in Japan but I am now retired from that side and am a writer. As I say in my paper on the WPF website, I came to what I call Universalism in the years before 1991, and I led a group of 12 Universalist philosophers in London in 1992–94, which may have been the first such group since the Vienna Circle. Universalism sees all disciplines in terms of the whole of humankind and all nation-states as being under a possible supranational, global authority. As a Universalist I wanted to act out Universalism, which is about the whole of all disciplines, and so I have written within seven disciplines, whose boundaries I cross: philosophy, history, literature, mysticism, comparative religion, international politics and statecraft, and world culture. I couldn't bring many books with me on the plane from London, but four of my 43

books are on the table over there, including *A New Philosophy of Universalism* (2009). Look at them by all means, but please do not take them away.

I am not here to dwell on areas where my Universalism's inclusion of metaphysics and my democratic World State differ from our agenda, but to be practical and pragmatic, to combine forces with the WPF and help launch a new approach to supranationalism. You will have seen the letter to Ban Ki-moon which calls for a special session at the UN General Assembly so the first ever supranational delegation can request UN delegates to support a new supranational authority to solve the world's problems – a new initiative in global citizenship education. More of this tomorrow. I understand I am to be Chairman of the Constitutional Convention, and today I shall want to meet you all so I can chair our discussion on the Constitution on Tuesday and Wednesday. The Constitution is very important but I shall try to make sure that we do not forget about the important letter to Ban Ki-moon which may signal the beginning of a new unified world. This is a very important conference.

Over pizzas and orange juice at a stand-up lunch in the shade of garden trees Raoul said the UN agenda is fixed a year in advance and that Ban Ki-moon was due to retire in December 2016. I pointed out that there must be some slack and flexibility to cope with new and unforeseen local wars which could not be timetabled in advance.

Igor spoke to me of the American Constitutional Convention chaired by George Washington in 1787, which established the United States of America. He said, "Washington's tombstone says he chaired the Constitutional Convention, not that he was President. To him chairing the Constitutional Convention was more important than being President."

I was not sure about that. The inscription over the entrance to Washington's tomb at Mount Vernon says, 'Within this Enclosure Rest the remains of Gen'l George Washington', and beyond iron bars only his name is visible on his marble tomb.

George Washington chairing the Constitutional Convention that created the
United States of America in 1787

I had a deep sense that we would be unifying the world sym-
bolically in a couple of days' time. Already, that first morning,
I was aware that I had to work on my concluding speech at the
end of a Constitutional Convention, the Declaration of a new
World State, and Junyan sat with me at a laptop Igor had made
available. I dictated four paragraphs and keyed in a fifth paragraph myself.

The afternoon session consisted of presentations on social education. A Greek priest with a long straggly beard, Father Christos Georgiou Zouros, stood and came to the microphone. Standing next to me, he fixed me with his eyes and spoke fiercely and
theatrically in Greek, saying (I was later told) that God is love
and books don't matter. He pulled a knife from his black cassock and brandished it on high, and waved it histrionically as he
spoke, rhythmically thrusting the air as he emphasised words.
For ten seconds I thought he was going to turn and behead me.
Then he turned and put the knife under his black cassock, embraced me and kissed me twice.

In the late afternoon we all went on to an art exhibition in a nearby building. There Igor opened his laptop and showed me an email he had received from a member of the Club of Rome who could not attend the conference, Mark Dubrulle, President and Executive Director of The Club of Rome's EU Chapter. Mark's email supported the visit to Ban Ki-moon and said that Herman Van Rompuy, until November 2014 the President of the European Council, should be in my delegation.

Igor then said, with Chinese Junyan at my elbow, listening: "When the Universal State of the Earth comes into existence on Wednesday, so will the Supreme Council of Humanity. I would like you to be Acting Chairman of the Supreme Council of Humanity. Ban Ki-moon will be Chairman, you will be Acting Chairman."

I looked at his list of the members of the Supreme Council of Humanity on his laptop. It included Pope Benedict XVI (the ex-Pope), Bill Gates and Ban Ki-moon. I wondered if they knew they were on Igor's list.

On my way out I slipped into the empty 'lecture theatre' downstairs and took a look at the room where I would be chairing the Constitutional Convention the next day. Igor had said the Mayor of Athens had donated the hire cost of this theatre for two days. (He said the hire of The City of Athens Cultural and Youth Centre's conference room had cost €600 for the first day.) I stood in a plush semi-circular 'theatre' shaped like the theatre at Epidaurus (modern Epidavros), with very comfortable armchair seats.

Then I braved the clusters of 'refugees' (I was told) smoking dope in the darkening garden, found a taxi and arrived back at the hotel in Phaleron Bay. I ate with Ann in the Tavern by the sea opposite the hotel under a clear night sky. I had moussaka and chips, yoghurt and honey and red wine.

We returned to our room and I wrote a twenty-minute presentation on the Constitution and on the proposed delegation to Ban Ki-moon. Igor had circulated a letter to Ban Ki-moon, which I would ask all to sign. Then I went to bed.

The two-day Constitutional Convention
The next day I arrived at the same time as Igor at the City of Athens Cultural and Youth Centre. We sat at a long 'counter' on the raised platform and discussed the day's program topics. He said, "I will speak and give my presentation, then I will give the chair to you and you will speak."

Igor's presentation was gripping. With the aid of Power-Point he went through the history of attempts to create a world government by force: by Alexander the Great, Julius Caesar, Genghis Khan, Napoleon, Hitler and "the Russian International linked to Marx and Engels" – he did not refer to Communism by name – and by the League of Nations and the UN, both of which

Nicholas Hagger (on left) chairing the Constitutional Convention (above) and making his speech on the Constitution (below)

failed to keep the peace "as have G7, G8 and G20". He spoke of world rule being imposed by force being replaced in our time by world rule by consent.

He spoke of UNESCO's strategy on global education in 2005 and Ban Ki-moon's 'Education First' policy of 2012, neither of which had been supported by world leaders. He spoke of UNESCO's medium-term strategy from 2014 to 2021. He said he supported Ban Ki-moon's policy of "global citizenship education". Raoul said, "It must be precise, in 'upbringing and learning'."

I then spoke about the Constitution. I had read through the Constitution and I have already said that I found it very materialistic. Igor had told me he was inspired by Engels and Lenin, and that his three philosophical works presented dialectical materialism. I had used the dialectical method of contrasting two opposites and reconciling them (thesis–antithesis–synthesis) in my works, but my metaphysical perspective was very different from Igor's materialistic perspective.

I said that in my writings, going back to *The World Government* (2010), I had seen the UN as the means of delivering a World State, and that as they could read in my paper online, my Universalism differed from Igor's Transuniversalism as it included a metaphysical dimension. But for the sake of the common cause I would set aside my own views and would concentrate on bringing in the Universal State of the Earth, leaving to one side how it would be adopted by the 7.33 billion world citizens. Igor's idea was that they would all sign up to it as members, but I thought that would take decades. It had to be adopted by the UN General Assembly on a representational basis to reach all humankind.

I dwelt on the "historical day" that would create the Universal State of the Earth and the Supreme Council of Humanity. I talked of the letter to Ban Ki-moon, requesting an opportunity for a delegation to address the UN General Assembly when the new World State had been created.

My speech was as follows:

Good morning, ladies and gentlemen. Thank you for appointing me Chairman of the Constitutional Convention. I want to talk on the Constitution and the letter to Ban Ki-moon. Because of their importance I want to follow a written record that can appear in print.

We are now considering a new Universal Constitution for the Earth. Plato wrote *The Republic* for his nearby Academy, and now we modern philosophers are writing a new '*Republic*' for a new World State. This new Constitutional Convention recalls the American Constitutional Convention of 1787 presided over by George Washington, which cemented the United States.

This Constitution[1] is to be known and used by all the earth's inhabitants. There are 61 articles in 14 chapters. Chapter 3 sets out a list of universal values and universal vices. Coincidentally, two of the three books I have being published in December focus on vices. My *Selected Poems* (a selection from my 1,800 poems) contains a section 'Follies and Vices', and the preface lists 150 vices. My *Selected Stories*, titled *Follies and Vices of the Modern Elizabethan Age* (a selection from my 1,001 stories, which echo *The Arabian Nights*) has a preface that lists 220 vices. My Universalist approach has covered the same ground as chapter 3 of the Constitution. I will leave a leaflet on each of these two books for you to look at.

We'll be looking at the Constitution in greater detail shortly. It is not often that a Constitutional Convention sets up a new state and gives it a Constitution with articles. As I said yesterday, this is a very important conference for that reason.

As I said yesterday, my Universalism is in seven disciplines, the seven bands of a rainbow. It includes all known concepts and therefore includes metaphysics (in *The New Philosophy of Universalism*) and it sets out a possible enlightened democratic structure (in *The World Government*). Political Universalism is one of my seven Universalisms – which are all one Universalism, seven bands of one rainbow.

In my historical Universalism, my study of 25 civilizations, I see each civilization beginning with a metaphysical idea round which it grows, and then turning secular. The rise-and-fall pattern of civilizations goes through 61 similar stages. Stage 43 is a union (the stage the EU has just entered). Stage 46 is federal (the stage the Byzantine-Russian civilization has just entered). There has been talk of civilizations. I point out that my study sees civilizations as passing through stages, and in the union-federal stages when the civilizations have turned secular they can be absorbed into a World State while the life of each nation-state in a civilization quietly continues. The Universal State of the Earth, the current World State, may be a stage that covers hundreds of years in the history of civilizations.

I now turn to the letter to Ban Ki-moon as an aspect of global citizenship education.[2] It asks for the first-ever supranational delegation to visit the UN General Assembly and request the delegates to consider setting up a supranational authority with the power to declare war illegal. Nation-states would sign a treaty, and once this is in force multilateral disarmament could begin to take place under another treaty. There are seven supranational goals in the letter. They are:

1 Bringing peace between nation-states and multilateral disarmament. All war can be declared illegal.
2 Sharing natural resources and energy.
3 Solving environmental problems such as global warming.
4 Ending disease.
5 Ending famine.
6 Solving the world's financial crisis.
7 Redistributing wealth to eliminate poverty.

In all these areas a global perspective can improve the lot of humankind, and only a supranational authority can make these improvements that will benefit the whole of humankind. (See Appendix 3.)

I know the UN agenda is allocated a year or two in advance, but slack is left for unforeseen crises and it may be that a 5pm–6pm slot for such a delegation could be squeezed in. If this cannot be fitted in, then (if the UN will give its blessing to the idea) there could be regional conferences in (for example, to cite places suggested) Peru, Malaysia, the Philippines and Hyderabad.

Igor and I are agreed that we should try to achieve a delegation's visit by December 2015 but there may be slippage until March. Ban Ki-moon retires in December 2016, so if we are doing it, we need to get on with it.

It's a generation thing. If we don't do it now an attempt may not be made for another generation. It's time to act now. Global citizenship education: the best way to educate is to set a project (a supranational authority) on which world leaders have to decide. Delegates will refer the question to their leaders, and 193 world leaders will undergo global citizenship education by reacting to their question. Yes, it will be difficult. But leadership is saying, 'We are going to get to the General Assembly. It looks difficult but we know a path.' And with that spirit the General Assembly *can* be entered.

If we succeed in leading a supranational delegation – the first ever – to the UN, it will be historic. The process of supranational government will be said to have begun in 2015. Signing the letter to Ban Ki-moon is therefore a historic act. Add that to the Constitution we will shortly be considering and endorsing and this conference may be regarded as one of the most historic conferences ever. Thank you very much. Now to the Constitutional Convention.

I had questions from the international philosophers, who all had copies of the Constitution: "How do you educate world leaders into accepting a supranational World State?" "Wouldn't it be better to decouple the supranational authority for the delegation to the UN General Assembly, wouldn't you have more success if you decoupled it?" I said "No, the idea should be placed before the UN in its entirety, part of the idea should not be withheld." Igor then announced that I would be Acting Chairman of the Supreme Council of Humanity.

We again lunched on pizzas and orange juice in the garden, and I found myself talking to the Greek leader of 'the Agrarian Party' (a party I could not find on any list, that was perhaps known by another name). He said he would arrange for me to meet the Greek Prime Minister Alexis Tsipras. This had been suggested the previous day, and the idea was taken up by Prof. Philippos Nicolopoulos of Greece's University of Indianapolis.

He told me, "I have already told Tsipras about you. He may see you in two days' time."

I said, "I am a Philhellene like Lord Byron and if invited will certainly discuss the future of Greece."

Tsipras had given an early indication of being pro-Russian, and he was having a new round of austerity imposed on him by the European Union. Greece was in a bad way with huge debts and unemployment and little sign that anything could improve. Byron would have done his best to help Greece, but even Byron could not improve Greece's deficit.

After the afternoon session Paris Katsivelos performed a one-man show, a dramatised version in Greek translation of *Avgerinos*, a poetic composition by Romania's national poet Mihai Eminescu. Paris wore a white suit and shoes and a white bow-tie, which all went with his white hair, and he struck postures and cried out fluently to a musical accompaniment. I went back and ate with Ann in the Tavern on the beach.

I pondered Igor's position. He had told me he had lived in Egypt for seven years and worked at Minister level. He had received four trade delegations a day. He told me, "I learned how to handle people." For nine years he had spent six months of each year in Athens and six months of each year in Moscow, where his daughter was in the Banque Credit Suisse. He told me again that the World Economic Forum at Davos had inspired him to start the World Philosophical Forum in Athens six years previously.

I was still not sure why he, a dialectical materialist, had sent his Constitution to me as soon as he had finished it and why he had made me Special Envoy to the UN and put me in charge of delivering the Constitutional Convention before I had arrived in Athens. I half-wondered if, unbeknown to him, the Russian SVR had had a hand in the promulgation of his Constitution, to sow confusion in the West, and was behind my involvement. But Igor seemed sincere about his supranationalism and I wanted to believe he had acted in good faith. I genuinely believed that the only way to bring order to the chaotic world of Russian expansionism and Syria was to turn the UN into a partly-federal World State with supranational powers to abolish war and control nuclear weapons. If the Russian SVR advocated this too, that should not matter. It should not prevent me from advocating the World State I had set out in *The World Government*.

The next day, Wednesday 7 October, before I left for the City of Athens Cultural and Youth Centre I pondered Igor's proletarian – perhaps Communist – approach to the World State. He had told me, "I don't want to go to world leaders, the masses will compel them to change." His view was that we should support the UN's program to bring global citizenship to the masses, and the masses would do the rest. But they wouldn't, that was the point. Without initiatives through the UN, nothing would happen. I wondered if the new World State should form a political party to lead the masses forward. I wrote in my diary, "The name of the WPF's party should be 'The Federation of the World'." I repeated this to Junyan as we sat on the platform waiting for the session to begin.

I had expected to go through the Constitution line by line and discuss each clause but Igor did not want that. The delegates all had the Constitution, it would be sufficient to discuss aspects of it, angles. John Moustos, the Greek owner of Greece's richest metal company, gave a PowerPoint presentation through his laptop on the Earth Bank he would be founding. The new international currency would be called 'the tero'. After his talk he said to me, sitting beside me at the 'counter' under the screen that had been linked to his laptop, "I understand that no lending can take place to world countries without it being approved by you and Igor."

I now had whispered conversations with Igor about the Constitution and about the Declaration that, with Junyan's help on the laptop, I had already drafted. Also about the contributors. He whispered advice on how to treat the more difficult philosophers. I noticed that he was very good at securing the course of action he wanted while appearing to do nothing. He was too pleasant to appear manipulative.

"Let him talk," he murmured to me of one philosopher I was about to interrupt. He did not seem interested in what the philosopher was saying but thought he would be more likely to have his support at the end if the philosopher had expressed his point of view to the conference. I was chairing the Constitutional Convention but he had an intimate knowledge of all the international philosophers and whispered advice.

During the usual stand-up lunch of pizza and orange juice in the gardens I found myself talking to the President of another Greek party in coalition with Tsipras. He told me, "I will be telling Tsipras about you."

Igor approached and we had a short discussion about his dialectical materialism – he again spoke of being influenced by Engels – and about the beginning of the universe. He said, "There was no beginning and the universe is infinite."

This was Hawking's position.

I said, "I see a Big Bang." Junyan was standing at my elbow and I said, "The *Tao*."

Later she said, "Yes, the universe began from the *Tao*. Igor is too materialistic. Conquests by force don't last, they have to be spiritual to last."

Junyan was a Chinese who gave the impression of looking back to the pre-Communist stages of the Chinese civilization.

During the afternoon there were more contributions from the international philosophers, including one from a Crimean lady on uniform electronic education.

Declaration of the Universal State of the Earth

In due course I circulated my draft Declaration and invited amendments.

At 5 I stopped the proceedings. To a Convention of about fifty I announced that the Declaration had been circulating and had been amended. I read the text of the Declaration for the Universal State of the Earth:

Nicholas Hagger (left) reading the text of the Declaration of the birth of the Universal State of the Earth

Athens, Greece, 7 October 2015

DECLARATION

We, the members of the Constitutional Convention and representatives of global (earth) citizenship, having carefully considered the current tense and hazardous situation on the earth and following UN appeals to foster global citizenship and the perfecting of global leadership, declare the Universal Constitution of the Earth approved on 7 October 2015.

The articles of this Constitution stipulate the order in which the supranational Universal State of the Earth (USE) will be founded.

Henceforth, from 8 October 2015, Citizens of the Earth are to commence activities to create and then establish the appropriate constitutional bodies of supranational USE governance.

We appeal to all 7 billion inhabitants of the earth to join our historic act and follow the UN global citizenship education initiative by means of universal, uniform civic education through upbringing and lifelong learning. We appeal to them to assume global citizenship to secure and ameliorate the life of everyone on the earth, and to protect its biosphere and environment.

This is the only way to save life on earth and preserve it from self-destruction, and to provide peace and progress for humanity on our planet.

On behalf of the participants of the USE Constitutional Convention,

Chairman of the USE Constitutional Convention
Nicholas Hagger

President of the USE and World Philosophical Forum
Igor Kondrashin

Athens City Hall
50, Academia Avenue
Athens
Greece.

I asked if the Declaration was approved and called for a show of hands. Some hands went up. There was a translation into Greek and then many more hands went up.

I had also brought in the Supreme Council of Humanity, the "highest body in the world", of which I was to be Acting Chairman. The Greek priest, Father Zouros, called out in Greek, and was translated into English as saying: "Sometimes a lot of seeds fall on the ground waiting to germinate."

I said, "Cosmic energies will make the seeds grow." And everyone laughed. I signed the text, and then Igor signed.

Now Timi said he wanted to sign the paper. Igor and I conferred. He could not sign the Declaration. At my suggestion we made available a copy of the Declaration for all the international

Nicholas Hagger showing the signed Declaration of the birth of the Universal State of the Earth, with Igor Kondrashin

philosophers and delegates to sign on the back. They all considered it to be a very important document, a descendant of the document that created the United States after the Constitutional Convention chaired by George Washington in 1787.

We were all aware that this was a historic moment. Igor said, "In a few years' time there will be a plaque on the wall outside with all your names on it."

The Declaration with Igor's signature and mine can now be viewed online.[3] The paper signed by the delegates can also be viewed online.[4]

Then Igor gave out certificates and there were photos. He had a word with me. He said, lowering his voice, "I shall nominate you to receive a Gusi Peace Prize in Manila next year. I shall make the Committee aware of your work. You will have to go to Manila to receive it. You can see online what you will have to do."

I did not know that Gusi Peace Prizes had been awarded each year since 2002, and that the Manila-based Gusi Foundation had an international network of nominators who put names through for a Committee to consider. I did not know that in the sifting process many names were rejected. I did not know that some of the nominators were of a very high level, including a prominent member of the Nobel family which funds the Nobel prizes, and that the Gusi awards had been called the Asian equivalent of the Nobel prizes. Eleven Nobel prizes are awarded each year, and between 11 and 16 Gusi prizes are awarded each year for excellence in different disciplines to nominees from all the world's

193 nation-states. I did not know that if my nomination was accepted I would be only the third UK citizen to receive a Gusi award since 2002.

I was not sure whether to take him seriously. I told myself that anyone could be nominated but that being accepted was another matter, and I put the question of a prize out of my mind.

UN to UF

We spilled out into the corridor and talked in an excited hubbub. I had questions from Junyan, who felt there should be a less materialistic, more spiritual Constitution.

I agreed with Junyan that there should be a new Constitution that could be laid before the UN, that would turn the UN into a UF, a United Federation of the World – the word 'federation' indicating and reassuring that in the transitional phase there would still be nation-states. The concept of a 'United Federation' had decoupled supranational authority from the UN General Assembly. The UF would be an interim institution. Only later would there be a truly supranationalist World State.

Junyan said she would help me produce such a Constitution. I said she could have the books I had brought and that I would send her more. Several of my past works had constitutional documents in Appendices. *The Secret Founding of America, The World Government* and *The Dream of Europa* contained the existing constitutional documents for the US, the UN and the EU which would help us draft a new UN Constitution.

Reflection on events

At 7 I slipped away and ate with Ann on the seventh floor of the Poseidon Hotel. George Washington had chaired the Constitutional Convention that brought in the United States of America in 1787, and I had chaired the Constitutional Convention that brought in the USE, a new World State. I could not see Igor ending up with 7.33 billion followers as World-Lord and so there was no question of my succeeding him as World-Lord if I outlived him.

In terms of the old Cold-War thinking, there was a case for re-garding Igor as a 'Dr No' figure trying to rule the world, and for seeing me as a James Bond figure who would sort the situation out. There was also a case for regarding the USE as a Russian-backed ruse to bewilder the West, spread division and dishar-mony and sow confusion. However, following new thinking I discounted such nation-state 'spoiler' views as a supranational-ist World State was necessary if war was to be abolished.

Then I thought of what had happened to me since my visit to St Petersburg. I had gone from 'Special Envoy to the UN' to 'Chairman of the Constitutional Convention', and then to 'Act-ing Chairman of the Supreme Council of Humanity', to 'Co-con-troller of the Earth Bank', and now possibly to 'Gusi Peace Prize Laureate'.

I had sought none of these titles. These things had just hap-pened to me. I thought of Keats' definition of 'negative capabil-ity', "when man is capable of being in uncertainties, Mysteries, doubts, without any irritable reaching after fact and reason". I decided I should just accept that these things had happened – and get on with the perspective I had developed in my writings, that a World State should be adopted as a way forward by the UN General Assembly.

Igor on coach tour
The next day there was a free coach tour for all the international philosophers to Mycenae, Nauplion (or Nauplia, modern Naf-plio) and Epidaurus (modern Epidavros) in the Peloponnese (paid for by Nikolas Bougiouris, General Secretary of ENELPA, Associations of Greeks for Culture and Development). Ann ac-companied me.

We took a taxi to Omonia Square and boarded our coach. I clambered in first and occupied a window-seat near the front and just behind Lidia, expecting Ann to join me. But Igor fol-lowed me and plonked himself firmly down next to me, and Lidia invited Ann to join her in the seat in front.

After the coach set off Igor talked to me about Aristotle's terminology, how Aristotle referred to 'citizens', 'monarchy', 'aristocrats' and *'politeia'*, all of which were good, and not to 'inhabitants', 'tyranny', 'oligarchs' and 'democracy', all of which were bad. In Aristotle's day the 'demos', the people who vote in a democracy, were a mob. He said that John Moustos would create an account in the Earth Bank and buy a yacht for the Supreme Council of Humanity. I was not sure how seriously to take this. He spoke of Citizens of the Earth, which might be the title of the USE's political party. I was clear that a 'federation' is an association of nation-states, and a 'Federation' therefore announces a transitional phase towards a World State.

As we travelled Igor gave me a long account of how he came to be a dialectical materialist. He had a country upbringing in Russia. He did not know his father and took his name from his stepfather. After working in cars and then trade he began a search from 1979 to 1981. He said, "My first book picked up a sentence in Engels' *Dialectics of Nature*: 'All living things in a chain of being obey the same laws of Nature, including humans.'" Although coming from my different perspective, I agreed.

He told me how he got his first pc. "A KGB man showed me his new pc. I said, 'Can you get me one?' He got me one and I didn't know what to do with it." He typed up his first book on it, *Dialectics of Matter: Part 1: Systematic Approach to the Fundamentals of Philosophy*. But then he fell foul of the Soviet committees which had to approve such writings. He eventually had his book published in 1997. He said, "My stance is on classical values: wisdom, morality, reason, responsibility and justice."

Igor said, "I would like you to work with me for one more year, and then write a book about what we have done."

While Igor talked we visited Mycenae and climbed up to the ruined foundations of what I reckoned was the bathroom where Agamemnon was stabbed to death. The last time I made this journey, from a cruise in 2001, I made a short ascent to the citadel with Sir Roger Bannister, who ran the first four-minute mile in 1954.

The coach took us on to Agamemnon's tomb. We went on to

the fortress of Palmidi and we lunched with Igor and Lidia in the open air in Nauplion (modern Nafplio), with a view of the sea. We chatted generally as we shared cheese, chips, smoked salmon, a ham-and-egg club sandwich and cokes.

The coach took us to Tiryns and the theatre of Epidaurus (modern Epidavros), where Paris declaimed a passage in classical Greek that contained ancient Doric words. Igor sat in the President's seat.

Nikolas, who had organised the conference and recorded the speeches, had wanted me to meet Tsipras, and had asked me to write out a potted CV for Tsipras's office. Now he reported that my meeting with Tsipras had been delayed by the Greek negotiations with Germany over Greece's chronic debts. He said that Tsipras could not see me on Friday (the next day), but could probably manage a later date. But we had tickets to fly home on the afternoon of the next day.

Georgian Centre

In the evening we returned to the Georgian Centre. As the international philosophers arrived, Igor took me into the office and on the Georgian Centre's computer found a blog he had written on disarmament. It showed pictures of a succession of events leading to the catastrophe of a nuclear explosion and a cloud that would blot out the sun for decades and create a nuclear winter of minus 50 Centigrade. Slipping back into old Cold-War thinking I half-wondered if Russia was trying to get the West to disarm while retaining nuclear weapons itself, and I told myself I should be wary.

Back in the main room at the Georgian Centre there were speeches, which were double-translated so they could be understood in English, Greek and Russian and filmed for Facebook (and any secret organisations on Facebook that had an interest in the live proceedings). I sat with Igor at an administration table and watched as he gave out certificates and medallions, which he had ordered. He presented me with a medallion of Pallas Athene and Ann with one of a Greek-looking owl. Three

Georgian children danced for us and finally the girl who sang for us the previous Sunday sang the Georgian national anthem.

Dream of a UN-based World State

On my last day in Athens, Friday 9 October, we breakfasted and packed. We vacated our room, left our cases with Reception and wandered over to the Tavern and sat by the sea in the shade. We drank Cola Light and had a light early lunch of feta cheese fried with sesame seed and then yoghurt and honey.

I reviewed the events of the last few days, first as a series of nation-states events with ulterior Cold-War motives and then as a series of supranationalist events that had to be taken at face value.

I wondered if the events could be linked to the earlier appearance of *My Double Life 1* and Nigel West's review – and his saying that the CIA had asked him to read my book. Igor had puzzled me by saying, when I drew attention to the display copies of my books, "I know what is in your books, I do not need to have them now." I wondered if I was caught up in an American plan to get the Russians to disarm or a Russian plan to get the Americans to disarm, and whether the WPF was somehow mixed up in a nation-state's plan to get one side of the East-West split to disarm.

Then I thought, 'I am not going to look for explanations for which there is no evidence. Supranationally, I accept the surface appearance of the events and choose to live in "uncertainties, Mysteries, doubts, without any irritable reaching after fact and reason".'

So I took the events at face value and looked at them from a surface perspective. I had chaired in the founding of a new World State. For this to be significant there would have to be followers. The masses of world citizens who had reached supranationalist consciousness would have to press their leaders to take note and accept what we had done. There could be a new world political party, Citizens of the Earth. Plato wrote of the ideal Republic and the philosopher-king, and the World State I had just chaired into existence was a modern version of his ideal Republic. Humankind now had to sign up to it.

But I had to admit to myself, I could not see this happening. It would take decades for humankind to raise its consciousness to a supranationalist level. A faster way would be to take over an existing institution, give it representational democracy and promote global consciousness from above. Deep down I regarded the USE as a dress rehearsal for the real World State. The formation of the USE had shown that it is possible to found a World State that can rule by consent.

The World State I wanted to see, the real World State, would be an interim institution based on the UN. The UN had always been 'inter-nationalist', 'between nation-states', a place where nation-states deal with nation-states. To be effective it needed to be reformed and replaced by a partly supranational and partly-federal democratic world government that can enforce disarmament and abolish war, poverty, famine and disease.

In its interim form it would be a United Federation of the World. I would now be working to convert the UN General Assembly into a partly-federal lower house, a World Parliamentary Assembly, of 850 elected Representatives and establish an upper house, a World Senate of 92 and a World Commission of 27, drawn from the regions I had set out in *The World Government* (2010). (See Appendix 3.) Such a World State would control oligarchs who have sought to enrich their families from the world's oil and gas, the dynastic families I revealed in *The Syndicate* (2004) – in the past the Rothschild and Rockefeller families. (See Appendix 4.)

I was clear that I now had to address the UN General Assembly to lay before it my scheme of turning it into a lower house of 850 elected Representatives. I would be calling on Ban Ki-moon and the UN General Assembly delegates to reform the UN. Many within the institution would want to preserve the *status quo*, even though the UN had been powerless to stop the Syrian Civil War, and would not want to listen to plans for a reform of the UN.

Nevertheless, addressing the UN General Assembly delegates was the way forward. I would aim to secure a slot to lay before them a new UN Constitution that would turn the UN into a UF, a United Federation, when, with Junyan's help, I had written the new Constitution. That was my way forward: to address the UN.

Soon after 1pm we drove to the airport.

PART TWO

6
Gusi Peace Prize for Literature

As a writer, I have always had an aversion to standing on a platform and being clapped. I saw myself as continuing the tradition and way of life of Wordsworth and Tennyson, who both lived apart from society and wrote long works (*The Prelude* and *Idylls of the King*) and shorter works out of their private inspiration, but also connected themselves to public issues, for example Tennyson's 'The Charge of the Light Brigade' and 'Locksley Hall' (1842), which saw a World State:

> When I dipt into the future, far as human eye could see;
> Saw the Vision of the world, and all the wonder that would
> be....
> Till the war-drum throbbed no longer, and the battle-flags were
> furled
> In the Parliament of man, the Federation of the world.
> There the common sense of most shall hold a fretful realm in
> awe,
> And the kindly earth shall slumber, lapt in universal law.

I shunned the literary world, preferring to live "in harmony with the Universe" (the title of volume 32 in *Life Cycle and Other New Poems 2006–2016*). Perhaps because I lived my life immersed in the production of books I was keen, at the level of tidy housekeeping, to hand over my papers and manuscripts to an archive. As a rule, prizes did not excite me. Many of them were awarded for political reasons rather than for the quality of the works. An award often coincided with the recipient's country undergoing a crucial stage in its development, like Heaney's 1995 Nobel Prize at a time when Northern Ireland's peace process was just beginning. So it was with mixed feelings that on 9 March 2016 I received an email from Igor asking if I would consent to his nominating me for a Gusi Peace Prize. At the time I was immersed in sorting my archive.

Archive of literary works
I had returned from Athens to news on my computer screen that
The Albert Sloman Library within the University of Essex wanted me to send a first *tranche* of my archive of literary works as
soon as possible. Correspondence with the Deputy Librarian,
Nigel Cochrane, established that it would be held on permanent
deposit as a Special Collection, for at least 125 years.

While the documentation was prepared I assembled, labelled
and catalogued an archive of 50 64-litre boxes of my papers and
manuscripts. I catalogued the folders within each box, and started four more boxes to cover the books that would come out in
2016. These boxes would be held back until December 2016. At
the request of the University of Essex I created The Nicholas
Hagger Literary Trust so my trustees could handle requests for
permissions and rights during the coming decades.

I delivered the archive on 22 March 2016. I hired a removal firm
and two strong fellows carried the boxes from the shelves in my upper archive room down two flights of stairs. I followed their loaded
van in convoy to Colchester and presided over the unloading. I was
then taken on a tour of the library and the Special Collections room.
The Special Collections were listed in alphabetical order and I was
intrigued to see that the Hagger archive was only three places away
on the list from the Harsnett Collection: the papers of Archbishop
Harsnett, who founded my school, Chigwell School, in 1629.[1] More
*tranche*s were to follow at the end of 2017 and of 2018.

During the drive back I felt a quiet relief that my papers and
manuscripts had gone to a good home and would be kept at a
constant temperature and be available to researchers who wanted to do research work on my books. My manuscripts were still
held in storage in the boxes they had been in for some while,
but now they were at the University of Essex they took on an
independent life and they felt like grown-up children that had
moved away and were living comfortably. Like a parent I felt
pleased for them.

Asa Briggs had died, aged 94, and his funeral was two days

after my delivery, on 24 March 2016, in Lewes. During the last
year I had communicated with him by emailing his secretary, a
Dutchman, Cornelis Schildt, known as Kees-Jan. He was then
a research student at Sussex University, drafted in to help the
ailing Briggs, and he had spent much of his time in a funded
project, scanning and uploading all Isaac Newton's manuscripts
online. He emailed me details of the funeral, saying he could
not attend as he would be in Holland, and my son Tony drove
me down. Edward Fox gave a theatrical reading from *Ecclesias-
tes*, and his sons gave addresses. I watched his interment by the
churchyard wall, beyond which was a view of the South Downs,
and told his widow, "He urged me to write *My Double Life 1* in
1978. Perhaps he was urging himself to write *Secret Days*."

"Yes," she said, "he wanted to start it then but had no time."

I wrote to Kees-Jan after the funeral. When he learned that
I had just deposited my manuscripts he offered to organise
scans of sample pages with printed text alongside, and incorporate them in a searchable version of my Catalogue. He visited me and chatted with my Dutch PA. He told me he would
be applying the skills he used in his Newton project to my
manuscripts.

I went along with this, and on 22 April 2016 I drove Kees-Jan
to Colchester and, working with the University, we spent a long
day from 8.30am till after 6pm in the old Special Collections
room, which we had to ourselves. Hunting among piles of boxes
I had requested to be in the room I extracted 139 manuscript
pages, which Kees-Jan scanned and numbered. We had to aver-
age three minutes a page.

The operation was successful and, working with the University, by August Kees-Jan had integrated the scans within
the Catalogue so they could be viewed online[2] as tasters of the
manuscripts in the boxes, samples of my 2,000 poems, my 1,200
short stories, my two poetic epics, my five verse plays and over
40 of my books. So, strangely, Asa Briggs' secretary seamlessly
assisted my archive.

News from Manila
On 5 April I received an email confirming my nomination for a
Gusi Peace Prize and saying that the Gusi Committee had asked
me to submit a CV. If I was awarded the prize I would have to
collect it in person in Manila on 23 November 2016, and the Gusi
Committee wanted me to declare that I would be available to be
in Manila on that day.

I reported the development to my two publishers. Although
I had only been nominated for the award, both my publishers
urged me to complete the books I was working on so they could
be out around 23 November. Proofs of *The Secret American Destiny* were sent for me to proofread. Its publisher, Watkins, would
reissue *The Secret Founding of America* at the same time with a
new cover, which I had seen on a wall at a Watkins party I attended in their London office on 16 March 2016.

For O-Books I had been compiling *Life Cycle and Other New
Poems 2006–2016*, my latest 210 poems; and *The First Dazzling
Chill of Winter*, my latest 201 stories. These had to be in by May.
I went to Cornwall by train soon after delivering my archive – I
had returned to Essex from Cornwall to see the delivery through
and was rejoining Ann by the sea – and I wrote the last fifty stories in seven days (25–31 March 2016).

With all this going on I was too busy to devote thought to the
World State. I had been aware of Obama's conciliatory policy of
appeasement to bring first Iran (in January 2016) and then Cuba
(in March 2016) into the diplomatic fold. Obama's policy towards Iran might avoid further interventions in the Middle East
and might improve the conditions that could bring in a World
State, a UF or United Federation – if Middle-Eastern war did not
spread to include regime change in Iran.

Then on 5 May 2016 I received a phone call about 8.30pm. The
voice was very faint and very hard to hear. At first I thought it
was an Ambassador to the Gusi Committee. Then I established
it was the Chairman of the Gusi Committee, "Ambassador Barry Gusi". He told me, "You have been awarded the Gusi Peace
Prize 2016 for Literature." He told me, "You will need to be in

Manila for events on 21, 22 and 23 November. You should arrive in time for 20 November and leave on 25 November."

He recommended that I should fly to Hong Kong and change planes. He told me, "You should pack two business suits and black tie." He said he wanted me to send him a package in July. It should include a video that could be sent to CNN International and used in a PowerPoint presentation, a profile and photos in colour and black and white. We talked for an hour and a half. After half an hour he said (Manila time being seven hours ahead of British Summer Time), "It's 4am here in Manila."

When I put the phone down I was excited. I had been nominated and now I was to receive an award. Igor had told me this would happen, but I had not believed it would happen. I found online that Barry Gusi had founded the Gusi Peace Prizes to continue the philanthropic work of his father Captain Gemeniano Javier Gusi, who had allegedly been a guerrilla against the Japanese occupation of the Philippines during the Second World War, and had then become a politician and championed human rights. I now found online that the Gusi Peace Prizes have been called "the Asian equivalent of the Nobel Prizes", and that eleven receive a Nobel Prize each year, and that at least eleven, and sometimes as many as sixteen, are awarded a Gusi Peace Prize. I found out that the awards are made to people from all countries and disciplines. Ambassador Gusi had confirmed that I was only the third UK citizen to receive a Gusi award since the awards began in 2002, and the first to receive an award for Literature.

From what I saw online the portraits of the Gusi Laureates were on gigantic hoardings in different parts of Manila, and on award day, 23 November, I would have to walk down an aisle beside a Philippine marine in uniform carrying a Union Jack on a long flag-pole. There would be 6,000–7,000 in the vast conference hall. The awards would not be officially announced until the last week of October.

Ambassador Gusi had said, "Outside our private conversations I will always be Ambassador Gusi and you will be Professor Hagger. You should always address me as 'Ambassador Gusi' in person and if you write to me."

Online I found that following questions about his title 'Ambassador' he had issued a statement in 2011 clarifying that the Governor and President of the Senate of the Northern Mariana Islands (a commonwealth of 15 islands in political union with the United States) had appointed him an "honorary ambassador" from 1996 to 1999 to promote tourism while he championed the welfare of Filipinos living in the Pacific island nation, and had not been a diplomatic envoy. This had been confirmed verbally by the President of the Senate.

Since 1999 he had continued to use the title as "once an ambassador, always an ambassador". In addition, in March 2008, through Proclamation No. 1476 which declared that every fourth Wednesday of November should be "Gusi Peace Prize International Friendship Day", the former Philippine President Gloria Macapagal Arroyo had conferred on him the title "ambassador of goodwill".

As the Northern Marianas had an American connection and as Ambassador Gusi left what seems to have been an honorary American position in 1999 and held the first Gusi Peace Prize awarding ceremony soon afterwards in 2002, I half-wondered if there was an American dimension to the awards, and if my American heroes in my two poetic epics (Eisenhower and George W. Bush) and my American trilogy had resonated. But I immediately discounted this view. I had been clear since my nomination that I was the only Western literary author to continue the call for a democratic World State begun after 1945 by Churchill, Truman, Einstein and Eisenhower and followed by Russell, Gandhi, John F. Kennedy and Gorbachev, and that that, along with my setting up of a World State, had triggered my nomination.

I thought of Marvell's 'The Garden':

How vainly men themselves amaze
To win the Palm, the Oke, or Bayes.

66

(The Palm being for victors, the Oak for rulers, the Laurel for poets.) The 17th-century values of the Metaphysical poets still held good, and my poetry looked back to their poetry. But if I was not wholly impressed by prizes, the publishers understandably welcomed them. And soon I was proofreading two more of the four books that would soon be coming out.

During the next three months Ambassador Gusi rang me from time to time, always in the middle of the night Manila time. In one of his phone calls he asked me to send him a box containing a letter of acceptance, a video, a profile, a Union Jack, photos in colour and black and white, publishers' leaflets and, we agreed, some books of mine which might be displayed.

All this took time and planning to assemble. My son Tony came with cameras and made a video and took a series of photos. I arranged for FedEx to collect the box on 25 July and was surprised when FedEx reported that the box had been refused at Ambassador Gusi's end. I established there was a customs charge of around $100, which FedEx had tried to make his Foundation pay. To prevent the box from being returned to England I created an account with FedEx and paid £54.25 for "original VAT" and "original duty", and the box was then redelivered successfully. Ambassador Gusi said to me in a telephone call regarding the Foundation's refusal of the box, "We're a Foundation." I understood him to mean that it was the charitable Foundation's policy not to incur unforeseen costs.

The Foundation's reluctance to pay appeared to confirm my view that it was run through donations on a shoestring, and I accepted there and then that his Foundation should not be presented with unforeseen costs. If Ambassador Gusi was running the Foundation through donations, there was something splendid about the way he had kept going on this basis since 2002, and was now into his fifteenth year. His struggle affirmed the charitable basis of the Foundation and made his efforts on behalf of his Foundation (which took all his days and half his nights, including phone calls at 3am or 4am) seem somewhat noble and even saintly.

7
The UK Referendum on the EU

It is not often that a nation-state takes a decision which deter-mines its direction for decades to come. Edward Heath's deci-sion to take the UK into the European Community on 1 January 1973 was one such decision. During the 1960s the UK had been unable to balance the books. The Conservative Government ran up a balance-of-payments deficit of £800 million and lost the 1964 General Election. Sterling was in crisis from 1964 to 1969. The hope was that by choosing a new European destiny the UK would become more prosperous, and by and large this hap-pened, although some control over its law-making and judicial system was surrendered.

David Cameron's decision to hold a referendum on whether the UK should remain in the EU was another such decision. And it had to be taken against a worsening situation in the Middle East and disquiet at the activities of Russia and China, when the West needed to be reunited.

The UK referendum on the EU was to be held on 23 June 2016, and I had been reflecting on the UK's membership of the EU for some while.

The Dream of Europa
Between mid-December 2014 and mid-January 2015 I had writ-ten *The Dream of Europa*, a masque. It was in the tradition of Ben Jonson's early-17th-century masques and it celebrated sev-enty years of European peace under the EEC, EC and EU. In my 1989 history chart I had predicted that the European civilization would pass into a secular conglomerate, a union that would be-come a United States of Europe. Churchill had called for a Unit-ed States of Europe in a speech to the University of Zurich on 19 September 1946: "We must build a kind of United States of Eu-rope." In the same speech he called for the founding of a Council of Europe: "The first step is to form a Council of Europe."

The European Union had been Churchill's post-war vision,

and having lived in his constituency as a boy and having implemented his Iraq policy of unity between Sunnis, Shiites and Kurds at the University of Baghdad, I had a special loyalty to Europe. This had been reinforced by my speech which was broadcast by the BBC World Service behind the Iron Curtain in 1986, calling for FREE (Freedom for the Republics of Eastern Europe).

The 'dream of the Roman goddess Europa' was that Europe would eventually include 50 states like the USA. The cover showed 50 yellow stars. The tree of European civilization I found in Berlin (see p.24) was in an Appendix. To me, this was the future, and nation-statehood was the past. I had sided with the future which I had foreseen in my history chart, and *The Dream of Europa* expressed this vision of the future which I knew would have had Churchill's approval. In my masque Churchill appeals to the UK Representative not to spoil Europe's celebration of seventy years of European peace.

UK referendum: Leave versus Remain

There had been no need for Cameron to call a referendum. He had announced it on 23 January 2013 to appease his right wing and head off a challenge by UKIP (the United Kingdom Independence Party), and he had expected to be in coalition and to be able to say that the Liberals had vetoed the idea. The Conservatives won the 2015 General Election and he was stuck with his rash strategy.

I had written at least four classical odes from a 'Brexit' perspective, the loss of UK sovereignty, between 1997 and 2005 – my 318 odes were written between 1994 and 2005 – but I was grateful to the EC and later the EU for taking in the Eastern-European nation-states that had been occupied by the USSR and for keeping the peace along with NATO for seventy years. England had regularly been involved in wars with our Continental neighbours for a thousand years, most recently in 1870–1871 (the Franco-Prussian War), 1914 and 1939. But since I was six years old there had been peace in Europe though there had been wars on the fringes of Europe, for example in the Balkans.

I could see three reasons for remaining within the EU.

First, I was aware that Putin wanted to divide the EU as part of his plan to recover Eastern Europe. He had created refugees to pour across the borders of Greece, Croatia, Hungary and Austria, and had succeeded in making Schengen-Area countries affected by refugees reintroduce border controls and in some cases border walls. I did not want a divided Europe. I had appealed to Eastern Europeans to leave the USSR in my speech in the Jubilee Room in the Palace of Westminster in 1986, which was broadcast on the BBC World Service (see p.11), and with great difficulty Eastern Europe had been prised away from the Soviet Empire to join the EU. I did not want all that work to be undone and parts of Eastern Europe to return to Russia.

Secondly, I did not want a divided United Kingdom. I did not want Scotland, Northern Ireland and eventually Wales to seek independence from the union on the grounds that the UK had voted to leave the EU and they wanted to retain their links with Europe. That would result in a Federation of England, Scotland, Northern Ireland and Wales, a decline from stage 43 to stage 46 on my history chart.

Thirdly, most importantly, nearly 44 per cent of British goods and services were sold into the EU's single market in 2015 – UK exports to the EU in 2015 were £220 billion out of total exports of £510 billion – and if the UK were denied that market of £220 billion or had to pay tariffs on that amount which would deter European importers, I could foresee low growth, unemployment, recession, the need to borrow and a mounting deficit. At a business level I could see a problem if we lost, or had to pay tariffs on, nearly half our income. I did not know where we would find £220 billion to replace our EU exports if we left the EU's single market.

The issue as I saw it was quite simply one of progress. Europe is moving forward to a more integrated regional conglomerate, a United States of Europe as forecast on my history chart. As we have just seen, I believed it was *en route* to collecting together 50 states that could be handed on to a coming World State. Would the UK move forward with it, or go backwards into nation-statehood, isolationism, Little Englandism and inevitable loss of world influence? I believed that the intelligence services of the UK, France, Germany and other EU nation-states needed to work together in combination to have the best chance of preventing IS from developing a radioactive 'dirty bomb' and letting it off in Europe or the US.

Russia wanted the Soviet territories back and was threatening seventy years of peace in Europe. The Russian invasions of Georgia and the Crimea and involvement in Eastern Ukraine – and the relentless Russian bombing of Syria that had contributed to the flow of the refugees into Europe that had undermined the Schengen Area – should not be allowed to escalate into an invasion of Estonia, as NATO feared.

I saw the nation-state as a transient, not a final form. There had once been ancient Greek and medieval city-states. The city-state was transient. The tribe had once been paramount (the Iceni in Boudicca's time), and is still important in the Islamic world. The tribe, too, is transient. The nation-state had evolved from city-states and tribalism, and the region (in Europe's case, the EU) has evolved from nation-states. The nation-state is also transient and is being superseded in our time by regions. Nation-states belong to an old order that has failed to keep the peace, and regions belong to the future, to a new order that can collect nation-states together and pass into a World State.

The UK referendum was a battle between Leave and Remain, between the backward-looking and forward-looking. Leave wanted control of borders and immigrants to strengthen the UK's nation-state and sovereignty, and it wanted to reject the Lisbon Treaty which it thought had undermined the sovereignty of the UK Parliament. Remain wanted the British economic success to continue. Since 1973 the UK's GDP had grown faster than the US's, thanks to its membership of the single market, and the UK economy was now the fifth-largest in the world with 2 million new jobs – which is why so many immigrants wanted to enter the UK. Leaving the single market would mean slower growth and more borrowing, which might discourage immigrants but could be expected to bring a lower standard of living to the British people.

There was a shock result on 23 June 2016. The British people voted to leave by 51.9 per cent to 48.1 per cent. The 'Brexit' decision caused immediate uncertainty. The Prime Minister resigned and the Leave leaders all failed to succeed him. The Conservatives pulled themselves together under the new Prime Minister Theresa May, who had voted Remain. The Labour Opposition was thrown into turmoil, and 172 Labour MPs rejected their leader Jeremy Corbyn's leadership. There was a lengthy leadership challenge.

Sterling fell 16 per cent against the dollar to £1/$1.31 and 18 per cent against the euro to £1/€1.18.[1] Over the year against the dollar sterling fell 19 per cent from 67.86p/$1 to 80.85p/$1; an effective devaluation which made foreign holidays more expensive but made exports cheaper. Some $2.1 trillion were wiped off shares. By January 2017 sterling had slid further to £1/$1.2160 and £1/€1.15. It was forecast by the Institute for Fiscal Studies that a slowing in growth would require the Treasury to undertake further borrowings of between £20 billion and £40 billion in 2019–2020, wiping out any planned surplus.[2]

Revival of UK's lost past and further decline
On my history chart stage 45 is when the "conglomerate causes yearning for and revival of lost past of civilization and revival of cultural purity". This was the feeling behind 'Brexit'.

Brexit represents a withdrawal from the union of stage 43 and the beginning of a federation in stage 46. It is a further stage in the process of decline. The EU remains in stage 43, the UK was on the verge of declining from stage 43 to stage 45 on my chart.

UK's nation-state isolationism
In July I turned back to the schools. I attended four prize days in four days. The schools were stable but the country's social stability had weakened.

It seemed that the UK electorate had chosen nation-state isolationism and possibly the break-up of the UK, with Scotland
and Northern Ireland immediately wanting to remain in the EU.
The referendum was only advisory, but the May Government
chose to regard it as binding. At first it was not clear when Article 50 of the Treaty of Lisbon (a formal request to leave the
EU) would be invoked, to begin the two-year leaving process, or
what Brexit would mean as there had to be a negotiation with
Europe. It was eventually announced that Article 50 would be
invoked before the end of March 2017, by which time the new
'Department for Exiting the EU' and 'Department for International Trade' would be properly staffed and briefed and ready,
and that the UK would not leave the EU until around 1 April
2019.

In August 2016 the UK Treasury pledged to replace lost EU
funding for farming, scientists, universities and local authorities
until May 2020 (election year), which, with Brexit due in April
2019, might only be in place for just under a year. It was soon
clear that after the funding for farming, scientists, universities
and local authorities there would be no funds left to give £350
million per week to the National Health Service (a day's extra
funding per week), a promise blazoned on the outside of the
Leave Campaign's double-decker bus.

In due course it became clear that the UK would withdraw
from the single market and perhaps the Customs Union while
asking for a no-tariffs deal with the EU, and would seek free-
trade deals outside Europe (to take effect after 2019), so that
immigration controls could be put in place and the UK could
break free from the European Court of Justice. To exit the EU
the UK could be forced to pay up to €100 billion in budget and
pension commitments, loan guarantees and spending on UK-
based projects, and just talking about trade deals before 2019 to
countries in negotiations with the EU could result in additional
hefty fines.

The final deal would be put to the House of Commons and
the House of Lords. MPs could shape the deal the Prime Minis-

ter wanted to seek and might now have the power to overturn Brexit. If they rejected it, then presumably the UK would continue to be a member of the EU in some form. However, it was understood there would be a snap election in 2019 if the deal was voted down (after the election called in 2017). For procedural reasons would there be a Universalist reconciliation of opposites, +A + –A = 0, Remain + Brexit = 0, a compromise?

(In October 2016 a legal challenge to Brexit had come to court and three High Court judges ruled that the Prime Minister did not have the power to invoke Article 50 unless Parliament's MPs voted first. The Government had to get a one-line bill through Parliament. The Prime Minister had been prepared to use royal prerogative, delegated power from the Queen as Head of State. The judges ruled that the Referendum was not legally binding and so Parliament had to vote. The Government appealed to the Supreme Court, and lost. The judges ruled that the making and unmaking of treaties is a matter of royal prerogative, but under section 2 of the European Communities Act 1972 the Government cannot use prerogative powers to change domestic law. They also ruled that devolution legislation did not require the UK to remain a member of the EU and that the devolved administrations of Scotland, Wales and Northern Ireland therefore had no veto over the UK's decision to withdraw from the EU.)

The deal with the EU was fraught with difficulty. The EU had ruled out 'cherry-picking' and 'having your cake and eating it' (leaving the single market and having no tariffs), and the EU's Visegrad group of Slovakia, Hungary, Poland and the Czech Republic threatened to veto any European deal that did not guarantee their citizens the right to work in the UK through freedom of movement. Canada's seven-year-long negotiations to reach a deal with the EU were torpedoed by a local council of Walloons in Belgium, and though this veto was reversed and the deal was signed, a UK deal with Europe could similarly be torpedoed by a small minority. The UK had only 15 trade negotiators in the Foreign Office, but needed 300 for its trade negotiations with the EU.

It stood to reason that the UK's deal with the EU would have to be inferior to the deal the EU members had, otherwise all the members would want to leave and have the same terms. It seemed unrealistic and illusory to believe otherwise. Withdrawing from the single market while expecting to continue tariff-free trading with the EU without making the payments to the EU required by the rules smacked of having it both ways, and of living in a fool's paradise.

In January 2017 the UK Ambassador to the EU, who was to be the UK's chief negotiator for a deal, resigned, accusing the Government of "muddled thinking", and there were reports that the UK Government was in chaos over Brexit. Boris Johnson had wrongly stated that freedom of movement was not in the Treaty of Rome (1957), but it is clearly stated in Article 3(c), which refers to "the abolition, as between Member States, of obstacles to freedom of movement for persons, services and capital".[3]

Europe looked to be going forward. The leaders of Germany, France and Italy meeting on Ventotene, the island off the coast of Naples where Altiero Spinelli wrote his manifesto for a united Europe, pledged there would now be common defence (a European army), security and economic growth in a continent without borders that was clearly moving towards a United States of Europe.

Islamic State and 'dirty bomb', and a Third World War
Islamic State's threat to Europe had escalated and 'Brexit' could not have come at a more difficult security time. It was reported that in 2014 IS had seized a high-tech laboratory in Mosul, Iraq and had used it to build bombs and chemical weapons; and that it had produced 40 kgs of uranium compounds.[4] Barely targeted by US air strikes, IS had provided jihadists with radioactive material. IS militants claimed to have developed a crude nuclear weapon using materials seized from Mosul University. A British extremist boasted of the damage a radioactive 'dirty bomb' would do if detonated in Iraq.

There were reports[5] (as we saw on p.xvi) that IS was attempting to develop a radioactive 'dirty bomb' that could be let off in a Western capital such as London, Paris, Brussels or Berlin, perhaps borne by a drone.[6] The two Brussels bombers who exploded bombs at Brussels' Zaventem airport on 22 March 2016 were stalking a Belgian nuclear scientist with a view to kidnapping him and forcing him to hand over radioactive material that could be turned into a 'dirty bomb'.[7]

The explosion of a nuclear bomb is millions of times more powerful than that of a dirty bomb. The radiation cloud from a nuclear bomb could spread tens to hundreds of square miles. The radiation from a 'dirty bomb' could spread a few blocks or miles.[8] A radioactive 'dirty bomb', assisted by a south-westerly wind, would have a much more limited effect but would still deliver a disastrous blow to the civilization where it was set off (the North-American or European civilization). Even so, if such a bomb were exploded in London (an eventuality for which the SAS have been preparing),[9] radioactive material released into the atmosphere and blown by south-westerly winds could contaminate swathes of south-east England.

The worst nightmare for Londoners is that a full nuclear explosion could make hundreds of square miles in south-east England uninhabitable for decades. Millions of south-eastern Britons would become refugees, heading where? To northern England? To the Continent? Would millions of British refugees be admitted to the EU following the British decision to leave the EU in the 2016 UK referendum?

A 'dirty bomb' would not lead to such extreme nuclear consequences. Even so President Obama was so concerned by the situation that he summoned fifty delegates of Western governments to attend a summit in Washington to consider a collective response from 31 March to 1 April 2016. The British Prime Minister David Cameron attended. Obama apparently asked the delegates what they would do if a drone-borne 'dirty bomb' exploded in their territory.[10] What plan did they have? I reflected that is the 21st-century nightmare: one bang and we are all refugees from our homeland for a while.

I reflected on 'Caliph' Abu Bakr al-Baghdadi, who was allegedly overseeing this Western nightmare. He was born Ibrahim
Awwad Ibrahim Ali Muhammad al-Badri al-Samarrai. On 21
April 2015 it was announced that he had been critically wounded in an American air strike near al-Ba'aj on 18 March 2015. He
had allegedly suffered spinal damage caused by shrapnel, and
was allegedly no longer in charge. However, it was confirmed
that he was still actively involved in December 2016. He had apparently believed in 2014 that making Western cities radioactive
had Allah's blessing.

When I lectured at the University of Baghdad from 1961 to
1962, through carefully chosen poems and novels within English
Literature I taught my students civilised Western values, to appreciate emotional nuances and to eschew violence. I had an impact, for students in one of my classes of mixed Sunnis, Shiites
and Kurds regularly discussed what I taught them in the eve-
nings and came to me with questions the next day. The legacy I
left Baghdad from my teaching there had evidently evaporated
before al-Baghdadi became a student at the University of Baghdad in the 1990s.

There was an internet rumour, wrongly attributed to the US

Nicholas Hagger with some of his students in the college cafeteria at the University of Baghdad, Iraq, in October 1961

whistle-blower and defector Edward Snowden, that al-Baghdadi had Jewish parents, that he was an actor, Shimon (or Simon) Elliot. The internet showed a photo of him in a room with Senator McCain in 2007, when McCain was a Presidential candidate.[11] At this time al-Baghdadi was with al-Qaeda in Iraq and the photo purports to show McCain meeting al-Qaeda in Iraq. Was the photo genuine? Was the leader of IS an Israeli agent? Or was the photo a doctored smear against al-Baghdadi? It seemed likely that it was a smear as he had been born Ibrahim Awwad Ibrahim Ali Muhammad al-Badri al-Samarrai.

To mark the 25th anniversary of his release, the former hostage Terry Waite added a final chapter to his republished autobiography reflecting on the current state of the Middle East, where he believed "a Third World War has already started".[12] If a Third World War involving the US and Russia was already in progress in the Middle East, were there signs that the Third World War was about to spread to Europe?

Russia 'mobilising for war' in Europe
In August 2016, following an attempted *coup*, Turkey (once the power behind the Ottoman Empire which ruled throughout the Middle East and North Africa) signed a defence agreement with Russia and joined forces to fight Islamic State in Syria. IS had already lost its Libyan stronghold in Sirte, and looked on the way to defeat. But Turkey's support for Russia would now assist the survival of Assad and of Russian influence in the Middle East, which would now be extended up into a NATO country, Turkey, a would-be member of the EU.

Russia had expanded its influence and the US nuclear base at Incirlik in Turkey, where US nuclear bombs were stored, now looked under threat. Although the US nuclear bombs required electronic codes to be activated, if Turkey were to leave NATO these nuclear weapons would have to be removed. Coming at a time when there seemed to be a new Cold War and Russia had just placed nuclear weapons in its exclave of Kaliningrad, this would be seen as a set-back to American strategy in the Middle

East.

Russia's decision to attack IS in air strikes had extended its influence throughout the Middle East. In fact, Russia's air activity was directed more against the rebels fighting Assad than the IS. As Russia had allied with Turkey against IS it had Turkish support for its drive against the rebels. A US-Russian plan for a cease-fire in September 2016 presented Russia on an equal footing with the US, which enhanced its influence in the Middle East. Russia was sending out a message that it could solve the Syrian problem without American help.

Despite its activity in the Middle East Russia was still active in Europe and the Russian threat to Europe escalated. From 7 to 17 June 2016 a NATO exercise involving 31,000 troops from 24 nations, including airborne troops, had been held on the Polish border.[13]

According to a Canadian intelligence report, the Russian military was modernising itself in preparation for a war for Eastern Europe. Despite spending one tenth on military expenditure of what NATO spends and having an economy one-twentieth the size of the American economy and on a par with Italy, Putin was building a 'super army' that could annex Eastern Europe, bringing the former Soviet states back into the fold of a 'Greater Russia'.

Reports of a Russian 'super army' had an effect on NATO, and a combined NATO force was assembled to protect Eastern Europe from Russia's grasp. The UK was asked by NATO to contribute troops to a NATO 'super army' of 4,000 troops based in Poland.

The Canadian report said of Russia, "The state is mobilising for war." The war would be a large-scale conflict, and according to the report Putin was readying Russia for a Third World War against NATO's 'super army'.[14]

Russia had 330,000 troops on its border with Eastern Europe out of an army of 800,000 troops and a military force comparable with that of France (if nuclear weapons are discounted). Russia had accused Washington of having a NATO-operated missile shield in Europe to enable it to launch a first-strike nuclear attack on Russia or China. Forty million in Russia's major cities were now receiving training in sheltering underground from an impending nuclear attack. Russia was trying to reshape the UN-NATO system and the structure of global security to restore the Russian empire.

In October 2016 Gorbachev told the State news agency RIA Novosti, "The world has reached a dangerous point."[15] He said, "We need to renew dialogue."

It was now urgent that Europe should unite against threats from across its borders. At a summit in Bratislava in September 2016 (to which the UK was not invited) the European Commission circulated a document heralding proposals for "a common military force", an EU army, which should be agreed by June 2017. This was seen by the UK as an unwelcome rival to NATO, but clearly a United States of Europe *should* have its own army with Russia pressing on its borders.

It was equally urgent that a long-term strategy should head off impending war. Beyond the nation-state (that the UK Brexiteers wanted to strengthen) and the regional union (that the UK Remainers wanted to strengthen) is the World State, which could be supported by ex-Remainers as it offers an elected region covering the whole world. The forward vision is now the World State.

China and a constitution for a UF and reformed UN

I now had a finished Constitution for a UF, a United Federation. My assistant, the Chinese lawyer Junyan Hé, had consulted all the constitutional documents I had sent her and many authorities, and had sent through draft paragraphs. I had amended both content and language and had assembled a document that could be shown to the delegates of the UN General Assembly.

I wondered if China would support my proposed conversion of the UN into a UF. The Chinese civilization is still in stage 43, the conglomerate and union state, on my history chart, but some commentators have said that there appears to be a historic shift in economic and geopolitical power that is bringing a 500-year period of Western dominance to an end – a shift to the East, to Asia, and principally to China.

Chinese maps already claim the entire South China Sea, where China has implemented an island-building program in the vicinity of the Spratly Islands, and China's military spending has increased by 12 per cent each year for a generation and could exceed America's by 2023. China was looking to establish military bases in strategic parts of the world, and has joint naval exercises with Putin's Russian ships in the East China Sea and there is a pipeline deal for China to receive gas from Siberia. China has launched the Asian Infrastructure Investment Bank (AIIB) with $100-billion capital for the building of infrastructure in the Asian-Pacific region.

US intelligence estimates that by 2030 Asia will have surpassed North America *and* Europe in population, GDP and military spending (a trend that the US-UK special relationship between Trump and May is seeking to challenge), and by then zero growth, falling military spending and an increased flow of migrants on present trends may make Europe a bystander to global events.

In 2014 the IMF reported that in purchasing power China has replaced the US as the world's largest economy – the US having held this position since 1871, when it replaced the UK – and China is already the world's largest manufacturer and exporter, and the world's largest market for vehicles, smartphones and oil. China is now the dominant economic power in Africa.[16] I recall single-handedly trying to neutralise Chinese power in Tanzania in 1972 by setting up a British loan to Tanzania to counterbalance Chinese influence,[17] and in the last 45 years China has spread its economic influence throughout Africa.

But my history chart showed that China would pass into a stage 46 federation sometime between 2020 and 2050,[18] possibly as a result of a coming upheaval and demand for regional freedom, a converse movement to that of the unifying Cultural Revolution I discovered in March 1966. Then I had gone to Peking

(Beijing) University expecting to see 40,000 students and only saw ten. I had found a 5th-year student who told me the 3rd- and 4th-year students had all been forcibly sent out to the countryside to learn from the peasants in what I was later told by the Vice-President of the University, Professor Wang, was 'socialist re-education', and this 5th-year student had been excused from having to go with them as he had a medical certificate.[19] I had seen from my own direct experience that a movement can suddenly arise in China and take everyone by surprise.

I reflected that the Chinese civilization is still in stage 43 and the North-American civilization in stage 15, and that much can change between now and 2030. There may be an upheaval that turns China into a stage-46 federation before then. But as American and West-European power appear to fade – and the appearance may be a temporary phenomenon – China may be able to take the lead in shaping a new world order. Despite its handicaps – a one-party system and democratic shortfall, lack of transparency and disregard for human rights, religious freedoms and international legal norms in the South China Sea – China may be able to help set up a system of regional representation in a lower-house World Parliamentary Assembly. A World State backed by the US and supported by China would be immensely beneficial to humankind.

A message from Ban Ki-moon
I had written to Ban Ki-moon and mentioned my Gusi award, which I had been told would not be announced until the last week of October. On 8 June – before the referendum vote – I had received an email from UN Secretary-General Ban Ki-moon's Scheduling Office. Benjamin Knight said that he was writing on behalf of Mr Chang Wook-jin, Chief of the Scheduling Unit of the Executive Office of the Secretary-General, who regretted that Ban Ki-moon would be unable to attend the Peace Prize ceremony in Manila on 23 November 2016 "in view of prior commitments and pressing demands already on his schedule on the said date". Chang Wook-jin was Ban Ki-moon's Special Assis-

tant, and the email was copied to seven senior officials in the Scheduling Office.

I immediately replied to Benjamin Knight requesting to visit Ban Ki-moon in July to show him my draft Constitution for a United Federation; to address the UN General Assembly on a World State; and to represent the UN as a Special Envoy to explain the World State to world leaders including President Obama and President Putin. I received a reply within half an hour saying that my email had been passed to the appropriate official, but then I heard nothing. And July slid into August, and then September.

I had challenged the UN with my reforming Constitution and understood that the UN might not want to hear the details. The UN might resist all fundamental reform. I now awaited an invitation to visit the UN to address the delegates of the UN General Assembly and explain my step-by-step approach to founding a UN-based World State, its structure and funding. (See Appendix 3.) I would show them a diagram of the structure of a coming World State (see Appendix 4) and the new Constitution for a United Federation. In short, I awaited an invitation to set out my plan for 'peace for our time'.

8

Athens Again: United Federation of the World and Speedy Action on Syria

I had been brought up to think of Russia as an aggressive nation-state that was dominated by the KGB, which after 1991 had partly morphed into the SVR. Wariness of the KGB or the SVR was nation-state thinking. But I had gone beyond that into supranational thinking so nation-state matters no longer concerned me at a personal level. I was beyond nation-states and their cloak-and-dagger spying activities and wars. I did not know the ins and outs and did not want to know. I was holding up a better way for humankind to conduct itself than through competing, warring nation-states, and so who was or was not in the KGB or SVR seemed as insignificant from the supranationalistic perspective as the movements of tiny people seen from a sky-high drone.

Syria under the Third World War

I had been in contact with Igor Kondrashin from time to time throughout the summer. I had emailed him that I would be coming to the Athens Conference in October, the Seventh Annual Conference of the World Philosophical Forum (WPF), and he had told me I would be chairing the embryonic Universal State of the Earth's "highest body", The Supreme Council of Humanity (SCH). He asked me for a paper for the WPF's website. He wanted my view of the current situation on the earth. I sent him 'Urgent Global Problems, Inactive Nation-States and Decisive Supranationalism' which said that the war in the Middle East looked like becoming "a proxy Third World War, with the US and Russia both involved in bombing different factions on opposite sides" (see Appendix 6).

The war in Syria had escalated. Following the 'Arab Spring' which implemented Zbigniew Brzezinski's Project for a New American Century (based on a book he published in 1997) there had been revolutions in Tunisia, Libya and Egypt. Gaddafi and Mubarak had fallen, and now the wave of 'liberation' had reached Syria. President Assad, who had inherited the country from his father, had stood firm and invited in the Russians, regarding the 'liberating Arab-Spring' rebels as terrorists. With Russian help he had retained a coastal strip of Syria, the interior having been abandoned to rebels, to Islamic State and to the Kurds. The focus had moved to east Aleppo, where 11,000 US-backed rebel soldiers were living among the civilian population of 275,000 (according to estimates in the British press) and were being besieged by the Syrian army, barrel-bombed by Syrian planes and bunker-busting-missiled by Russian planes. There had been horrifying and seemingly deliberate bombings of hospitals and schools, which could be regarded as war crimes.

Peace negotiations based on a Kerry-Lavrov plan for a cease-fire had taken place in early September 2016 but had broken down when Americans bombed the Syrian army, killing 62 soldiers, and Russian planes allegedly bombed a hospital. Putin was challenging America's international hegemony, wanting to recover the territories Gorbachev lost, and Russia and the US seemed to be heading for a new Cold War. It looked as if a Third World War had already started in Syria.

Conference registration
It was against this background of US-Russian hostility that I returned to Athens with Ann on Monday 3 October 2016 for the Seventh "Dialectical Symposium". We were up at 4.20am and again flew from Stansted. While waiting to board, sitting beyond Departures I wrote a story, 'Barley-Risotto', about my visit to Oxford for a reunion the previous Saturday, when the Provost of Worcester College Jonathan Bate told me he had been reading my poems. On the plane we sat in the same seats as in 2015 (2E and 2F).

We landed at 2.20, having put our watches on two hours, and took a taxi to the Poseidon Hotel and checked in to the same room we stayed in during our visit in 2015 (room 304). Leaving Ann to unpack, and wearing a light-weight suit and a blue open-necked shirt, I rejoined the taxi and drove past the Temple of Zeus, columns half-hidden behind trees, to the City of Athens Cultural and Youth Centre to register in the same room where I registered in 2015.

Igor, in a jacket and tie, greeted me warmly with a bear-hug and Lidia embraced me. Not many others were present, but I was introduced to a Canadian, Ricaardoe Di Done, who had flown in from Montreal, and to Hendrik Hol, a youngish Dutch photographer with long hair who was talking to Junyan.

We all stood and talked. Hendrik said he had written a book on Greece, and that he had found out that the amount Greece spent on buying arms from Germany was equivalent to Greece's total indebtedness.

Since the Turkish invasion of Cyprus in 1974 Greece had

spent at least €216 billion on armaments, and nearly 15 per cent of Germany's total arms exports were made to Greece.[1] Germany had charged interest on its loans. Greece had been sunk by disastrous arms purchases. I pointed out that when Germany's foreign-owed debt was 25 per cent of its national income after the war the UK had convened a London conference in 1953 and had forgiven Germany half its debt in what became known as the London Agreement on German External Debts.[2] I said, "Germany now needs to remember the help it had from the UK."

I said nation-states lead to economic bullying and war, and mentioned Plato's Republic as an ideal World State. Junyan said, "Plato's Republic has become a Universal Republic," which I thought very true.

I talked with Igor about the coming week. He said, "Please speak your greetings and message tomorrow, and on Wednesday please speak before the Supreme Council of Humanity." I found a taxi outside the City of Athens Cultural and Youth Centre and returned to the Poseidon Hotel.

I changed and Ann and I crossed the road and ate at The Place, the Hotel's restaurant on the beach (which had been called The Tavern the previous year), with the Aegean Sea near our table. We had moussaka and then yoghurt, honey and walnuts as the sun set and the crescent moon rose in the clear twilight and early dark. Then we returned to our room and, focusing on the international situation, I worked on my two conference addresses.

Conference: day 1, the Universal State of the Earth
The next morning I got up at 7.15, had breakfast and in a white shirt, tie and suit took a taxi at 9 back to the City of Athens Cultural and Youth Centre, past the Temple of Zeus. Following the printed agenda I went up to the room where I registered and found the door locked. I sat in a comfortable chair in the corridor and almost immediately Hendrik joined me. We talked effortlessly for about twenty minutes about globalism and a World State, and, realising we must be in the wrong place, went downstairs to the theatre where I had brought in the Universal

State of the Earth.

Lidia was sitting at a table by the door. She greeted me with a warm hug, and I left two of my books and some leaflets for her to guard on the table.

Lidia said, "I looked you up on the internet last night. There are many things about you in Russian. One person says, 'Nicholas Hagger is a genius.' Another says, 'Nicholas Hagger is very romantic.'" (Or did she mean 'Romantic'?) I smiled and pulled an amused slightly-disbelieving, modest face.

I was greeted warmly by Paris Katsivelos, Jeffrey Levett and others I had met last year, who were sitting or standing chatting in groups.

Igor was sitting by the microphone, and after I had greeted him he said, "Today we need interpreters up here so please sit in one of the seats. Tomorrow you will be up here, chairing the Supreme Council of Humanity." Then he said, "Not many are here. Sir James Mancham, your Acting Chairman for tomorrow, has had a stroke and cannot do any chairing. He may not come at all." He was the First President of the Seychelles from 1976 to 1977, when he was overthrown in a *coup*. Igor said the Malaysian delegation had accepted but not arrived, and that the Philippine delegation had left applying for their 45-day visas too late; their visas were for two weeks after the conference.

Igor told me that Nikolas Bougiouris had "separated" and gone off on his own. His boss Ionnis Galanis was now doing the recording and the video of the conference. I spoke with Ionnis, who had not much English and spoke through an interpreter he found. He immediately said, "You need to see Tsipras" (the Greek Prime Minister Alexis Tsipras), "I will arrange it. Someone will come this afternoon who will do that."

The theme of the Symposium was "from diversity of beliefs to human unity". As it was a Symposium in the tradition of Plato's *Symposium* everyone present was called on to speak in order of seniority, those who had been linked to the WPF a long while having precedence over more recent attenders.

There were between twenty and thirty present, and Paris Katsivelos and Jeffrey (who had letters on his head like a headband from Ionnis's projector) interpreted into and from Greek. The Deputy Mayor spoke, a young Greek in jeans with long hair. He had authorised our use of the theatre for free. A Russian lady, Larisa Zelentsova, interpreted into English for the Russian ecologist Svetlana Chumakova-Izmaylovskaya.

Paris himself spoke, invoking Mnemosyne (Remembrance), the Mother of the Muses, reciting his Greek words against a film of himself reciting the same words. There was a flame-lighting ceremony in the film and Paris lit a candle held in a metallic hand. Igor said, "This is the Flame of Reason." But as Paris knew, it was the Light which is beyond Reason. Jeffrey Levett said, "Man is an endangered species, like the elephants."

Perhaps because I was Chairman of the Supreme Council of Humanity the next day and therefore deemed one of the organisers, I was called to speak last, shortly before lunch. In my address I raised the way forward. I indirectly placed my contacts with the UN alongside the USE and began an appeal for something to happen immediately, regardless of the membership of the USE.

My speech was as follows:

Greetings from the United Kingdom. I am very pleased to see so many familiar faces from last year when after the Constitutional Convention we issued the Declaration that brought in the USE. It made a statement about supranationalism and global citizenship education that looks back to Plato's *Republic* and of course Aristotle's *politeia*. The events during the last year – in Syria and the massive increase in refugees – show that the world is crying out for a global, Universalist solution to its problems. Yet at the UN on 20 September (two weeks ago) we heard nothing of a supranationalist nature, just leaders of nation-states talking from the perspective of their own national interest and borders, and Ban Ki-moon powerless to control events in Syria. The Western world is looking backwards rather than forwards, and supranationalism and the USE Constitution are ignored amid the clamour of populism.

Last year we planned to take the first-ever supranationalist delegation to the UN. You will recall that our letter to Ban Ki-moon identified seven goals that a supranational authority could work for. They are:

- bringing peace between nation-states, and disarmament;
- sharing natural resources and energy so that all humankind can have a raised standard of living;
- solving environmental problems such as global warming, which seem to be beyond self-interested nation-states;
- ending disease;
- ending famine;
- solving the world's financial crisis; and
- redistributing wealth to eliminate poverty.

All of these are better solved by a supranational authority than by nation-states defending their borders.

I have repeatedly reminded the UN about a supranationalist delegation and had a message from Ban Ki-moon's Special Adviser, but an invitation to address the General Assembly is still being considered and Ban Ki-moon leaves office at the end of December. As a general rule institutions don't like to be reformed, they prefer the status quo. And although Ban Ki-moon has spoken out for global citizenship education he may not want the system to change while he is in office so he can hand the status quo over to his successor. We may soon be writing another letter to Ban Ki-moon's successor.

Tomorrow there will be the first meeting of the Supreme Council of Humanity, which was created at the same time as the USE. This is an important development, and as Chairman I will keep you informed. You can find the seven goals and some of the things I have to say in my paper which is on the WPF website, 'Urgent Global Problems, Inactive Nation-States and Decisive Supranationalism'. I have one general question I would like to raise now.

The question for us Universalists and supranationalists is, how can we speed up the civic education of the masses so there can be a supranationalist *politeia* sooner rather than later? Should we just jog along as we are and wait for our membership to increase, which may take decades? Ideally there would be global publicity about the USE, but during the last year in the West the surge of nation-state populism – representing the wishes of the *demos* – has gone in the opposite direction and thrown up Trump in the US and Brexit in the UK and a similar outlook in many other European countries. Trying to get publicity for supranationalism is like swimming against the tide. In this prevailing climate should we limit our aim for now, to get supranationalism established?

In my books since *The World Government*, which came out in 2010, I have called for an interim phase, for a world federation of nation-states based on a reformed UN which can eventually become a supranationalist World State. I have called for the UN General Assembly to be turned into a lower house of a world government with 850 Representatives. Nation-states would survive, and once the new system has been established it could be turned into a fully-fledged World State. Raising the supranationalist awareness of the masses could then be encouraged – insisted on – from above during this interim time rather than left to grow by word of mouth as now. I said last year I am leaving my books to one side to make common cause with the WPF and I am still doing that now, but I can't help wondering if we can speed things up by encouraging a partly-federal World Federation that can later be assimilated into a supranationalist World State.

Talking of my books, I have three more literary works coming out in November and another book being reissued. I've brought *The New Philosophy of Universalism* and *The World Government* for display. Please ask if you would like to have a look. There is a leaflet about my most recent book, *The Secret American Destiny* (out in November). I was asked to present the seven disciplines of Universalism in terms of what America can do in the future, and in this book I am saying that America's secret destiny is to help create a universal state. It's like taking our supranationalist, Universalist message to the UN, only taking it to the US public.

No arrangements had been made for lunch. Two hours were set aside for us to find something to eat on our own. Together with others I trooped to a restaurant two doors away and sat with Hendrik. Junyan came and sat opposite us, and Lidia was on the next table, but not Igor, who was working on his laptop. We discussed the international situation and Syria.

Hendrik said, "Syria is part of the Project for a New American Century, PNAC, Brzezinski's plan."

I knew of Zbigniew Brzezinski's *The Grand Chessboard* (1997), which said that to maintain global supremacy the US needed to gain control of Central Asia and its vast petroleum reserves, and that a new Pearl Harbor would sway the US public to support the US's imperial effort to establish a global *Pax Americana* (the US dream that revived following the collapse of the Soviet Union). The "new Pearl Harbor" was 9/11.

Hendrik continued, "The American plan was to take out Afghanistan, Iraq, Lebanon, Syria, Iran, Russia and China. They've already done Russia – that was the Berlin Wall coming down – but Putin got it back. China's been postponed for a while."

I said, "China will become a federation, like Russia."

At this Junyan was thoughtful. Then she said, "My name, Hé, is also Han, one of the seven kingdoms or Warring States in the 3rd century BC. The Han was the first to be absorbed by the Qin state which created 'China'. I have been into my family records, some written and some oral. We can trace our family back to 230BC."

"So you are from a former royal family," I said. "You're an aristocrat."

"Yes," she said.

"Your family would know about being in a federation, having run one of the seven kingdoms and joined Qin."

"Yes."

I saw Junyan as a pre-Communist looking towards a China not long after the time of Confucius and Lao-Tze that would enshrine the spiritual royal values her family used to embody.

Later I asked her if she had family or contacts in China who could advance our Constitution for a new United Federation. She said, "I am on my own in Greece and have no family, but I have contacts with the government in China who may be able to help."

Back in the theatre I spoke to Prof. Philippos Nicolopoulos, who had just arrived, tall, bald and bearded. He said in English, "I remember you from last year. I couldn't get you to Tsipras because he was so busy, I will try again this year. I can't influence him. I know him, but I can't influence him. It's hard to make an appointment. You should write him a letter." He later said that the EU and US would put their own interests before those of all humanity.

During the afternoon there were more presentations. The Slovenian, Timi Ecimovic, made a speech and said he wanted to make a presentation – "to Nicholas". I had to stand and he presented me with a memory stick containing 50 years of his research into Nature, which was on a ribbon he hung round my neck, saying: "I give you my medal." Later he came to me and said he had taken *The New Philosophy of Universalism*, would I sign it for him? After his presentation to me I could not say it was for all to read. So I duly signed, depriving others of access to my display work on Universalism.

A video was shown on screen of a greeting by Federico Mayor Zaragoza, the Spanish ex-Director-General of UNESCO from 1987 to 1999, who would be heading a War Crimes Committee under me in the Supreme Council of Humanity. Everyone spoke.

At 5 we went upstairs to the registration room to look at paintings which reflected the unity of humankind. There were speeches about the artists. Igor said wine would be served, but there was no sign of any wine.

I had been speaking to a portly Syrian who had links with the

Syrian army, Motasem Takla. He had said to me, "I have videos at home, sent from Syria, I would like you to see. I have something to tell you about Syria that will surprise you. But I want my wife to be here – she can translate. Her English is better than mine."

Now his wife had joined him, a thin bespectacled intelligent-looking young Syrian lady. Standing in the registration room before the platform I asked him to tell me now.

Through his wife he said, "Assad is a good man and is loved by his people but the Americans have moved against him as a pipeline is to carry natural gas from Qatar across Syria to connect with a pipeline in Turkey."

I knew that a new gas field had been discovered in 2009 and that Qatar and Turkey wanted to remove Assad, who had opposed a pipeline crossing Syria, so the pipeline could carry natural gas from Qatar to Turkey and eventually to Europe.

Motasem continued, "And Islamic State must be Saudi or Israeli as the Americans could have defeated them over six years. It's the New World Order."

I nodded. I knew that oil and gas pipelines backed by the New World Order had featured in the Afghanistan and Iraq wars. I said, "Our World State is beyond the New World Order, a fresh start. The New World Order is controlled within the structure of our World State."

Hendrik was by my elbow. He repeated what he had said at lunch-time: "It's the Project of the New American Century. Brzezinski. America plans to turn countries into democracies. Afghanistan, Iraq, Lebanon – "

"Egypt?" Motasem asked.

"No, not Egypt. Syria, Iran, Russia and China."

Motasem said, "America's already lost, it's bankrupt."

Hendrik said, "The Americans got the UK to assist with their plan. The UK fired some depleted uranium rounds at Fallujah in 2003 with radioactive consequences worse than Hiroshima."

I knew that the US had fired 782,414 depleted uranium rounds during the 1991 Iraq war, and that US jets and tanks fired more than 300,000 depleted uranium rounds in Iraq during 2003, according to the Dutch peace group Pax. They fired DU rounds in the assault on Fallujah, and UK tanks fired a small number of DU rounds. The co-ordinates were provided by the UN Environment Program.[3] The toxic legacy of the DU rounds was greatly-increased infant mortality and cancer.

Hendrik continued, "The New World Order is behind Brexit. The Queen let slip she was pro-Brexit. They want the dollar, pound and euro to draw together. The Americans are very strong in the UK. You must know the CIA controls the literary world in the UK."

I was startled and thought of what Nigel West had told me at the end of our interview: "The CIA asked me to write my review. They asked me to check whether the book is... genuine."

"Is Israel involved?" Motasem asked.

Hendrik said, "Before Afghanistan, 9/11 was internal and twelve Israelis were involved."

Motasem said, "And Islamic State is Western-backed."

I said, "According to websites on the internet al-Baghdadi of Islamic State may be an Israeli."

"He is, for sure," Motasem said. "That's what we think. That's why Islamic State is still there after six years. America wants it there. In Syria America wants to divide and rule. America wants the whole country. But it will fail. Assad and Russia will succeed. America and Islamic State will fail."

Hendrik said, "Syria was too secular. It allowed all nations to live there. The Americans did not want that."

Motasem said in Arabic for his wife to translate, "There is a Third World War happening in Syria right now." He and his wife turned away to talk.

"Who do you think is behind it all?" I asked Hendrik.

He looked at me.

"The World Philosophical Forum was based on the World Economic Forum that has met at Davos since 1971," I said. "Who's behind the World Economic Forum?"

"The Bilderbergers," Hendrik said without hesitation.

"And the World Philosophical Forum?"

"I have no idea. But you must understand where Igor is coming from. What Putin wants."

He meant that Putin or Putin's interests were behind the WPF. I was not sure I believed this.

I said goodbye to Hendrik and Motasem and headed out to the door. Igor and Lidia were sitting in the comfortable chairs in the corridor where Hendrik and I had been sitting that morning, and there were two opened bottles of wine and some snacks on the table. People I did not recognise were sitting in the other chairs.

"Nicholas," Igor called, "come and have some wine."

I thanked him but declined, saying I had some work to do for tomorrow. He understood. As I turned to leave he said, "Tomorrow, please deal with the speed issue in what you say."

I was back at the Poseidon Hotel before 7. Ann was leaning over our balcony and watched my taxi go beyond the Hotel and do a U-turn in a traffic filter and draw up outside the Hotel entrance. I wrote for half an hour and changed, and we crossed the road to eat in Edem, the restaurant next to the one we had eaten in the previous night. It had a fuller menu and we sat nearer the sea, a couple of metres from the edge of the water. The Aegean in the Argo-Saronic Gulf (or Gulf of Aegina), like the Mediterranean, has no visible tides or waves when it is tranquil, and resembles a lake.

We ate mullet and yoghurt, honey and walnuts under a pink and pale-blue sunset and a crescent moon. Then we returned to our room and I wrote out my address to the Supreme Council of Humanity in longhand, and (at Philippos's suggestion) a letter to Tsipras to hand to Ionnis's contact, which I took down to Reception and had copied. I wanted Tsipras to write to Ban Ki-moon urging him to invite me to address the UN General Assembly, and in my address I was resolved to make an urgent appeal for action to stop the killing in Aleppo.

Conference: day 2, chairing the Supreme Council of Humanity, plant-

ing an olive tree
The next morning, Wednesday 5 October, I showered and breakfasted and sat on our balcony overlooking Phaleron Bay and
read through my address. At 9 the taxi I had ordered came to
the Hotel.

As we drove to Athens the driver asked in immaculate English, "Can you explain how there is a perfect triangle between
the Temple of Aphaia in Aegina, the Old Temple of Athena on
the Acropolis in Athens and the Temple of Poseidon in Sounion?"

I thought and then gave him my reply as we approached and
passed the Temple of Zeus: "It's an equilateral triangle between
the temples because Pythagoras met the builders. The temples
were all begun by around 510BC."

I knew that the Old Temple of Athena on the Acropolis can be
dated to 529–520BC. (The sculpture of Athena in the Parthenon
holding a spear that glinted in the sun was begun later, around
447BC.) The Temple of Aphaia in Aegina dates from around
510BC. The Temple of Sounion was built in the 6th century BC
and was destroyed by the Persians in 490BC. Pythagoras lived
from around 570BC and died in 501BC.

I continued, "Pythagoras was alive before they were built
and he had got the equilateral triangle from the stars. He looked
at the stars and saw a triangle. He had the idea for a triangle
of temples and had a plans meeting. He met the builders. The
scheme was approved. He had Marathon runners run the dis-
tances from the Acropolis to Sounion and from the Acropolis to
Salamis and count the paces."

I knew that Philippides, sometimes referred to less correctly
as Pheidippides, ran as a messenger from Athens to Sparta and
back and in the same week ran to fight at Marathon and ran
back from Marathon to Athens with news of the Athenian victory over the Persian fleet in 490BC and collapsed and died as he
gasped out the news: "*Nenikekamen*," "We have won."

I continued, "From Salamis to Aegina and from Aegina to
Sounion were measured by counting the number of oar dips

made by rowers in a boat. Pythagoras's theorem was on the equilateral triangle, he presided over the operation."

"A very plausible and convincing answer," he said. "But I think they had help. From another planet through UFOs."

I, being evidential and not speculative, was not impressed.

I found Timi and Ricaardoe already in the theatre. Timi said to me, "The WPF is not making progress, it exists on paper but not in actuality. The same is true of the Universal State of the Earth and the Supreme Council of Humanity."

Igor began the meeting of the Supreme Council of Humanity by apologising for the no-show of the Malaysian and Philippine delegations and of Sir James Mancham, who we had already heard was ill (and who died the following January), and of Federico Mayor Zaragoza who was at another conference. There was no mention of others who were supposed to have attended: Bill Gates and Pope Benedict XVI. He said, "People say they will be here and they are not here." He then said that all attending the Universal State of the Earth yesterday could listen to the presentations by the Supreme Council of Humanity and handed over to me as Chairman. I announced the agenda and duly asked Igor to speak on item 1, 'Current Global Problems and Challenges and their Solution'.

Igor was set to give a PowerPoint presentation on screen from his laptop but he had a technical problem. He struggled to open his text but it would not open. To give him time I spoke of the nuclear problem. I headlined how Islamic State had captured 40 kgs of nuclear material from Mosul University and was trying to manufacture a 'dirty bomb' and perhaps deliver it by drone. I said that Obama was so concerned he had called 50 world leaders to Washington to ask them what they would do.

Jeffrey Levett asked to speak. He spoke of the dreadful damage a 'dirty bomb' could do to the earth.

I said it would not be as bad as a nuclear explosion, but it could still contaminate and cause areas to be uninhabitable for decades.

Igor was struggling. He asked me to start my presentation.

And so I passed to item 2, 'How to Speed up the Global Education Process'. I had Syria in mind and had decided that if the Supreme Council of Humanity could not precipitate immediate action on Syria, which included the possibility of addressing the UN General Assembly, then I would walk away from it. It would be better to say what should happen and fall out with the WPF than to go along with waiting for 7.33 billion to become members. I had decided to be outspoken so they could all know where I stood. I said we could not wait seventy years, we could not even wait seven days as the situation in Syria was too urgent. My address was as follows:

In my paper 'Urgent Global Problems, Inactive Nation-States and Decisive Supranationalism', which is on the WPF website [see Appendix 6], I spoke of the urgent need to solve the world's problems. I said that Syria, the refugees and the tide of populism and nationalism in America and Europe have taken us in the opposite direction from supranationalism, and it is very difficult to get publicity for supranationalism. The nuclear situation is very dangerous. There are 15,350[4] nuclear weapons according to the Federation of American Scientists, 2016. Islamic State has obtained 40 kgs of nuclear material from Mosul University and is trying to turn some of the nuclear material into a 'dirty bomb' (a bomb with some nuclear material in it). In Brussels bombers were stalking a nuclear scientist to try and obtain nuclear material with a view to creating a 'dirty bomb'. Obama was so concerned he convened a meeting in Washington for 50 Western leaders including the Prime Minister of the UK on 31 March and 1 April to ask them what they would do if a 'dirty bomb' exploded on their territory. The situation is really urgent; something must be done to resolve it very soon.

How can we speed up a solution to the world's problems? At present we are spreading the Universal State of the Earth by word of mouth, and global citizenship education is linked to Aristotelian educating of the *demos* of 'democracy' into global citizens with awareness of supranationalism. This cannot take decades. In view of the urgency we want action now. The Athenian city-state in Aristotle's day contained some 250,000 people, many of whom were illiterate. We have to reach 7.33 billion urgently. How? Social media?

I wonder if we should be looking at an interim phase of a world government by taking over an existing institution. In my books since 2010 I have called for a Federation of nation-states based on a reformed UN which can eventually become a World State. As I said yesterday I have called for the UN General Assembly to be turned into a lower house of an elected world government of 850 representatives. There would be an upper house of 92 World Senators and a World Commission of 27, drawn from the countries I list in *The World Government*. Nation-states would survive. The UN may be comfortable with turning itself into a United Federation, a UF, knowing that a federation is for nation-states. During this interim process global civic education could be directly pursued by the new central authority, and the supranational awareness of the masses would be lifted. The World Federation would be a partly-federal United Federation that can later be assimilated into a supranationalist World State. This idea of a democratic world government was called for by many great men in the 20th century, including Churchill, Truman, Einstein, Eisenhower, Gandhi, Russell and Gorbachev, but I seem to be the only Western literary author calling for it in the 21st century.

As I see it, the SCH's role is to bring in a functioning supranationalist authority that can begin to implement the seven goals we put in the WPF's letter to Ban Ki-moon last year. They are:

- bringing peace between nation-states, and disarmament;
- sharing natural resources and energy so that all humankind can have a raised standard of living;
- solving environmental problems such as global warming, which seems to be beyond self-interested nations;
- ending disease;
- ending famine;

- solving the world's financial crisis; and
- redistributing wealth to eliminate poverty.

All of these are better solved by a supranational authority such as a United Federation than by nation-states represented in the UN and defending their borders.

So what is the way forward? To carry on as we have been doing, raising the consciousness of those who come to us? Or go out and supranationalise an institution such as the UN to advance awareness of the need for supranationalism? Institutions don't like being reformed and may resist our proposal. But if we can get to the UN General Assembly and appeal to the 193 Representatives, they will consult their governments independently of the UN Secretary-General.

The present precarious state of the world requires global problems to be solved as soon as possible. What is the best way to speed up the global consciousness of the 7.33 billion people in the world?

What I said initiated a discussion. Ricaardoe and then Timi came to the microphone to speak. Timi said the conference was about the planet earth, not humanity on it.

I said, "The two are inextricably interlinked. One nuclear bomb can damage the earth and destroy all humankind." And: "The theme of the conference is 'From diversity of beliefs to human unity.'"

Others spoke. By and large the urgency of the international situation and the need for speed was accepted.

Igor now gave his presentation, having overcome the technical problems. He was setting out the world's problems without any reference to the need for speed. He spoke of philosophy coming out of the tradition of Aristotle.

I interrupted to point out that there are two traditions in philosophy, both covered at the beginning of *The New Philosophy of Universalism*, the scientific tradition of Aristotle and the metaphysical tradition of Plato whose philosophy saw society as shadows thrown by the light of a Fire on the walls of a cave.

He spoke of the need to raise humankind's consciousness to achieve peace.

I said, "How would you speed the process up?"

He said that humankind was doomed: "We are on the *Titanic* heading for an iceberg."

I said, "So the pilot's been trained and shouldn't prevent us from hitting the iceberg?" I shocked Igor into taking a more positive view of our predicament.

At that point Paris Katsivelos interrupted: "We have to leave for the Acropolis at 12.20, for our planting of an olive tree. There will not be time for Igor to finish his address."

I had been led to believe that we would leave at 1. So I proposed that we should adjourn until 3.30, the time on the agenda for the next session.

We gathered outside and one of the delegates, Athena, who was in her early seventies and lived in Athens, had a car and offered me a lift along with Igor and his wife. Igor conferred with her. I was swiftly disinvited and the Russian lady Svetlana took my place. Three Russian speakers went by car, the rest of us had to walk to Panepistimio metro station and go by metro to Akropoli.

The station was very modern and I was told by Paris that it was completed a month before the 2004 Olympics, on EU money at a cost of €1,600m. Paris bought the tickets (€1.40 each) and after two stops we got out and walked under the towering Acropolis and past the Theatre of Dionysus where Aeschylus, Sophocles and Euripides all sat to watch their plays in the 5th century BC and where Paris had performed in 1978 (he proudly told us).

On our left was an olive grove of tightly-packed olive trees that almost made a tall hedge. We stopped at a gap, near a waist-high olive tree by a square hole. The Deputy Mayor of Athens, who had greeted us at the conference and now looked about twenty-five in his jeans and sweater and with his long hair, made a short speech.

I also had to make a short speech. I said to camera: "The ancient olive tree is sacred to Athena of the Acropolis, and Plato and Aristotle would be proud of the WPF."

Then we were all filmed shovelling small heaps of dusty earth into the hole with a spade. The film was later edited by Ionnis for Sky Go Extra, the way of watching a Sky channel in Greece. I do not know on which channel the film was shown. There were many photos of different groups of WPF members touching the olive tree.

A tall man in a suit, white shirt and tie addressed me in English. He introduced himself as Lucas. He said Ionnis had spoken to him, that he understood I had a letter for Tsipras, and he wanted a copy so he could "process" it. I gave it to him later at the conference and Ionnis returned it to me at the end of the day.

Paris led the way back and somehow lost everyone except for the Greek priest, Father Christos Georgiou Zouros, and me, probably because the three of us looked in on a Byzantine church. Paris took us by metro back to Panepistimio metro station, and the three of us lunched in an arcade opposite the university.

Paris told me he lived with his mother on €840 a month, his pension. He gave his mother's pension to a live-in carer as his mother needed twenty-four-hourly supervision and the carer allowed him to leave his home and do his acting.

Father Christos showed me a diamond-shaped pendant he wore round his neck and recited the four faces: Apollo, Dionysus, Venus and Demeter. And he pointed out two Pythagorean triangles that connected them.

Back in the theatre Igor continued his presentation. He ended by referring to all the grades his Aristotelianism required.

Athena, his chauffeur to the Acropolis, a Greek lady who had emigrated to Australia when seven, spoke out at the end: "I don't like your hierarchy. I'm a democrat." She said, "I'm spiritual, and *all* people have something to recommend them."

Igor made a general reply.

Ricaardoe then asked if we could debate the question of speed for an hour, which we did.

For an hour we had a Symposium in which many spoke on

the speed with which the Universal State of the Earth and Supreme Council of Humanity could be got across. Ricaardoe suggested there should be 40 to 50 Ambassadors to take the message to their countries. Hendrik proposed writing to 30 living world leaders. There were calls for funding so there could be an office and back-up, particularly a secretary who could write accurate English. There was a call for a place to meet.

Athena said that globalism was disliked by some as it suggested the export of American brand names and that I should write a book in which I stated very clearly what the world government of a democratic World State would mean and how it would differ from past globalism and from the 'world government' of the exploitative New World Order.

We finished just after 6. Motasem came with his wife to tell me more about what was happening in Syria. He said, "Islamic State were responsible for the attacks on hospitals. The children were made up to look as if they had been wounded. Islamic State did this to end the peace progress and blame Syria and Russia for ending it." I asked, "Who are Islamic State? Who do you think they are?"

At that moment the cultural program (which always followed a Symposium in classical times) began in the theatre. A woman declaimed 'Hymn to Orpheus'. Dancers in traditional dress lined up to dance. I whispered my goodbyes and slipped away.

Ann was again sitting on our balcony as my taxi passed below her and swung round. I changed and we again ate in Edem. There was a cloudy sunset and we ate on the beach very near the quietly lapping sea and were served moussaka, baklava sponges and yoghurt, honey and walnuts.

We returned to our room where I reflected that I had gone out on a limb, that Igor and I were in coalition, that the cracks were showing and that I might not be in Athens next year. I looked forward to returning to my writing. I should be talking about Universalism and promoting peace in the Middle East. I should not be promoting what might be a front behind which concealed Russian interests might work.

9
Athens Again: World State and Plan for Peace Talks at Delphi

Sometimes in life there is a surprise round the corner. My address (see pp.98–100) had laid down the reasons why I would be leaving the Supreme Council of Humanity, because I could not wait for the membership to reach several billion before beginning to stop the war in Syria, I wanted speedy action on Syria. I did not understand how or why, but what I called for and wanted was suddenly pushed my way. I was taken aback, but found myself in a position in which I might contribute to averting a Third World War. My lone call for universal peace seemed to have struck a nerve.

Conference: day 3, chairing the Supreme Council of Humanity
The next morning I was off again at 9am. I thought again in the taxi that I should be giving two-hour talks on Universalism, not promoting Igor's imperialistic and hierarchical ideas that would take decades to become fully established. In my own mind I had already broken away from the philosophers and would not be returning to Athens next year.

Timi and Ricaardoe were sitting in the theatre when I arrived at 9.30. Timi tackled me: "Yesterday you allowed blah blah blah and did not stick to a scientific, objective agenda so I did not know where we were going."

I said, "Igor drew up the five-point agenda, not me, and because of the technical issue in the morning item 2 preceded item 1. He asked me to focus on the speed issue. It's a Plato-style Symposium, everyone gets to speak, and there will be some blah blah blah when everyone speaks."

He said, "We are discussing the sustainability of humanity."

I said, "We are discussing the points on the agenda. We have done items 1 and 2, in reverse order, and we still have items 3, 4 and 5 to do."

He said, "We are arriving at truth and that is scientific and objective."

I said, "Pilate said, 'What is truth?'" (*John* 18.38.) I said, "There are different traditions of truth: one metaphysical, holding that Reality is invisible; one secular, holding that reality is social and scientific."

Others, including Igor, had arrived and had overheard the end of the exchange. I sat behind the microphone next to Igor to begin the morning session. Igor told me (taking his cue from Timi) he had helped himself to *The World Government* on the way in, would I please sign it for him.

Then Timi approached and had a guarded conversation with Igor in English which I could not help overhearing. He mentioned the chairmanship of a philosophical body. Igor thought Timi was proposing that *he*, Igor, should become the Chairman, and he began explaining why he kept a distance from that body. Timi interrupted and said, "No, me. Will you recommend me for Chairman?" Igor looked stunned and said, "We will talk about this later."

The morning session began with item 3, approving staff for the USE Supreme Council of Humanity. Igor said they should all be Citizens of the Earth and therefore members of the WPF. From the floor there was a request by Hendrik for an objective procedure. There was supposed to be a presentation on the Earth Bank by John Moustos but he was in Istanbul on his way back from Asia and unable to attend.

We passed to item 4, adopting four documents Igor had produced as Universal Declarations. One of them was on "Equating crimes against Nature to crimes against Humanity". I said that it could be inferred from the language that cutting trees was equivalent to killing people, that deforesting was equivalent to bombing Syrians in Aleppo. I said Igor did not mean this, he wanted to make acts against the environment criminally prosecutable.

Jeffrey Levett (a Professor in Athens) came to the microphone and spoke. He agreed with my interpretation and said, "It's a linguistic thing."

Timi came to the microphone and said, "We are talking about planet earth, not humankind. The two are completely different."

I said again, "The two are inextricably interlinked. One nuclear bomb can damage the earth and destroy humankind. They can't be treated separately." And there were many nods within the audience. Item 5 was approving the future working program of the SCH online and at the WPF meeting next year.

At lunch-time Hendrik and I walked to the Paul *boulangerie* nearby for a quiche-like snack. Hendrik told me, "I like the diversity of nation-states, and nationality is good and interesting."

I pointed out that in the World State there would be diversity within unity, that all nation-states would retain their internal independence but would be partly federal in external policy, especially in matters of war and disarmament.

Athena joined us. She said she had lived in Greece until she was seven and in Australia until she was twenty-one. She then visited the UK and worked in Harrods, selling bathing-costumes in 1967–1968. I said there was a demonstration against the Greek *junta* in London in 1968, and that I stood near Kingsley Amis in Trafalgar Square. She said, "I was there." We had been at the same demonstration and our paths would not cross again until nearly fifty years later in Athens.

In the afternoon there were bitty presentations from Athena and Paris (on his acting in relation to Aristotle's *Poetics*), from Svetlana (on ecology, translated by Larisa) and from a Greek, Georgios (on mythology). Georgios (translated by Athena) spoke of the 147 maxims that used to adorn Delphi's original Temple of Apollo, including *'gnothi seauton'* ('know thyself') and *'meden agan'* ('nothing too much'), meaning 'moderation in all things'.

Globe Center: Supreme Council of Humanity's headquarters
Then Igor announced, "An architect has designed the building where the Supreme Council of Humanity will meet in the future. Here is his design of the Globe Center." He clicked on his laptop and a video played on screen showing a huge building, a globe with countries clearly visible, dominating the skyline and

roads leading to it from all directions.[1] I could see Africa. We approached the building and went inside and saw the central lifts and narrow bridges in tiers to north, south, east and west. We saw the hotel, an office, a swimming-pool. It was a building as tall as the UN building in New York, possibly the Twin Towers, and befitted a world centre and the centre of a World State.

"The architect has done the work," he said, "we have to decide where to put it." To me he said quietly, "It could be in Athens or perhaps Malaysia."

I was staggered. "When can building start?" I asked publicly.

"Who knows. Ask John Moustos. Two months maybe. That will be our headquarters." He said quietly to me, "Your headquarters, for you are Chairman of the Supreme Council of Humanity. You are above me. You are Head of Humanity. I want to keep a low profile. I don't want to be seen in the front of what we are doing."

Globe Center, from architect's video showing possible headquarters of the Universal State of the Earth and the Supreme Council of Humanity

That is what a Russian SVR officer would say.

Igor was full of surprises. I had not expected an iconic building on this scale.

At the end of the video there was a credit: "Produced by International Real Estate Center."

"Who is the architect?" I asked quietly.

"A Russian, a Russian firm."

I thought how long it must have taken to come up with this
video. All the measurements and all the accommodation must
have been worked out. Months of work must have gone into
this. It may have been started after the setting-up of the Universal State of the Earth the previous October. I thought this likely
as 'the Globe Center' showed 'the Earth'. I did not connect the
Globe Center with the golden Russia Globe building planned for
Moscow's Park Russia as I had not seen the artist's impression
of that Globe building.[2]

Then Igor gave out certificates recording admissions to Aristotle's hierarchy, mostly to Aristotle's level of Aristocrats (meaning the best rulers with level-5 awareness of global citizenship).
The Venezuelan delegate refused to accept her certificate as she
was against the principle of aristocracy and for the people, like
Hugo Chavez (President of Venezuela from 1999 to 2013). I had
similar misgivings but accepted my certificate and a Diploma
stating that I was now a Professor of Civic Knowledge.

I spoke with the Syrian Motasem through his wife. He told
me, "Islamic State is led by a Mossad spy, Shimon (Simon) Elliot, also known as al-Baghdadi, who has been asked to create
a Sunni-Shiite war that will benefit Israel – by destroying countries that threaten it and allowing it to expand into Greater Israel between the Nile and the Euphrates and control the Middle-
Eastern pipelines – and also the USA."

Then, still reeling from the size of the Globe Center so casu-
ally dangled in front of us, I left and found a taxi. Ann was bending over the balcony of the Poseidon Hotel and waved to me as
I got out by the entrance. I changed and we crossed the road to
Edem and ate watching the sunset. The crescent moon flecked

the still Aegean with moonlight until it passed behind a cloud. We were served salad, moussaka and yoghurt, honey and walnuts with red wine and returned to our room at 9.15pm.

Conference: day 4, Universalism and World State
I was haunted by the Globe Center and the next morning I told Jeffrey about it. He had not been present when it was shown and he wanted to see it. I said, "The cost must be colossal, you might ask Igor about it. And where it's to be built. The planning authorities in Athens won't allow it to detract from the Acropolis."

I asked Igor as we sat together before the start of the session, "Could you show the video of the Globe Center again?" And as he fiddled on his laptop, "Who paid for the film?"

"It was paid by the Order of Malta," he told me. (He pronounced it 'Mall-ta'. It took me a moment to understand what he meant.) "They're like Freemasons, the Knights of Malta. They want to be invisible. They paid for the video."

"And the International Real Estate Center?"

"A group of my Russian friends. They were the architects and they made the film."

I said, "Don't get into trouble with Putin."

"No. If you say, 'Putin is stupid' or do something to take his job, you will be in trouble, but to talk about banning war won't get you into trouble, it's all right."

I nodded.

We then began the session with a re-showing of the film, which I announced. There were gasps at the scale of the project from those in the audience who had not seen the film. At the end there was applause and Jeffrey asked to speak. He said he knew of a smaller project in Chicago which cost in excess of $100 million, and he said, "This can't be in Athens, the Acropolis is the centre of Athens."

Igor said, "It may be in Malaysia."

Athena suggested the Old Airport in Athens which was by the sea and now housed 3,000 Syrians. We had passed it on our way from the airport to Phaleron Bay. The site could be cleared and levelled for this building.

Quietly Igor said to me, "You and I will decide where. We may build it in Crimea."

My initial thought was, 'No way.' Putin had invaded Crimea, the world would not accept a supranational building in Crimea, so anyone who visited it would be accepting the Russian occupation of Crimea. I wondered if building the Globe Center was Putin's plan to win acceptance for the Russian occupation of Crimea by building a rival UN there, a Russian-backed 'UN'. If Hitler had built the Globe Center in Nazi-occupied Sudetenland in 1938 there would have been an international outcry and no one would have visited it. But then I thought that in a world peace deal, Crimea, which had long historical associations with Russia, could be in a Russian sphere of influence and Afghanistan, which had long historical associations with the UK and more recently with the US, could be in an American and Western sphere of influence.

As Chairman I said to the conference, "That's where we may be meeting in three, four or five years' time."

Igor said publicly, "Maybe two months."

Privately he whispered to me, "The Knights of Malta are serious. They want to make a large deposit. It will be placed in the Earth Bank under the Supreme Council of Humanity, under you and me."

I reflected that as Chairman of the Supreme Council of Humanity I would be overseeing the large deposit.

I then announced that further to a presentation the previous day we could now see a six-minute video, *Delphic Maxims*, on some of the 147 maxims carved into the original Temple of Apollo. I said, "We are going to Delphi tomorrow, so this will be useful background." The video showed about sixty of the maxims and sometimes a bust of the Greek philosophers who had said them, with their names and dates.

After a final vote, which concluded the business of the Supreme Council of Humanity, Igor asked me to talk about my Universalism and World State, the topic of my first WPF paper (see Appendix 1) which I had been pondering the previous morning.

I said that Universalism is seeing the unity of the universe and humankind and that this perception has an impact on all disciplines. I said that philosophical Universalism is seeing the universe and humankind as within a Oneness that contains order. Philosophy is about man's relationship with the universe, not the logic and language of the Vienna Circle. I said that historical Universalism sees the history of humankind as a whole, 25 civilizations which go through 61 stages, and history has to be regarded as a whole, not as bits or national histories.

I said that literary Universalism sees all world literature since the 'Epic of Gilgamesh' (c.2600BC) as having one fundamental theme: a quest for Reality and immortality like Gilgamesh's that alternates down the Ages with social condemnation of the follies and vices of humankind, as in the odes of the Roman poet Horace. I said that I had reflected both in recent books, *Selected Poems: Quest for the One* and *Selected Stories: Follies and Vices of the Modern Elizabethan Age*. I said I was being interviewed on this theme for an American TV and online site. I pointed out that my manuscripts were in the archives of Essex University.

I said that political Universalism sees the whole of humankind as being under one political system and democratic World State with a world government. I said that in the 20th century many great men had called for a democratic World State, including (as I had said in one of my addresses) Churchill, Truman, Einstein, Eisenhower, Gandhi, Russell and Gorbachev, and that I was the only Western literary author to continue this tradition in the 21st century. I said that before 2010, before I knew Igor, I could not see how there could be a supranational Universal State without taking over the UN General Assembly. And so in *The World Government* I see a lower house based on the UN General Assembly of 850 Representatives and an upper house, a World Senate, of 92. I said I had listed the world constituencies for these seats in *The World Government*.

Timi asked to come to the microphone. He said, "You don't

accept that you know nothing. We all know nothing and you don't accept that you know nothing."

I said, "I know *something*, that's why I've written *The New Philosophy of Universalism* and *The World Government*."

"Don't interrupt me."

"If you are misrepresenting me I have to put the record straight."

Igor interrupted and took my side. "Look, Nicholas has seen things are wrong and he has tried to put things right with supranationalism. He is right to do this."

Timi returned to his seat.

There was a lively discussion during which Igor said, "In two years' time we will have our own General Assembly, there will be a General Assembly in the Globe Center."

And I realised the Globe Center might indeed be a rival Russian-backed UN. Was Russia setting up a new UN with me in charge of the transition? But then I dismissed the idea as nation-state thinking. I took a supranational view.

During the discussion I was supported by all except Timi. I could see that he had presented me with the memory stick of his own research because he was trying to superimpose his own nihilistic world-view on mine.

In summing up I put it to the conference: "We have two ways of proceeding. We have supranationalising the UN, and we have creating a rival to the UN. Which avenue should we pursue, should I go to the UN and even though they won't supranationalise it they will receive our message and think about it? Or should we just build a rival to the UN?"

There was a silence. Then Hendrik said, "You should pursue all channels."

I smiled. I had placed my UN strategy alongside the Universal State of the Earth and had the conference's permission to pursue both approaches. I could see Junyan smiling and nodding.

I now closed the conference. I spoke of the good week we had had and of the Universal Declarations we had approved.

I stressed that speed was still a problem in view of the urgent world situation in Syria and elsewhere.

In the lunch break I thought again about the Globe Center and wondered if it would be built with recycled Russian money, via the Order of Malta. I wondered if Putin was behind the Globe Center. I asked myself questions about the WPF, and Igor. Was he a great man, a genius, who had seen the need for supranationalism so clearly without putting it in books and who had come up with the dream global centre? Or was he a bumbler who had founded the WPF to promote his three philosophical works online despite his inaccurate English? Or was he a genius who was promoting both supranationalism and his philosophical works?

Or, in nation-state rather than in supranationalist thinking, was the WPF acting as a front for the SVR, as a meeting place to assemble dozens of thinking people who would supply information and unwittingly co-operate in implementing hidden Russian policies? The Globe Center made me wonder if it was a front for Russian money laundering, perhaps an alternative UN based in Crimea, a beacon for Putin's aggressive outlook on the West.

'Hymn to Peace': lyre and Pan pipes
In the afternoon we were all to attend a performance by Paris Katsivelos, who was to recite a 'Hymn to Peace' written by Vasilis Nousias in Doric dialect. It would incorporate a ceremonial invocation to peace. At 3 we all walked with Igor to Panepistimio metro station and went two stops to the Metaxourghio metro station and walked to Stathmos Theatre. It was a small theatre with perhaps a hundred plush seats. I was shown to a front seat and was immediately greeted by Paris.

Igor and I had to go up on stage with Paris, and Igor gave out certificates to helpers who were in the audience. I had to shake hands with a procession of men and women (announced through a stand-up microphone in Greek by Paris) and then Igor had to make a speech, followed by me.

"Please sum up the conference," Igor said.

I said we had had a good conference and explained what we would be doing. A lady interpreter had come on stage and she interpreted. I said we were supporting Paris who had contributed a paper to the conference and had translated, "and who acted at the Theatre of Dionysus in 1978, where Aeschylus, Sophocles and Euripides sat and watched their plays". There was appreciative applause.

Then the priest, Christos, shouted out from the dark auditorium. The lady translator said, "He says there were good minds at the conference but he could not understand them as there was not enough translation from English to Greek."

I said, "Last year everything was translated into Greek, Russian and English. This year we did not always have someone to translate. I'm sorry if the Father was at one of these sessions, and we'll try and get translators for next year." Igor nodded approvingly and there was a ripple of applause. Igor and I returned to our seats.

Lucas was sitting in my seat in a white shirt and tie and dark suit, the man who had promised to deliver my letter to Tsipras. I bent and whispered that he could stay there and picked up my bag. He understood that he had sat in my seat and insisted on moving, so I sat down. A Russian lady behind me who spoke English petitioned me as Chairman of the SCH. She said she wanted to build a stadium for children at Delphi but had been refused permission by the EU, even though the Russians would pay all costs and the stadium would not intrude on any view of the ruins. I said I would consult Igor, and reflected that my role in the SCH meant that I was now looked on as being able to solve difficult problems.

The performance began with a musician, Pakis Taksoulas, strumming an ancient lyre shaped like a U. I relished the beauty of the music and thought of Apollo and Orpheus. Paris, wearing white, strutted about the stage declaiming in Doric Greek. The musician now blew down into double pipes and then down into a cluster of pipes side by side like miniature organ-pipes. I thought of Pan. Paris's declaiming turned into invoking peace. After half an hour the performance was over.

After the applause I stood up and Paris bent from the stage. I asked him about the musical instruments and he beckoned me up on stage and led me to a room in semi-darkness where the musician was bending over his instruments. I admired them and he told me that Apollo's lyre had three strings, Orpheus's had seven strings and his own had twelve strings. He told me the double pipes were classical and that Pan blew down on seven clustered pipes whereas he blew on eight or eleven.

As I came out I saw Lucas and asked him about the letter. He said it should be typed before going to Tsipras. He would try and type it from my handwriting and would bring it to the coach the next day for approval before delivering it to Tsipras. He did not come to the coach the next day and the letter never reached Tsipras.

Romanian Cultural Centre
We all walked to the Romanian Cultural Centre nearby and were served wine in a ground-floor room. There were *canapés* on a central table. I talked to the Syrian Motasem through his wife, and to Igor, who said that Svetlana had said after my talk on Universalism, which Larisa had interpreted for her, that I knew everything. We went downstairs to hear singing: a mixed choir in traditional costumes. There were two free high-backed and rather splendid chairs, and Igor said, "One of those is for you. You're now Head of Humanity, you are higher than Ban Ki-moon." He sat on the other chair.

His wife Lidia was in a chair behind me, and after hearing some songs, including a Russian song that the Russians all sang along to and clapped, I whispered to Lidia to take my place and told Igor I was going. I slipped out and was back at the Poseidon Hotel around 7.20. I changed and Ann and I crossed the road to Edem.

It was cloudy with distant lightning. We ate cod, salad and chips by the water, and just as my pudding arrived (yoghurt, honey and walnuts) there were spots of heavy rain. We de-camped to under an awning, and with one eye on the coming storm as the lightning drew closer I gobbled the yoghurt, paid and crossed the road to the Hotel just before it poured.

Rain lashed the French windows of our room and water spread across our floor. I mopped it up with a towel. There was no movement from Edem, all guests were trapped under the awning until the rain stopped. I thought again about Igor and resolved to ask him some questions during our outing to Delphi the next day.

Igor on the coach: peace initiative
We were up at 6.45am. As we sat and waited for the taxi just be-fore 8am Ann discovered she had had an email late the previous evening saying our flight home the next day had been cancelled. Ann emailed back and later attempted to text our eldest son for further information.

The coach was parked opposite the City of Athens Cultural and Youth Centre. It was a white Mercedes-Benz with a middle door. Ionnis had provided it and filled it with those at the con-ference who had not left and some of his own clients. Paris in-sisted that Ann and I should sit in the front seat "as you are the most important" and that Igor and Lidia should sit behind the driver. Igor and I were beside each other, separated by the aisle. Natasha, Igor's cheerful-looking banker daughter, had flown in from Moscow for a two-day visit and was seated behind Svet-lana and Larisa, who were already immediately behind Igor and Lidia.

As soon as the coach set off for Delphi Igor leaned over and began talking: "Enough papers, action now. I want you to chair a meeting between all the fighting parties in the war in Syria. The talks will be in Athens. The UN Secretary-General retires at the end of December, and the new man, a Portuguese, announced two days ago, does not start until next year, so no peace talks can happen in the UN. The US Presidential election is next month, so the US cannot do much for peace. The situation in Syria is urgent as you said in your presentations. We are committed to abolishing war, which is illegal, based on the values of classical philosophy. We will aim to get representatives from Russia, the US, Assad and Islamic State and other fighting groups over here, and we will seek a cease-fire. We will hold the first meeting in Delphi and we will ratify an agreement in the Old Parliament building in Athens."

There had been none of this until now. Then I thought, 'He has reflected on my appeal to do something over Syria.' My addresses had precipitated this action. Then I wondered if the idea had arrived with his daughter Natasha, and immediately dismissed the idea.

Thinking quickly I said, "I will fly back to Athens for peace negotiations. We will secure a cease-fire, and a no-fly zone over Aleppo during the talks." I added for the second time: "Don't get into trouble with Putin."

Igor said, "Look, Svetlana who is sitting behind Lidia is friendly with him and can visit him and explain everything we are doing. She has already explained everything about us, he knows everything you did last year and this year. And Larisa, sitting next to her, has known Sergei Lavrov for fifty years. They were students together. She meets him four times a year and can explain everything to him."

Lavrov was the Russian Foreign Minister, and I knew he had been at Moscow State Institute of International Relations (MGIMO), which was set up in 1944. I knew it had been run by the Soviet Ministry of Foreign Affairs and was now run by the Ministry of Foreign Affairs of the Russian Federation. It had always been the most *élite* University in Russia, the main Cold-War university. It taught 56 languages and prepared students for careers in international relations and diplomacy, and had been a place that trained future KGB operatives in those early Cold-War days. That was where Larisa had also studied.

I looked back at Svetlana and Larisa and said, "So Putin knows about the USE and SCH?"

"Yes. He knows everything we've been doing. It's all right."

Later I leaned across and asked him about the funding of the Globe Center.

He said, "The head or almost the head of the Order of Malta is a Russian who knows me. He told me the Knights of Malta have been going since the eleventh century. They have invested in Europe for centuries. But now Europe is becoming unstable and they want to take their money out of Europe and make a deposit. He has said to me, 'We are very serious about this and it will be soon.' Don't think we are doing nothing."

I pondered. In 1966, in Moscow, during a visit to the Cathedral of the Archangel I had glimpsed a future World State with a World-Lord and had put it in my poem about Communism, 'Archangel'. Now in a sense I had become the World-Lord as I was being called the Head of Humanity, had been asked to hold peace talks regarding Syria and would be in co-charge, perhaps even in direct charge, of the Earth Bank.

We stopped for coffee at a large roadside store. After I bought cappuccinos Ann shopped for presents to take back for our children and grandchildren and I found a small inexpensive notepad with pictures of all the Greek philosophers on the front and bought two, one for Igor and one for me. We returned to the coffee area and I showed it to Igor and said, "I got you one" and I gave it to Lidia. Then Natasha appeared and I stood and we had a chat.

She was a round-faced young lady who spoke English well. She said she had flown in from Moscow and sometimes went to London for five days. I asked her what she did in London and she told me she visited the First Merchant Bancorp Ltd at 27 Old Gloucester Road, a merchant bank. She worked upstairs out of sight of the customers. She said, "In Moscow I work in Credit Suisse so I can send money to my father to help him attend the conferences he needs to attend." I thought, 'What a nice, dutiful daughter.' I only later found out that she too had been a student at Moscow State Institute of International Relations, the Cold-War university where Lavrov and Larisa had studied.

We returned to the coach. As it drew towards Delphi the Syrian couple, who were sitting behind us, spoke through a gap between the high-backed seats. Through his wife Motasem commented on a ruby ring Ann was wearing. He said he worked in stones and he came and stood over me and shone a light on Ann's stone to show it was of good quality. He showed pictures on his phone of expensive stones he had for sale and said, seeing Ann as a potential customer, through his wife's translation, "You must come to our house. I will show Nicholas my videos from Syria and you can look at my stones."

At Delphi

We passed through Arachova and parked beneath the slope of Mount Parnassus and Delphi. All round us were mountains and plunging valleys. A guide was waiting for us, and we climbed steps as a group and walked to the entrance. Ionnis gave out tickets and we went through railings into the upper site.

We followed the guide, a young Greek who spoke good English, to the shopping *agora* where visitors to the Oracle gathered in classical times. Delphi was for *all* Greeks from *all* city-states. The guide explained that in classical times the Pythia, the Priestess of the Temple of Apollo, was available only one day a month. At dawn she bathed in the Castalian spring to purify herself and sacrifice an animal to study the omens in its entrails. If the result was favourable she accepted questions (mostly concerning marriage opportunities or events in daily life) in the Temple of Apollo. Otherwise visitors had to wait a month for her next appearance.

Ann, who was waiting for a knee operation, elected to remain at that level. I took the Sacred Way up to the *omphalos*, the navel or belly-button of the world, the Centre of the Earth. The guide said the round waist-high stone had rolled down from the original Temple of Apollo that held the engraved maxims when it was destroyed by fire in 548BC or again by rockslide in 377BC.

At this point Igor asked, "Is there a meeting place in Delphi, for meetings today?"

The guide said, "The European Cultural Centre of Delphi.

Down there."

Igor repeated, "The European Cultural Centre of Delphi." He turned to me and said, "That's where we will have the peace negotiations."

"We'll talk to the representatives on the coach and get to know them before the talks," I said, agreeing with him.

We carried on up the original Sacred Way past the Athenian Treasury, built from spoils from the battle of Marathon (490BC) and passed a stoa built from spoils from the battle of Salamis (480BC). We passed a laurel tree and reached the ramp up to the entrance to the Temple of Apollo, which was now a few columns and a fragment-strewn stone base. Near it was a small upright stone slab with three holes, perhaps originally the stone base for the tripod on which the Pythia sat.

In an underground room she breathed gases from a nearby fissure in the earth and chewed laurel leaves to drug her mind and open her soul so she channelled the words of Apollo. Her answers were always enigmatic. When King Croesus of Lydia asked if he should cross the River Halys, his border, he was told: "If Croesus goes to war he will destroy a great empire." He crossed the river and his own Lydian empire was destroyed.

Nicholas Hagger and Igor Kondrashin (right) by the ramp of the Temple of Apollo, Delphi

The underground room was to the back of the Temple, I could see the sides of the passage that led down to it.

I looked at the ruined Temple and imagined how it was in the early 6th century BC and thought of the 147 maxims carved on its stone walls (including 'Know thyself' and 'Nothing too much'). I knew that if I were approaching the Oracle I would ask, "Will the fighting in Syria lead to the Third World War or will a peace initiative succeed?" I later put my trek up to the Oracle, and question, in a poem, 'At Delphi'.

The guide said, "The Inextinguishable Fire burned near the entrance of the Temple, the Eternal Flame."

Igor said to me, "Fire, what was the Fire?"

I explained that 'inextinguishable' meant that it was never extinguished or put out.

"It was the Flame of Reason," he said.

"No," I said, "it was from Apollo, god of the sun. It was the Fire of Apollo, the invisible Light beyond reason. The Pythia spoke Apollo's words and the Inextinguishable Fire was Apollo's Fire."

But Igor, with a sense of the 18th-century Illuminati, still wanted to see it as the rational Flame of Reason.

We climbed on up to the theatre and looked down at the valley. Then we descended. I found Ann and we walked into the museum. (Our entrance tickets gave us free admission.) Ann had been sitting with Larisa, who had told her she had a son with cerebral palsy and so had worked for a charity. She would be attending a charitable conference in Edinburgh in December.

We returned to the coach and drove back towards Athens. On our way out of Delphi we stopped at the roadside Castalian spring where John Milton, in his imagination while reading Thomas Young, "thrice sprinkled [his] happy lips with Castalia's wine".

Our eldest son Matthew texted and (when there was a signal) phoned to say there was a strike of air traffic controllers and no planes would be leaving Athens airport for a week. I relayed the news to Igor, and at his request to Larisa and Svetlana, who had to fly back the next day. There were more texts from Matthew, which I shared with the Russians. Then we heard that the strike had ended but that our flight was still cancelled. Matthew texted that he would work on getting us moved to another flight.

Caucasian Cultural Centre
The coach took us to the Caucasian Cultural Centre in Athens. In 2015 it had been called the Georgian Centre but had been renamed, presumably to distract attention from Russia's occupation of the Georgian regions of South Ossetia and Abkhazia in August 2008. We sat on chairs round the walls and watched a young girl dressed as a bride with a square head-dress and veil dance with a young boy dressed as a bridegroom. Wine was served and we helped ourselves to a buffet of meatballs, sausage rolls, pastry puffs and chocolate-topped shortbread.

I talked to Motasem, the Syrian, and his wife. I told him the SCH would be conducting peace negotiations over Syria. I said, "The war is longer than the First and Second World War and must end. We will ask for a cease-fire and no-fly zone while talks last. Talks will take place in Greece. We will ask each conflicting party what they want and explain what they can have."

Motasem said through his wife, "I agree with your principle. But how can you stop a war when everyone wants the whole cake?"

I said, "We will explain they can't have the whole cake. They can have a slice but not the whole cake." I meant that there would be elections and all conflicting parties would be represented.

He said, "It is a good idea, but how will you get all the fighting parties to Athens when the WPF can't get the delegates from Malaysia because of the visa problem? Visas will be a problem for some of the Syrians."

I said, "We will have representatives who are here in Athens or who are outside Syria and can get here for negotiations."

Motasem nodded and said, "I will support it."

I said, "We have to try. There has to be a fresh start. For the 275,000 who are trapped in Aleppo under siege." (I was using the number that had appeared in the British press.)

He nodded.

I talked to Svetlana. With Larisa translating she said, "We are going to Edinburgh in December, via London. We want to meet you in London to give you a package, a present, and there will be a package for the Queen. Please deliver this package to the Queen."

I wondered what the package would contain and why I had been singled out to deliver it. In the event I was not asked to meet her in London.

I spoke to Lidia, who said she was very happy with how the week had gone.

On the coach I had told Igor he needed a bodyguard and he had said, "Lidia is my bodyguard." I had said, "Last year Father Christos produced a knife at the microphone and spoke seriously in Greek about me and I thought he was going to behead me." (See p.38.) Igor had said, "I remember that. Lidia said she was all ready to rush down from the door and take the knife away from him." I had not been sure if he was joking. Lidia was very buxom and it would have taken time for her to waddle down the steps to the microphone from the back of the theatre. By then my severed head would have been facing the audience near the microphone.

Igor came out with us to find a taxi. He said, "Your task for next year is to bring Obama and Ban Ki-moon to the Supreme Council of Humanity." I smiled. He said Natasha would be going to London, and that I should meet her there.

I thought how nice the Russians had been. I recalled reading that Philby had said how nice his Russian contacts had been in the 1930s. I could understand how he felt. These Russians were very nice people. Philby had lost his perspective and had gone to live in Moscow and had spent the rest of his life there. I was in among the Russians but had retained my perspective. I was clear that I must not allow myself unwittingly to become a Philby. But I had warmed to Igor and his family and his influential friends, and was pleased we were able to have a warm supranational friendship.

Flight home

We returned to the Poseidon Hotel after 8. Almost immediately Matthew rang Ann's mobile. He said he was looking on screen for an alternative flight and there was nothing.

Then he gave a cry and said, "A Ryanair flight has just come up at 6.30am tomorrow. I'm booking it now." We waited, and he said, "There's no extra charge. You've just switched from 16.05 to 6.30am, same seats. I'll send confirmation and boarding passes to the Hotel." It would mean getting up at 2.45am but the alternative might be to be stranded for several days.

We packed. Then I went down to Reception, paid the bill by card, booked a taxi for 3.30am and waited until the confirmation and boarding passes came through. We went to sleep about 11.15pm.

We checked in at the airport soon after 4.30am on Sunday 9 October. Ours seemed to be the only flight going. No other windows were open and there was a long queue at a closed window to re-book tickets for cancelled flights. There were only three airport staff, all on our check-in desk, and only a handful at Departures X-raying our hand luggage. Ours was the only Departure lounge open and the only two Departure-lounge staff in the building were in ours. We could see this as we boarded a bus and were driven past rows of Departure lounges and Gates in darkness.

Our plane was the only one lit and ready to go. There were 60 empty seats which could have been re-booked had people known. We had been very fortunate, we had returned to our room at exactly the right moment to enable Matthew to re-book our flight.

We were met at Stansted airport by our driver. In the car on the way home I reflected on how much of the week had been spent in running an embryonic World State and setting up a peace initiative for Syria – in aspects of international politics and statecraft – and how little of the week had been spent on philosophy, the *raison d'être* of the World Philosophical Forum. The previous year I had gone to Athens to deepen my knowledge of Plato and Aristotle in relation to my Universalism, but now I was promoting my Universalism in peace talks at Delphi, of which I was in charge, and in institutions such as the Globe Center, which would be under me, and in the Earth Bank, of which I was in co-control.

I was still not sure how it happened, but it had all come about because Igor had involved me piecemeal in what was now a considerable interconnected operation. Every day something new had been added, and I now found myself involved in more than I had originally imagined. And I did not know if I was doing all this for Igor or for the Russians at a time when the Cold War had been revived and a Third World War had loomed in the Middle East. It was weird that all this had happened, seeing that I had been a British intelligence agent known to Philby, as set out in *My Double Life 1: This Dark Wood*.

10
Peace Initiative: Urgent Statement

It is not often that a private individual who is not a diplomat or a politician finds himself involved in peace negotiations, and in such a situation it may not be clear whether this is a result of an entanglement with the whim of another private individual or whether there is State power behind the entanglement. Neville Chamberlain had at least been a politician and had not had to cope with an ambivalent situation.

What I found really strange was to be involved in peace negotiations while being in the advanced stages of preparing to receive a Peace Prize that had not yet been announced. Somehow two parallel tracks were converging, and I was not sure if this was accidental. But surely there was no way it could have been planned? Surely I was not an unwitting actor in a script that had been written without my knowledge many months previously? As there is ambiguity in political alliances and the borderline between war and peace is indistinct and in "uncertainties, Mysteries, doubts" (Keats' words), I can only narrate the events and leave their interpretation to others.

Preparations for Literature award in Manila
The night before I left for Athens Ambassador Gusi had rung me again about 6.30pm. He had told me there were now eighteen receiving awards. He wanted me to send him two British Union Jacks, which I had acquired and planned to take to Manila with me. I now arranged for them to be collected by FedEx. He had told me he had spoken to Prince Andrew about me. He had said I should invite the British Ambassador to the events on 22 and 23 November.

I now emailed the British Ambassador, Asif Ahmad. He replied promptly saying his diary was full for those days, implying that he needed more than five weeks' notice, and saying he would unfortunately be travelling outside Manila during the time I would be there.

The following Saturday, 15 October, at 4pm I was interviewed via Skype by Dan Schneider, an American literary critic who had a TV/online website and had put nearly 150 interviews with writers on YouTube. I was supposed to be talking about *A New Philosophy of Literature* but the interview widened to include my Gusi award for Literature and Bob Dylan's Nobel Prize for Literature, which Dan said was an insult to writers like me who wrote serious literature.

I said I did not begrudge Dylan his prize: Elizabethan poets like Campion and Donne had written songs, which were admittedly slight in relation to Donne's metaphysical questioning, but were still in the canon. I said the mainstream of Literature included Shakespeare's soliloquies (Hamlet's musings on life and death), Donne's profound wrestlings, Milton's questions about God, Keats' odes about life and death and Wordsworth's glimpses of the One in *The Prelude*. I pointed out that Ricks (in *Dylan's Visions of Sin*) had found all the seven deadly sins (and four cardinal virtues and three Heavenly Graces) in Dylan's work, and that my *A New Philosophy of Literature* stated the fundamental theme of world literature as a quest for Reality (to which Dylan had not contributed) and social condemnation of follies and vices, to which in Ricks's estimation Dylan *had* contributed. In fact Ricks was soon on record as pointing out that the art of song involves voice, music and words, and that it is dangerous to reduce songs to words only, as 'literature'.[1]

The interview widened through my literary works to my Universalism and my World State and to the international politics and statecraft of running the world. It lasted two and a quarter hours without a break.[2] Throughout my film-director son Tony was hiding off camera in case there were technical problems my end.

Urgent Statement on peace talks

The peace initiative was now under way. Igor had published a long version of an 'Urgent Statement' online, which we had both signed. It said:

> Earth Citizens appeal to fighting parties in the Middle East
> to stop the beginning of the Third World War
> 16 October 2016
>
> Every passing day the current situation on the earth is growing worse. For more than five years, longer than both the First and Second World Wars, there has been a war in the Middle East that looks like the beginning of a proxy Third World War, with the US and Russia both involved in bombing different factions on opposite sides. The Arab Spring that was started in North Africa now involves different conflicting groups and states fighting each other, including Islamic State.
>
> We live in a troubled time in which economic competition between nation-states and domination by some nation-states over other nation-states have led to local hybrid and proxy wars. One consequence of this chaotic disorder has been the refugees. Some 65 million displaced people from war-ravaged and poverty-

stricken countries are on the move, and many desperate families have left behind the dreadful situations in their own countries and reached Europe. The lot of those displaced by war is indeed wretched.

The current world system is based on the sovereignty of nation-states. The UN is 'inter-national', 'between nation-states', and has no authority or jurisdiction to end the wars. There have been 162 wars since 1945 on the planet which the UN has been unable to prevent or to end. The G7, G8, G20, UN General Assembly and Security Council are unable to do anything to end this war in the Middle East that has already started and is turning into a Third World War. It is obvious to every thinking person that the ongoing fighting may end in a global catastrophe. Nuclear explosions can cause a nuclear winter of minus 50C everywhere that would last for decades, or can even split planet earth into several asteroids. A colossal war that has already begun and to which we seem indifferent could culminate in a huge nuclear catastrophe that would terminate all life on earth, and of course the existence of humanity.

People all round the earth are crying out for something to be done now to prevent a coming nuclear holocaust, but the governments of nation-states and the UN seem powerless to do anything to end the misery.

Taking account of this precarious global prospect and following UN Secretary-General Ban Ki-moon's 'Education First' global citizenship initiative of 2012 and the UNESCO Medium-term Strategy 2014–2021, the World Philosophical Forum has begun the establishment of supranational Earth Citizenship in accordance with the principles and values of ancient Greek classical philosophy, notably: reason, morality, justice, wisdom and responsibility (including global responsibility). These principles can create a new social order in which humanity can extend its life on a secure planet.

In 2015 a special Constitutional Convention set up by the Citizens of the Earth adopted the Universal Constitution of the Earth, see http://glob-use.org/eng/use/convent.htm.

In accordance with this Constitution, in October 2016 the Supreme Council of Humanity (SCH) was established, the first supranational administrative institution of the Universal State of the Earth (USE), see http://glob-use.org/eng/use/sch/index.htm.

The first act of the Supreme Council of Humanity was to adopt the 'Universal Declaration on the Illegality of Wars on the Earth', see http://glob-use.org/eng/use/decl/war.htm.

Only this new supranational institution, which has been authorized by Earth Citizens, can effectively assist in negotiations to end the war that has already started in the Middle East, the Third World War. Only the Supreme Council of Humanity can bring the conflicting parties, the combatants to a peaceful agreement within the framework of the Universal State of the Earth, see http://glob-use.org/.

On behalf of all Earth Citizens the Supreme Council of Humanity appeals to all conflicting parties and combatants in the Middle East to end all armed clashes; declare their national, economic, political or ideological interests and claims in the region; and inform the Supreme Council of Humanity's Secretariat (through its e-mail address info@glob-use.org) of their readiness to observe a cease-fire and send their representatives to negotiate a peace agreement in the Middle East under the auspices, supervision and participation of the Supreme Council of Humanity and the World Philosophical Forum, on the basis of ancient Greek principles and common values of the World Philosophical Forum.

The Supreme Council of Humanity and the World Philosophical Forum propose to negotiate the peace agreement in the European Cultural Center of Delphi in Greece. (In ancient Greece, Delphi was considered the Centre of the Earth and a sacred place. It was used for settling disputes.) If a Peace Agreement on the Middle East is reached, the final signing of the agreement will take place in the Old Parliament House in Athens.

Everybody on earth should know that all those combatants in the Middle East who do not respond positively to this Urgent

Statement of the Supreme Council of Humanity within three weeks of the date of its publication on the website of the Universal State of the Earth (http://glob-use.org/) will be regarded as war criminals, named and shamed (with particular names being mentioned) as inhuman murderers and killers of the civil population in the region (men, women and children), and will be prosecuted under due process. They will be considered common enemies of the whole of humanity by all peace-loving humans on the earth.

The Supreme Council of Humanity appeals to all inhabitants of the earth to support this Urgent Statement not just by empty talk but by action – by becoming true Earth Citizens, see http://glob-use.org/eng/socr-sch/wcznrq.htm.

Otherwise, it will be widely understood that in fact they support the common enemies of humanity and wish to die in the nuclear nightmare of a Third World War, and doom to certain death all their relatives, children, parents, friends and co-citizens.

Let us together immediately end the war on the earth that is already taking place in the Middle East and maintain peace in accordance with the 'Universal Declaration on the Illegality of Wars on the Earth'.

Albert Einstein once said: "We should demand a fundamentally new way of thinking if mankind wants to survive. The fundamental problems we face cannot be solved at the same level of thinking with which we created them".

Let us raise our thinking and social life to the supranational level.

Nicholas Hagger
Chairman of the USE Supreme Council of Humanity

Igor Kondrashin
SCH Secretary-General
President of the World Philosophical Forum

Igor now uploaded a shorter, unsigned version calling for a

cease-fire and peace talks over Syria and listing thirteen conflict-ing parties.[3] The deadline for making contact was put forward a week to 15 November, and I wondered if that was to give time for a Russian attack on Aleppo after the US Presidential election on 8 November and before 15 November. (In fact Russian cruise missiles were fired at Aleppo from 15 November.)

The shorter version of the 'Urgent Statement' said:

Earth Citizens appeal to the fighting parties in the
Middle East to stop the beginning of the Third World War

On behalf of all Earth Citizens the Supreme Council of Human-ity appeals to all conflicting parties and combatants in the Mid-dle East:
1. To end all armed clashes and start peace negotiations;
2. To declare to all Humanity their national, economic, political or ideological interests, or claims in the region they wish to reach by war;
3. To inform the Supreme Council of Humanity's Secretariat as soon as possible in writing (to info@glob-use.org) of their readiness to maintain a cease-fire and send their authorised representatives to negotiate a Peace Agreement for the Middle East region under the auspices, supervision and participation of the USE Supreme Council of Humanity and the World Philosophical Forum, on the basis of the updated ancient Greek principles and universal values of the World Philosophical Forum.

The Supreme Council of Humanity and the World Philosophical Forum suggest holding the negotiations for the peace agreement for the Middle East in the European Cultural Center of Delphi in Greece. (In ancient Greece, Delphi was considered the Centre of the Earth and a sacred place. It was used for settling disputes.)

If a Peace Agreement on the Middle East is reached, the final signing of the agreement will take place in the Old Parliament

House in Athens.

The fighting parties in the Middle East:
1. The United States of America, with President Obama at its head;
2. Russia, with President Putin at its head;
3. France, with President Hollande at its head;
4. Turkey, with President Erdoğan at its head;
5. Syria, with President Assad at its head;
6. Syrian opposition;
7. Islamic State of Iraq and the Levant;
8. Kurds;
9. Iraq;
10. United Kingdom;
11. Iran;
12. Qatar;
13. Saudi Arabia; and
14. Who else? Please write to info@glob-use.org.

All those combatants in the Middle East who do not respond positively to this Urgent Statement of the Supreme Council of Humanity before 15 November 2016 will be regarded as war criminals, named and shamed (with particular names being mentioned) as inhuman murderers and killers of the civil population in the region (men, women and children), and will be prosecuted under due process.

Using my MP, Eleanor Laing, Deputy Speaker of the House of Commons, as an intermediary, I had sent her two emails about the peace initiative and my coming Gusi award, both of which she forwarded at my request to the new British Foreign Secretary, Boris Johnson. During the weekend of my interview there had been a Kerry-Johnson attempt to obtain a cease-fire and no-fly zone in Syria, which had failed, and I now indicated that our Athens initiative would be a new attempt. I sent Eleanor Laing a third email requesting UK and US support and a promise to send a representative to the talks, and wrote about bringing the conflicting parties to a Greek table. I then wrote a combined email to President Barack Obama, Secretary of State John Kerry, Senator Hillary Clinton and UN Secretary-General Ban Ki-moon asking them to support the peace initiative and send a representative.

On 20 October I attended a dinner in honour of the former British Chancellor of the Exchequer George Osborne, and, introduced by Eleanor Laing, chatted with him about Brexit. He told me there would be three negotiations: the divorce, which would take two years; the transition; and then the negotiation with the EU, which would not start until after the transition and take four to five years. He said the whole process could take ten years. (The UK's Ambassador to the EU, Sir Ivan Rogers, resigned in January 2017 after warning in an email leaked in October 2016 that the process would take ten years, which Brexiteers did not want to hear.)

I had no doubt that George Osborne was now a major political figure in the UK. I told him, "You don't need to do anything very much. As time goes by we will be in mounting deficit and people will turn to you as the politician who was right and saw it coming." He nodded.

I knew he was in touch with Henry Kissinger and soon afterwards he became the first Kissinger Fellow at the McCain Institute of International Leadership in Washington DC, an institution founded by the Republican senator John McCain.

Eleanor Laing confirmed to me that she had passed my latest email to the Foreign Secretary.

I wondered if there would in fact be support for our peace initiative as the US and UK were committed to expelling Assad from Syria so the Qatar–Turkey natural-gas pipeline could cross Syria. Assad had opposed this pipeline to protect Russian interests, Russia being Europe's top supplier of natural gas. Hence the US and UK were backing 11,000 rebels in Aleppo who Russians described as 'terrorists'. They were on the same side as al-Qaeda-linked extremists and were fighting Syrian, Russian and Iranian-backed forces. Assad, as the incumbent President, whose third seven-year term did not expire until 2021, had invited the Russians into his country to help him oppose the rebels. The US and UK needed a cease-fire in Aleppo to protect the 11,000 rebels, and Assad and Russia were prepared to bomb the 275,000 Syrians reported to be besieged and trapped in east Aleppo. (This figure dwindled to 50,000 during the next few weeks, and nobody really knew how many were holed up in east Aleppo.)

It was 'the 275,000' I was trying to save with our peace initiative. But I could see the US and UK going through the motions of peace talks, as had happened with the Kerry-Johnson effort, and failing to reach agreement because they wanted to continue the struggle against Assad. I could also see the Russians doing the same and failing to reach agreement because they wanted to take Aleppo and besiege the rebels. I could see Russia wanting a peace agreement that left Assad in place and blocked the Qatar–Turkey pipeline.

Syrian solution

As I saw it, Assad should step down, perhaps in 2021, to allow a fresh start. Removing dictators like Saddam and Gaddafi had led to the disintegration of their countries, Iraq and Libya, and I was happy that Assad should remain in power in the short term to hold Syria together while the peace plan was implemented. Russian and American interests in Syria should be guaranteed: a Russian base and continued Russian supply of natural gas to Europe, the Russian-backed Iran–Syria pipeline and the US-backed Qatar–Turkey pipeline. All bombings should cease. There should be an amnesty for all Syrian army soldiers and rebel fighters. War crimes should be prosecuted if there was evidence but this should not override the spirit of the amnesty. There would be elections, and all conflicting parties would be represented as soon as practicable. Saudi Arabia should not impose a strict Wahhabist government on Syria, and Qatar should not impose a Muslim Brotherhood government on Syria. American and Russian funding should assist the reconstruction of Syria. It would be down to me to explain that the situation of the last five years could not be allowed to continue and must be unjammed, and that no one can be an outright winner.

I pondered what I had read about US policy in the Middle East. *American Free Press* had asserted that the US wanted a Greater Israel from the Nile to the Euphrates, which would accommodate the Qatar–Turkey pipeline in Syria, and that it was achieving this by driving Islamic State (IS) out of Mosul into an escape corridor into Syria, where it could push back the Assad regime and make a Greater Israel possible.[4] Donald Trump was pro-Israel and would drive IS eastwards, and I wondered again if, although his Arabic birth name was known, the leader of IS was in fact an Israeli Mossad agent, whether al-Baghdadi was in fact Shimon (Simon) Elliot who was creating a Greater Israel between the Nile and the Euphrates with the help of Islamist fighters in a deception program that aimed to control all the Middle-Eastern pipelines (see pp.27, 78, 108).

But it was a development in Russian policy that gave most grounds for concern. On 31 October *The Times* carried a front-page headline that according to intelligence assessments there was about to be a "huge attack" on Aleppo from the Task Force led by the Russian aircraft carrier *Admiral Kuznetsov* that had passed through the English Channel. It now seemed that Aleppo would be flattened and the rebels vanquished before 15 November, and that our peace talks might in effect rubber-stamp a Russian military victory.

Earth Bank and UN

Meanwhile, starting on 19 October, Igor had sent me successive versions of a paper by John Moustos on the Earth Bank. He had told me in Athens that Moustos had attended the World Economic Forum several times. Igor said, "John mentioned the WPF but they didn't want to know as we had no money. But now we have a large deposit being made, perhaps they will want to know." Moustos, I now discovered, was based in London, at the

First Merchant Bancorp Ltd, where Natasha visited (see p.118). I thought that Natasha had introduced Moustos to Igor.

There was now a timetable to set up the Earth Bank. It would commence trading on 15 October 2017. It would deal in its new currency, the tero, and would grant loans connected with the environment, for example for projects relating to forestry, energy production, recycling, water resources and agriculture, which would support and protect the global environment. Igor wrote and re-confirmed that he and I would be deciding what loans the Earth Bank made. The question was: would the tero be a proper currency with an exchange value against pounds, dollars and euros? Moustos wrote offering a teleconference between himself, Igor and me to discuss the setting up of the bank. In my reply I asked that question.

On 25 October I had had an email from Mark Dubrulle of the Club of Rome, copying an email he had sent to Daniel Schaubacher congratulating him on being associated with a Brussels-based think-tank that was being set up to explore the constitutionality of the UN with a view to making it more effective in solving the world's problems. I replied outlining my idea of turning the UN General Assembly into the lower house of a democratic world government and saying I had already prepared a new Constitution that would turn the UN into a UF, a United Federation. On 29 October I had a reply from Shahryar Sharei, saying I would receive a response from Dr Roger Kotila, Vice-President of the San-Francisco-based Democratic World Federalists (DWF) and a founding member of the Center for United Nations Constitutional Research (CUNCR), the think-tank to which Mark had introduced me.

In due course Roger Kotila emailed me at length and said that from what he knew about me he wanted me to appear before the UN General Assembly. Soon afterwards a couple of books arrived from him, one of which contained 'A Constitution for the Federation of Earth', and in a handwritten note inside the cover he wrote: "We have much in common. I feel we can work together."

However, I knew that the new Constitution for a UF that I had prepared with Junyan should appear in print before it went to the CUNCR as the group behind the Federation of Earth had been working to promote their constitution for many years – it was first drafted in 1977 – and as they only had a page on the rights and freedoms of world citizens I was confident that our Constitution should be placed before the UN, not theirs.

Junyan emailed me with her support for this stance, saying I should present the Constitution for a UF on my own as: "You are one of the best humanists I have met." She meant 'Renaissance humanists', for the humanists in the Renaissance time operated in several disciplines as Universalists and were concerned with good governance.

Oil-painting of stag

I was now getting ready to go to Manila to receive my Gusi award. While coping with the practicalities of undertaking a visit to the Far East I reflected on my perspective, on what I stood for, and what I would say in my acceptance speech.

I had known Gillon Aitken, the main partner in the literary agency Aitken Alexander Associates, for nearly twenty years. We had sent each other many emails and letters. He was never my literary agent but we were in regular contact and he often gave me advice. His views on literature spurred me to write *A New Philosophy of Literature*, as that book's Acknowledgments make clear. I was shocked when within five days in 2011 his ex-wife died and his daughter, his only child, committed suicide. When he heard about my Gusi award he suggested I should set out the themes that had preoccupied me during the last few years, and he inspired the present book. I knew he was working from home rather than his office, and he now told me he was battling cancer, and later that he had lesions in his mouth. He told me he would fight "the rascals". Then I read his obituary in *The Times* and the next day his obituary in *The Daily Telegraph*. He had died on 28 October before hearing about my peace initiative.

On Saturday 5 November I recorded a podcast on *The Secret*

American Destiny.[5] Steve Nobel interviewed me. For half an hour I talked about the World State and Universalism. I was asked if a World State would mean McDonald's and Nando's spreading from America to every corner of the earth. I said, "No, a World State would liberate humankind from war, nuclear weapons, famine, disease and poverty." I said globalism would not swamp the world with American features. I talked about the consequences of Universalism in the seven disciplines. I talked about my peace initiative and said the UN and US were in no position to host peace negotiations as they were both changing their leaders: their Secretary-General and President.

The following Monday, 7 November, Ambassador Gusi rang about 8pm. It was the middle of the night in Manila and he was whispering, and his voice was so faint I could hardly hear him. I heard him say he was busy, and I heard him mention the Peninsula hotel where we would be staying. Perhaps he was saying that the hotel was busy. He said, "There are now sixteen Laureates." I was not sure what had happened to two of them.

I asked him, "When will the announcement be made?

He said, "November 14 or 15, on the Gusi Foundation website."

I said, "The announcement has been delayed."

He said, "Yes, for security reasons. Please do not put it on your website until after then."

I knew the Philippines had pro-IS jihadists, and I was not sure whether the security measures to narrow the time between the announcement and the award so Laureates like me would not be a target had come from the Philippine police or from Western intercessions. I was pleased that Ambassador Gusi had the Laureates' security uppermost in his mind, but the delayed announcement would delay the press releases my publishers had lined up and therefore the publicity surrounding my new books.

I continued my preparations for the Gusi award. I brought down suitcases from the loft, and our driver came by and checked that they would all go in the boot of his car. I bought Philippine pesos and Hong Kong dollars online.

Ambassador Gusi had several times (and again in his most recent telephone call) asked me to donate an oil-painting reflecting the countryside – "Nature" – around my hometown to the Gusi Museum. He said, "I ask all Laureates to donate an oil-painting. It must be an oil-painting. The Gusi Museum does not have anything but oil-paintings as they are for ever. For ever, Mr Hagger, for ever." He had said, "It will say underneath, 'In memory of Nicholas Hagger.'" 'In memory of' was a phrase that suggested someone had died, and I wondered if he knew something I did not know.

After several unsuccessful combs through the internet and consultations with several prominent local dignitaries who knew what oil-paintings were available, on Wednesday 9 November I found online a framed oil-painting of a stag titled 'At Fiddlers Hamlet, Epping Forest'. Fiddlers Hamlet was near Coopersale Hall, the school I founded in 1988. The painting was priced as £950 and the frame was an extra £150, but my offer of £500 for the lot was accepted. The stag was my literary trademark – as some stags have antlers with seven branches – and I wrote a poem 'Epping Forest Stag' saying as much, seeing myself as a stag bearing with me always, antler-like, my seven-branched works.

Privately I saw one of my antlers as my works in seven disciplines: mysticism; literature; philosophy and the sciences; history; comparative religion; international politics and statecraft; and world culture. I saw the other antler as my literary works within seven branches of literature: poems and poetic epics; verse plays and masques; short stories and novellas; diaries; autobiographies; letters; and my statement of the fundamental theme of world literature.

I collected the painting from the Euroart Studios in Markfield Road, Tottenham Hale. Ann drove me there on a wet Saturday morning, 12 November, the Saturday before we were to fly to Manila. The Studios consisted of seventy rooms like prison cells rented out to artists. The artist, Phaedon Constantin, wore a flat cap. He took me up to his anchorite's cell where I shook hands

Oil-painting of a stag in Epping Forest whose antlers symbolise the branches
of Nicholas Hagger's works; acquired for the Gusi Museum, Manila

with his wife. A propped-up *résumé* of his life gave the year of his birth, and I calculated that he was seventy.

My painting was on one of the walls with about twenty others. On the back he had written as a title 'Peaceful Day' and along the top: "Landscape Epping nearby High Street, Epping Forest – Fiddlers Hamlet." I complimented him on his beautiful paintings.

He said, "I paint from my feelings."

I said, "You were born in Istanbul to Greek parents."

He nodded.

I said, "Phaedon is a Greek name, how do you pronounce it?"

He said, "'Fay-don.' It's an ancient Greek name. Phaedon was a disciple of Socrates, and Plato wrote about him."

I knew of Plato's dialogue *Phaedo*. I thought of Paris and Athena, and now a disciple of Socrates. Three Greeks I knew had been named after a legendary hero, a goddess and a philosophical disciple who today might have attended the World Philosophical Forum.

American election and Russia
The American election on 8 November had been fought bitterly and had reached a new low in its denigration and vituperation: Donald Trump's record of groping women, his avoidance of tax and his racism; and Hillary Clinton's emails, which were investigated by the FBI towards the end of the campaign and whose disclosure was later blamed on Russian hacking directly authorised by Putin.

Trump won and was set to reverse many of Obama's policies, including Obamacare. Russia welcomed his election as he had said that NATO should not support small countries like Estonia as they did not pay enough contributions, a repudiation of NATO's Article 5 which pledges collective defence. Russia saw his remarks on NATO as a green light for a possible invasion of Estonia by Russian forces.

Trump's victory in the US Presidential campaign raised the question of how aggressively the pro-Trump Russian leadership would continue to act in Syria. He announced that his new Secretary of State would be Rex Tillerson, a friend of Putin's who while working in oil as CEO of Exxon Mobil (a company created by John D. Rockefeller and now in dispute with the Rockefeller family) had received the Order of Friendship from Putin; and he announced that Henry Kissinger (now 93 and a former employee of Rockefellers) would be involved in repairing relations with Russia. Rockefellers had always had a good relationship with Russia, having funded all Stalin's five-year plans since 1926.[6]

Immediately after Trump's election victory Russian Mikoyan MiG-29 and Sukhoi SU-33 jets began flying sorties from Russia's aircraft-carrier fleet seeking targets for cruise missile strikes around Aleppo. Russian bombers attacked rebels on the outskirts of the city (the approaches to Aleppo), who were trying to break through to relieve comrades surrounded in the east of the city. It seemed that Putin regarded Trump's victory as *carte blanche* to finish the war quickly in favour of the Assad regime. Iranian-backed troops and militias of Pakistani and Afghan Shia immigrants helped regime forces retake ground in the south-west of Aleppo.

The peace initiative had been thrown into confusion by the election result as it now seemed that there might be a new American-Russian alliance and that new thinking by Russia, Turkey and Iran might bring peace to Syria.

PART THREE

11
Manila: Peace Laureate and Invitation to
Visit Assad

'The Gusi Peace Prize 2016 for Literature' sounds very grand, especially as there were several references online to the Gusi awards being the Asian equivalent of the Nobel Prizes and I was only the third UK citizen to win a Gusi award since the Gusi awards began in 2002, and the first UK citizen to win a Gusi Literature award. Having been a Professor of English Literature in Japan and travelled through Asia, including the Philippines, on my way back to the UK in 1967, being known throughout Asia in the company of some great achievers meant a great deal to me, and I was pleased that my books would be promoted in both Asia and the West as a result of the prize.

Mission and vision of Gusi Peace Prize Foundation and
prizewinners
The Gusi Peace Foundation is a non-profit-making body that confers awards of recognition to individuals or groups who have contributed to peace and respect for human life and dignity. It recognises achievements in a wide range of skills. Its logo states "Awards for Great Achievers of the World".

The Foundation's stated mission is "to honor individuals and organizations who have given exemplary contributions to global peace and progress, through international brotherhood and friendship, and by using their God-given talents for the benefit of mankind; to champion human rights and maintain governance, democracy, equality, international peace and goodwill". Its vision is "a world of peace and prosperity due to the Gusi Peace Prize ideals (godliness–unification–service–internationalism) totally embraced by all nations".[1]

Ever since 2002 the fourth Wednesday in November has been the Gusi Peace Prize International Friendship Day, and the awarding ceremony has been held on that day at the Philippine International Convention Center in Manila, which can apparently seat 6,000–7,000. Recipients must be present.

Normally the recipients are announced on the Gusi Foundation's website. In 2016, however, there was no prior announcement as one of the recipients was the Philippine National Police's Director-General, Ronald Dela Rosa, who according to *The Guardian* was the man behind the death squads that had in extrajudicial killings killed nearly 6,000 suspected drug dealers and criminals without any trial – a claim he denied – and who would be running the country in President Duterte's absence in Peru. "For security reasons," Ambassador Gusi told me, the announcement of the awards was delayed. Contrary to what I had been told the announcement was *not* on the Gusi Foundation's website. The security issue meant that the 16 Laureates would be travelling before they had been formally invited.

Their names and awards were in an email of 7 November sent by Ambassador Gusi and Rosario (Rose) Gonzales of Gusi Peace Prize International to the British Ambassador asking him to present me with my award, and also in the awarding ceremony program. The email, which was copied to me after I arrived in Manila, began: "We would like to invite you to attend the activities of the Gusi Peace Prize as follows: Welcome Dinner at The Peninsula Manila on November 22, 2016 at 6 PM and as a presenter on November 23, 2016, 6 PM, during the 15th Annual Gusi Peace Prize International Awarding Ceremonies, at the PICC Plenary Hall. We are sure that the laureates, especially those from the United Kingdom and the British delegation will be greatly honored with your presence. Looking forward to your immediate and favorable response. In God We Trust." According to this email and the program of the awarding event on 23 November the Laureates were as follows:

1	Australia	Hon. Dr Kingsley Faulkner, for Medicine (Surgery), Anti-Smoking and Environmental Advocacy
2	Bosnia and Herzegovina	Atty. Amor Masovic, for Humanitarianism (Human Rights and Research for Missing Persons)
3	China	Prof. Baoguo Jiang, for Medical Research (Peripheral Nerve Injury Regeneration)
4	Egypt	Dr Khalid Ismail, for Innovation and Technology
5	India	Hon. Kanahiya Lal Ganju, for International Diplomacy and Philanthropy
6	Iran	Hon. Nemat Bani Adam, for Philanthropy
7	Japan	Hon. Daisaku Ikeda, for Peacebuilding through Education and Religion (Buddhism)
8	Libya	Hon. Ahmed Kashadah, for Economics
9	Philippines	Police Director-General Ronald Dela Rosa, PhD, for Peace (Fight against Drugs and Crime)
10	Romania	Health Minister Nicolae Banicioiu, for Governance and Social Services

11	Saint Kitts and Nevis	Prime Minister Timothy Harris, for Outstanding Statesmanship
12	Sudan	Sheikh Abdalla el-Badri, for Social and Educational Services
13	Syria	Architect Mousallam Sakka Amini, for Architecture and Historic Preservation
14	United Kingdom	Prof. Nicholas Hagger, for Literature
15	United States of America	Dr Philip Fidler, MD, FAC, for Medicine (Burn Surgery)
16	United States of America	Dr Vincent Giampapa, for Medicine (Cell Ageing Research)

In the event 13 Laureates attended, and two were represented by relatives (the Japanese and Sudanese Laureates). The Libyan Laureate, Hon. Ahmed Kashadah, could not attend as he was ill and his representative was not allowed to collect his award. He did not appear in the awarding ceremony's program.

Journey to Manila
On 17 November, the day before I left for Manila, *The Secret American Destiny* was published. My publisher sent me a celebratory hamper.

During the afternoon of Friday 18 November Ann, my son Tony and I, and three large green suitcases, were driven to Heathrow, and after a wait in a VIP lounge flew to Hong Kong by Cathay Pacific at 5.15pm.

We sat as a three in premium economy to have extra legroom. We 'slept' from 8pm till 2.30am, and gained eight hours. Breakfast was at 10.30am (Hong Kong time). We landed in Hong Kong at 12.15pm (4.15am GMT) and in heat transferred to our

2.15pm flight to Manila. The last time I was there, in 1967, Hong Kong was inefficient and chaotic but now everything worked perfectly.

I picked up a free newspaper, *The Philippine Daily Inquirer*, and in the air read about the Philippines. The news was dominated by the burial of the former Philippine leader Ferdinand Marcos in the Heroes' Cemetery early in the morning. The burial was authorised by President Duterte and carried out by Dela Rosa, my fellow Laureate, and all the stories in the newspaper only mentioned their two names. No names of any ministers appeared, and it was clear to me that the Philippines were being run by Duterte and Dela Rosa.

We landed in light rain in Manila around 4.30pm. We were met by a large limousine from the Peninsula, welcomed by a dark-suited greeter, wished a pleasant stay and then driven to the hotel in early dark. The traffic was stationary and it took an hour and a half to complete a journey that normally takes 15 minutes.

The hotel had Christmas lights: angels with trumpets. There was airport-style security outside. Our suitcases were sniffed for drugs and explosives by sniffer-dogs and passed through an X-ray machine, and we were screened by a body scanner.

The air-conditioned Lobby was marble and retained its pre-war (1936) splendour. A huge sun with rays dominated the ceiling and there were tables and chairs on both sides of a central aisle.

A lady with a clipboard was waiting for us inside the door and, having arranged for our cases to be brought up separately, led us to the lift and up to the ninth floor. She asked for our passports and checked us in within our spacious and modern room, 938, which connected with Tony's room, 940, by an internal lockable door. Our cases arrived before she left.

We unpacked and the three of us went down to the Lobby and had a late light supper of wantoon soup with dumplings and a platter of fruit while a Palm-Court-style live orchestra played Western music (Beatles and Sinatra songs) above us on a balcony. I gathered that the hotel was occupied by the Japanese during the war, and like the marble the mood was of the 1930s.

Before we returned to our rooms I asked Reception if there was a co-ordinator for the Gusi Laureates, who were all supposed to be staying at the Peninsula. There wasn't. So I emailed Ambassador Gusi from Tony's laptop to report our arrival and ask if we were involved in the next day's 'International Peace Summit' as listed on an 'itinerary' I had found online.

International Peace Summit

I slept soundly from 11.45pm to 6am and dozed until 8. It was now Sunday morning. We had breakfast and sauntered to the pool in heat. All the hotel's corridors were air-conditioned.

I worked at my desk on the possible speeches I might have to make, collecting my thoughts, and went down to the swimming-pool. There were palm trees on one side under a blue sky and it was distantly overlooked by tall buildings. We sat under an umbrella in shade and ate crab-and-lobster bridge rolls.

Suddenly there was a squall. Rain lashed. I vacated the chair I had been sitting on and a whirlwind blew my padded seat into the pool. It floated to the other side. Then calm weather and hot sunshine returned. Tony went to the gym, which faced the pool, and Ann and I sunbathed for ten minutes in a temperature of 32C until the sun moved behind one of the tall buildings.

I left Ann dozing and returned to our room. I rang Ambassador Gusi but there was no reply. At 4.30pm I went back to the pool to report that we were presumably not going out in the evening. I went back to our room and as I opened the door at 4.50pm I heard the phone ringing. It was Ambassador Gusi.

He said, "You are being collected at 6. All of you. Smart clothes."

So I returned to the pool and told Ann she had to change and found Tony in the gym's locker-room. When I got back to our room a lady rang and said we would be collected at 6.30pm.

We all went down to the Lobby at 6.10pm and voluntary co-ordinators introduced themselves and took me to meet some of my fellow Laureates. I talked at length with a Syrian who was based in Qatar but was still in touch with Syria, Mousallam Sakka Amini. He had a sallow face and white hair and a close beard and spectacles, and I liked him. I said I wanted to bring peace to Syria and explained how I would go about it, and he said, "I will get you to Assad." I was surprised but said, "I will go."

I met a Chinese from Macau, Dr Billy Chan, who spoke impeccable English. He gave me his visiting-card – they all had cards to hand out – and I saw he was a Vice-President of Gusi Peace Prize International besides being Director of Macau-based medical bodies. He said, "I'm so pleased you are a Laureate. I knew your work, and when I saw your name on the list I said, 'Wow, we must have him, I know his books.' I was thrilled it was you, you have such a big name." I met his publicity manager and assistant, Chris Cottrell, an American who had married a Chinese girl, lived in China and wrote for the *South China Sea Magazine*. I knew that not all the Laureates had yet arrived, but I met Laureates from India and Iran.

We boarded a coach and sat until 7.15pm, and I gradually became aware that in the Philippines a stated time could have massive slippage. We eventually drove through the dark to Viviere Hotel in Alabang, Muntiniupa City. We were shown up to a large room filled with round laid tables before a stage.

Ann, Tony and I were guided to a table with the Indian Laureate Kanahiya Lal Ganju, a Consul and benefactor, and his family, and also one of the two American Laureates, Dr Fidler, a burns specialist. There was a notice on the stage making it clear that we were being hosted by a Rotary Club and that the theme was 'sustainability'.

Ambassador Gusi and his wife entered. They had a permanent group of people standing round them.

This was my first meeting with him after our phone calls. I went across and joined a queue and waited until several women and young ladies had finished their conversations with him. He was small in stature with slow, astute eyes and an intent look, and had considerable ambassadorial bearing. I smiled and shook his hand and introduced Ann and Tony. I shook hands with his wife and smiled at his four children who were nearby. But there was no time to talk as two compères asked us all to return to our tables as dinner was being served. He did not ask about our journey or whether we were comfortable in the Peninsula.

During the four-course meal – shiitake mushroom, salad, sea bass and a combination of crème brûlée, chocolate parfait and cheesecake – compères introduced the five Laureates present and

Nicholas Hagger speaking at the International Peace Summit on 20 November 2016

we all had to stand in turn and acknowledge applause. There were several dancing displays by Philippine dancers.

Then the Laureates were called up to speak. I was after the Indian, Iranian and Syrian Laureates and before the US Laureate – speeches were in our countries' alphabetical order – and I climbed onto the stage and gripped the lectern and addressed the room.

Free-wheeling, I began, "I am a Universalist." I said that a Universalist believes that the universe and humankind is a unity, and I mentioned some of my books. I said, "There have been 162 wars since 1945, and that's too many." I said, "I want a World State that can abolish war." I told them about the think-tank to examine the constitutionality of the United Nations to make it more effective in solving the world's problems and bringing peace. I talked of the earth's sustainability under a new world structure.

What I said seemed to go down well and Ambassador Gusi stood and shook my hand as I made my way back to my seat. His wife and four children were sitting on his table, and each came and had a word as we were leaving. I walked downstairs with the youngest, a boy of about ten, and asked him, "Do you want to do what your father is doing one day?" and he said very maturely, "Yes. I want to do what my father is doing."

The coach brought us home and as we walked up to the hotel entrance Chris, the American journalist, said he would like to interview me. So Ann and Tony went up to their rooms and Chris found a free table in the Lobby. His boss Billy Chan found us and sat opposite me. Chris produced his mobile and recorded me. He asked me questions about the World State I envisaged and my Peace Plan for Syria. Billy Chan asked, "What will happen to the Commonwealth?" I said it could be bolted on to the World State like the EU.

The conversation turned to President Duterte and the Director-General of Police, and I said I thought the two were running the country.

Chris said, "That's a very astute comment." He said he would like to get to President-elect Trump.

So I said, "Send him your recording of this interview."

He said, "I will. And I'd like to get to the Chinese leader."

I said, "Send it to him as well."

Again Chris said, "I will."

I gathered that as an American living in China he wanted access to the leaders of the US and China.

I asked how they saw Ambassador Gusi. I said, "He is very devoted to the Gusi Foundation and enormously respected. I've heard he's a billionaire, is that your impression?"

Both men were silent. Then Billy Chan looked at his watch. Now I realised the time was 12.30am, and ended the interview, which had gone on for well over an hour. I went up to bed.

Peace-Tourism Summit: lunch with Mayor

The next day, Monday 21 November, we were up at 6.30am and finished breakfast at 7.30am to assemble for 8am to be taken to a 'Peace-Tourism Summit'. We had been told in the coach the previous evening that the dress would be smart casual, so I wore a fawn linen jacket and open-necked blue shirt. Then the lady volunteer co-ordinators came and said there would be a delay as some of the Laureates were still having breakfast and that Ambassador Gusi would be travelling with the coach and was on his way.

While we waited I talked with the Iranian and Syrian Laureates. Both men were very wealthy. The Iranian, Bani Adam, spoke little English but from his wife and grown-up daughters I learned that since the 1970s he had been a philanthropist and had created schools and universities out of his own funds throughout Iran.

The Syrian, Mousallam, had had a kind of museum in Damascus, which he had moved to Qatar for safety. It contained many valuable 18th-century *objets d'art*, and he said Ambassador Gusi had befriended him with his Gusi Museum in mind. Mousallam said, "We never had war in Syria. Six years ago everything was peaceful. The superpowers need to get out and then the Syrian conflict is manageable. There is enough money in Syria to rebuild the country in five years."

In the end the coach left at 9.50am. We had a police escort as we would be going outside Manila where kidnapping was rife, and hundreds of police stood at every junction, holding up traffic and waving us through. Most of the police were armed. We left built-up Manila and passed through frondy jungle, and still the police were at every intersection, making sure we kept moving. It must have taken a lot of co-ordination as Manila has 16 cities, each under a mayor, and the traffic regulations differ in each city.

Eventually we arrived in the city of Santa Rosa in Laguna, and with police guarding the coach exit we clambered down and walked up a slope to a glassy entrance, where there were many photographers.

We walked through to a large auditorium filled with students and a vast stage. The Laureates were given garlands (necklaces of beads holding a red-petalled yellow badge of the city) and were then introduced – we had to stand and nod – and then we sat in the front row and watched some dancing (a 'doxology', liturgical praise to God) and then stood for the national anthem.

The Philippines flag was shown on a large screen. Some of the Laureates were in suits and I made a mental note not to listen to guidance to wear 'smart casual'.

The Vice-Mayor welcomed us at 10.50am, and we were then welcomed by the Mayor, Dan Fernandez, a young man with long hair who looked as if he was still a student. We then watched several groups of dancers and listened to a quintet, and then four of the Laureates had to go up and speak: the US Laureate Dr Fidler; the Indian; the Iranian; and then me.

I walked up to the platform when it was my turn and, holding a microphone, talked about humankind's being a unity and how tourism helped people appreciate its different cultures.

Nicholas Hagger speaking at the Peace-Tourism Summit in Santa Rosa City, Laguna on 21 November 2016

The speeches and Ambassador Gusi's final words took until 1pm. I noted that Ambassador Gusi had a saintly image. He was regarded by everyone with huge respect, as a kind of Gandhi figure who had devoted his life to the values of the Gusi Foundation and to the annual awarding ceremonies and all the organisation they entailed. But he was also something of a mystery. No one knew much about him or his wealth.

We went out to a crowded area where all those who had attended sat at round tables and waiters squashed between. I was on the same table as Ambassador Gusi and the Mayor, and the Syrian Laureate. We were served pumpkin soup, salad, Angus beef, cake with mousse and fruit, and iced tea. From the top of the menu protruded two round 'diamonds'. Ambassador Gusi was silent and kept getting up and talking to people between tables. He occasionally whispered to the Syrian. He had his own agenda and was very watchful.

Nicholas Hagger (left) lunching with the Mayor (centre, back), with (to right) Mousallam and Ambassador Gusi, and (foreground) Ann and Tony

I talked at length with the Mayor about his city. He told me 180,000 voted in the mayorial election, he employed 3,500 and had been in power 100 days. He looked after seventy to eighty schools and a hospital. His main problem was 'homeless settlers'. I asked, knowing about the death squads that targeted drug suppliers after dark, "Are drugs a problem in your city?" He said tersely, "Yes," and stood up and went to talk to somebody who was standing nearby. He did not want to talk about the death squads.

We returned along a road through the frondy jungle back to the suburbs, at one point going against the traffic which was held up to speed up our journey. In the hotel Lobby Ambassador Gusi sat with an assistant over a laptop, and I asked him if he could take delivery of the oil-painting of the stag I had brought in my suitcase.

He said, "Yes, go and get it now."

I went up and fetched the painting from our room. I cut the tape that held protective cardboard in place front and back and returned to the Lobby in the lift and put it on the next table and opened it.

He peered at the stag and said, "Ah, it's oil."

"Yes."

"Is it oil?" he asked suspiciously. He held the painting up and squinted so he could have a close look. "Not film?"

"No," I said, "an oil-painting."

"I like it," he said. "It will go in the Gusi Museum."

I showed him the manuscript poem that accompanied it. I told him he could frame the poem and the typed text. "One day that manuscript may be of value."

He read the first line, "An Epping Forest stag", and said "Oh" and packed it away in the wrapping. He said, "Can I change the frame? And put glass on it?"

Nicholas Hagger presenting Ambassador Gusi with the oil-painting
of the stag

I thought he was asking whether this was technically possible rather than asking permission. "Yes," I said. It was a good
double frame.

Tony was with me, holding his camera. Ambassador Gusi
held the painting and consented to two pictures with me standing alongside handing it to him. "And on this camera," Tony
said.

Ambassador Gusi said, "No more photos, I have run out of
time. I have to go home and change to be back for 5."

He was clearly very busy. He placed the re-wrapped painting
on a chair and turned back to the laptop he had been looking at.

Later in our visit Ann saw Dr Fidler and his wife hand over
a painting they had brought. She said Ambassador Gusi took it
and put it to one side without looking at it, probably because he
was busy at that particular moment.

"Tonight," he said as we were leaving, "Laureates only, not
family." To Tony he said, "You cannot come."

I said, "Someone said that as it's a medical forum, only the
medical Laureates should attend."

"No, you come," he said to me. "Suit and tie."

Sino-Asia Pacific Medical Forum
I changed into a suit and white shirt and tie and found the
room on the second floor where the Sino-Asia Pacific Medical
Forum were dining. Tables were laid with white tablecloths and
half a dozen marines in uniform were waiting in the wings to
march flags. I spoke to the Chinese Laureate, the President of
the Peking University People's Hospital Baoguo Jiang and his
deputy Tianbing Wang, and then passed the American Laureate
Dr Fidler, who was talking with the Australian Laureate Dr
Kingsley Faulkner and another Australian to the Syrian Laureate
Mousallam.

"Here's a philosopher," said Dr Faulkner with a twinkle in
his eye, "we have a conundrum for you. Our Syrian friend de-
signs buildings and approaches them through architecture. We
are saying that the design of the human body leaves much to

be desired. The sex parts and bowels are too near each other. So what does philosophy say about the design of buildings and the body? You can adjudicate for us." And I found myself talking about the symmetry of legs and arms and fingers and toes, which could not be bettered, as they agreed, and the symmetry of windows in buildings. I came away with the other Australian, Ross Hytor. We were guided to a table and sat and talked, and no one else joined us.

Ambassador Gusi welcomed us from a microphone, and he thanked Michael Nobel of the family that funds the Nobel prizes for being with us, a lean Swede with silver hair and reddish cheeks. He introduced Dr Manson Fok, a Chinese whose late father had been a non-Communist Vice-Premier. Then he stepped off the platform and came to me, looked at the empty places on our table and said, "Where's your wife?"

I said, "We were told 'Laureates only'. Not their families, for this dinner."

"Go and get your wife and son."

Nicholas Hagger at the Sino-Asia Pacific Medical Forum dinner, 21 November 2016

So I went down to the pool and told Ann she was expected to change and join us, and I found Tony in the gym. He said he would come when he had finished his work-out. I returned to the dinner and we were now joined by the Libyan Gasim, who was attending on behalf of the Libyan Laureate who could not travel as he had cancer; by the Romanian Laureate (the Romanian Minister of Health); and by some Chinese.

There were on-screen presentations. Ann and Tony slid in at different times and caught most of them. The Chinese Laureate spoke about his work in China, where he had cut trauma death rates from 27 per cent to 17 per cent. Dr Fidler spoke on burns and showed graphic illustrations of naked bodies with 80-per-cent burns and broken limbs, and slides showing how the limbs were reconstructed. The Australian Laureate, Dr Faulkner, spoke on medical progress in Australia. Another American Laureate, Dr Vincent Giampapa, who had been twice nominated for a Nobel prize, spoke on his stem-cell work which, he claimed, was arresting ageing. Others spoke.

Ambassador Gusi now announced and presented the new Gusi Peace Prize International Committee. Dr Manson Fok was the new President, and Ambassador Gusi then called out names of around twenty, and one by one they came up on stage, including Dr Fidler; the Indian Laureate; and Gasim, the Libyan deputiser. The Syrian Laureate was among them and I understood what Ambassador Gusi had been whispering to him at lunchtime. Ambassador Gusi announced that each would be expected to attend three meetings during the coming year, and to be present at next year's Peace Prize awards in Manila.

I was clear that I could not be making the visits because of my heavy schedule for the coming year and was ready to decline, but to my relief my name was not called. We left as soon as we could and went to bed as we had to be up at 5.15am the next morning.

Wreath-laying in Rizal Park
The next morning, leaving Ann asleep, Tony and I breakfasted at 5.30am and were ready with the other Laureates in the Lobby to leave for a wreath-laying ceremony in Rizal Park. Jose Rizal, a national hero, had been executed in 1896, and wreath-laying at his memorial is embedded in Philippine culture.

We were taken in two coaches through traffic full of slender and brightly-coloured 'jeepneys' (local buses that could navigate narrow streets). We parked in the wide Taft Avenue, on the other side of which was a high billboard with the inflated images of 16 Laureates, including me.

The Park's spacious lawns were encircled by police standing

every hundred yards. A rectangular area before the monument had been cordoned off. It was surrounded by a small crowd several deep, including a number of police. Large flags of all the Laureates' countries were at the road end, held by marines in uniform, and we Laureates took our places in front of our flags. We stood in two rows for a ceremony, the Laureates in front

Billboard showing (left) the Gusi Laureates with Nicholas Hagger standing beneath his image (bottom row, third from right) and (right) next to the Syrian Laureate Mousallam

of their flags and members of the Gusi Peace Prize International-al Committee in front of them, including Ambassador and Dr Gusi, and before us all, on stools, stood a marine and the Indian

Nicholas Hagger at wreath-laying ceremony in Rizal Park, walking third from right (left) and standing before British flag (right)

Laureate. The two of them marched to the monument bearing wreaths and, having laid them, returned. The marine saluted the Indian Laureate, who returned the salute. There were a couple of dozen photographers and a TV camera.

Then we all walked towards the monument and stood facing it with our flags behind us while three shots were fired. The marines now took up positions with their backs to the monument, holding the flags, and we turned and stood facing the avenue and were photographed and filmed. Then we walked back and dispersed.

Many came and spoke to us Laureates and we were photographed many times with different groups of people. On the way back to the coach I talked with the new Chinese President of the Gusi Peace Prize International Committee, Dr Fok. He told me his father had been one of the first Chinese modernisers.

We climbed aboard our coach and were driven across the avenue to the billboard. We dismounted and I stood under my picture to be filmed by Tony, and was then photographed over and over again as the photographers gathered. The other Laureates joined me and we stood in a long line for more photographs.

We returned to the coach and were taken through the Spanish town, Intramuros, which I visited in 1967, past San Augustin church, and Fort Santiago, which housed Japanese-controlled dungeons during the Second World War. The guide told us that as Manila is composed of 16 cities with 16 Mayors there are 16 different sets of regulations for many civic functions; and that the sun symbol, which was on many buildings as well as on the national flag, has eight rays (sometimes eight double-rays) which represent the eight provinces where the Philippine language was first spoken. We returned to our hotel around 11am.

Welcome dinner
In Tony's room I dictated my speeches for the welcome dinner that night and the awarding ceremony the following night. He printed them off on a printer downstairs in Reception. Short of sleep, I then drew the curtains, got into bed, read that night's

speech and fell asleep for a couple of hours. When I woke I lay in bed and looked at that night's speech until 4pm. Ann came up from the poolside and made a few suggestions on the speeches, requiring manual changes.

I put on a suit and at 5pm I went to the Peninsula's Rigodon Ballroom on the ground floor for the Laureates' 'press conference'. From the deserted foyer I peeped through the open double doors and saw a huge empty room and many tables laid with white tablecloths, cutlery and glasses; and chairs.

Then one of the co-ordinators said, "There has been a change, come at 6.30."

Someone else said, "No, Laureates at 6."

So I returned upstairs to our room.

There I found a letter addressed to me that had been pushed under the door. It was from Ms Rosario (Rose) Gonzales, the volunteer co-ordinator, and said: "There is a delay of the media coverage due to an emergency at Camp Crame." That was the HQ of the Director-General of Police. "Media coverage is moved to 6.30. Program starts at 7."

I had been told that the Laureates should gather at 6pm so I returned downstairs and found Chris, the journalist, in DJ. He said, "It's formal, we've been told DJ."

I said, "Well news of that hasn't reached the Laureates. I've got DJ upstairs."

He said, "It's Laureates at 6.30 now, you've got time to go up and change."

So I returned to my room and changed into DJ and joined the other Laureates, most of whom had also been up and changed into DJ. Then we hung around in the Lobby, standing, until 8pm, waiting for the Director-General of Police. Someone told me, "He caught a fugitive and had to appear on television, and now he is held up in traffic."

There was a five-minute photo opportunity before a couple of dozen journalists but no interviews. Ambassador Gusi stood before us and spoke to a national-television camera. There was a reduced version of the billboard by the Reception desk, and the

Laureates were photographed against their pictures. From one of the receptionists I was able to establish that most countries had representatives from their embassies, but not the US (still smarting because Obama had been called "the son of a whore" by President Duterte) or the UK – despite the formal invitation from Ambassador Gusi. I noted that there was no sign of the box of books I had sent by FedEx, but as all the volunteers knew of the books and had obviously seen them it had been worth sending. Then we were shown to round tables near the stage.

Nicholas Hagger sitting next to Vincent Giampapa (left) at the welcome dinner

Ann, Tony and I were seated next to Dr Vincent Giampapa, the American Laureate whose stem-cell research had earned him two nominations for a Nobel prize. He looked very young – he had no wrinkles and looked as if he had had Botox – and he told us: "I've arrested ageing in animals, and I want to arrest ageing in humans. They won't allow me to do this in America, so I'm relocating to Costa Rica where I will be allowed to experiment on human volunteers."

I asked, "Have you experimented on yourself?"

"Yes," he said, "of course."

I said, "It's like a story by Robert Louis Stevenson."

He said, "The one on Dr Jekyll and Mr Hyde.[2] Dr Jekyll experimented on himself and became Hyde, but I don't become Hyde. How old would you think I am? I'm sixty-seven, but my biological age is thirty-seven. I've had no surgery. What you see is just arrested ageing. I can give seventy-year-old humans the quality of life of twenty-year-olds."

I thought he would not be able to arrest the ageing of their brains.

Tony leaned forward and said, "I'd like to make a film on that."

"Sure," Vincent said. "You can come to Costa Rica and I'll do it. You have higher consciousness," he said to me. "What you were saying in one of your speeches, that everything is one, reminded me of Hesse's *Magister Ludi*. Do you know that book? All disciplines are one. It's all there. I would be interested in experimenting on *you*. You can come to Costa Rica with your son? I want to find out if higher consciousness makes a difference to the cells. You already seem to have some age-arresting."

I told him I went to the gym once a week, was careful with my diet and worked every day on my books from 8am till after midnight, which kept my mind active.

He nodded. "I'll welcome you both to Costa Rica."

Beyond him, listening, was Michael Nobel, and I brought him into the conversation. I told him my view of Universalism and the World State, and said I had a Syrian Peace Plan in mind. He agreed with everything I said. Not having Googled him and not knowing he was the Swedish-Russian great-grandson of Alfred Nobel's brother Ludvig, who was the richest man in the world in his day, and that Michael was therefore Alfred Nobel's great-grand-nephew, I asked if he was the head of the Nobel family. He said, "I was, but I am not now."

Nicholas Hagger (centre) between Ann and Vincent Giampapa, with Michael Nobel (third from left), Philip Fidler (far left), Issam Eldebs (second from right) and Mousallam

I did not know he had been the elected head of the Nobel family and served as Vice Chairman and Chairman of the Board of the Nobel family from 1991 to 2006; or that in 2007 he was deselected for attempting to start a new Nobel prize with three other members of the family (Gustaf, Peter and Philip Nobel), the Michael Nobel Energy Award for developing clean energy.

There was now a new 'head of the family', Michael Sohlman, Director of the Nobel Foundation who was a descendant of an adviser to Alfred Nobel and was not of the Nobel family itself. He allegedly disapproved of the use of the Nobel name in the Michael Nobel Energy Award and Michael Nobel's Nobel Charitable Trust, which contributed to conflict resolution programs and peace education, and the Nobel Family Benevolent Society. I did not know that Michael Nobel was at present Chairman of the Nobel Sustainability Trust to accelerate the development of clean energies, and was supported by his Serene Highness Prince Albert II of Monaco.

He said, "I am Swedish, and I funded the Nobel prizes for 15 years. I don't nominate people."

I asked what he thought of Bob Dylan's refusal to attend the awarding ceremony to collect his Nobel Prize for Literature.

He said, "It is very disappointing, we are disappointed."

I said I could see there was a tradition of song in literature going back to the early Greeks and that his early songs criticised the Vietnam War and civil rights abuses, but if T.S. Eliot and Hemingway could attend, proper writers, then he should attend too.

Both Michael and Vincent said simultaneously, "I completely agree."

I asked, "Will the initial investment last?"

He pulled a face and expressed doubt. He said, "I am having to subsidise it."

I could sense that Michael was still an important behind-the-scenes figure in the Nobel prizes.

I gathered he was a Professor in Osaka. He was interested in my literary works, and I gave him a publisher's leaflet I had in my pocket, which he said he would read.

While I was talking to him Tony had got up and vacated his seat to put his tripod in the right place for filming. And a man I did not know came and sat next to the Syrian Laureate, and his daughter sat next to him – in Tony's seat. I had not seen this as my back was turned while I was talking to Michael Nobel. With eminent good sense Tony accepted the situation and decamped to a nearby table, not wanting to make a scene.

The welcome dinner started and lengthy conversation was no longer possible. There was a doxology and the Philippine national anthem was played on a screen while all stood and the Philippine citizens placed their right hands on their hearts. There was a dance troupe and the new President of Gusi Peace Prize International, Dr Fok, spoke on the platform, introducing each of the Laureates in the room, so we all had to rise and bow in turn. During the first two courses of the meal – parsnip soup and beetroot salad – the Laureates were called up to speak in the alphabetical order of their countries, starting with the Australian Laureate. Many spoke a few lines only, off the cuff.

Eventually it was my turn. I stood, strode to the microphone, looked at the 500 diners and followed my text from memory, occasionally glancing down for a prompt. I said:

Ambassador and Dr Gusi, fellow Laureates, ladies and gentlemen, greetings from the United Kingdom.

I am grateful to the Gusi Foundation for awarding me the Gusi Peace Prize for Literature. I've been an author for most of my lifetime, and my literary works have reflected my experience of the world's diverse cultures.

I was a Professor of English Literature in Japan and was private tutor to Emperor Hirohito's second son, Prince Hitachi. I lectured at the University of Baghdad and the University of Libya, and was an eyewitness of the Gaddafi revolution. I was also in China at the beginning of the Cultural Revolution. When I was a journalist for *The Times* I visited Africa and saw the building of the Tanzam Railway.

During my wide travels I have observed the tolerance and respect that people of all cultures generally show each other in their daily lives. I have also observed the darker side of human nature when national self-interest gets in the way and results in war and destruction. Self-interested nation-states have been quick to declare war, often without adequate justification. Wars have caused great inequality, poverty and suffering.

In more than 40 books I have tried to reflect the growing disharmony in the world, which seems to be escalating into greater conflict. Now is the time to do something about it before it turns into a Third World War. We Laureates in our various disciplines are striving to improve people's lives and make the world more peaceful. I believe that we can make a difference in our own ways.

The Gusi Foundation has been seeking to counteract poverty and inequality by its charitable works and by recognising individuals who are working for the greater good within their fields. Let's hope we can all make a difference as we strive to make a better world for the coming generations.

Thank you.

My speech was very well received. I seemed to have struck a nerve. The Syrian Laureate, Mousallam, stood up as I returned to the applauding table and came and shook my hand. He said, "That was excellent. May I introduce you to the Syrian Consul General, Issam Eldebs?" And I shook hands with the man whose daughter had unwittingly taken Tony's seat.

Issam, a pleasant, smiling man with fair hair, said, "I can get

you to Assad. I have heard that you need to get there."

Elated at his interpretation of my speech and that he was indirectly asking me as a Peace Laureate to undertake a peace mission, I sat with

Nicholas Hagger speaking at the welcome dinner

him on one side of the stage, which was a couple of feet off the main floor and ideal for sitting on, and talked with him.

He said, "Your next book will be titled *Assad and Me*. And they'll be talking not about Assad but 'me'. You."

I said I wanted to meet Assad and then Putin, and then Trump.

He said, "You can fly to Putin from Damascus. Assad's people will arrange that."

I returned to my seat as Vincent was speaking and I wanted to be respectful. When he finished he lingered at the microphone and I leaned across the empty chair and, not knowing that his Nobel Charitable Trust contributed to conflict resolution programs, said to Michael Nobel, "We were talking about Syria. That man has just offered to get me, as a Peace Laureate, to Assad."

Michael misunderstood. He thought I was asking that Assad should be given a Nobel prize. He said, "No, that can't happen. That's too controversial. He cannot receive a Nobel prize."

I said, "I wasn't saying Assad should get a Nobel prize. He will arrange for me to meet Assad to try and bring peace to Syria. It's happened at our table."

Now he understood. He looked at me and said, "If you solve Syria, you will receive a Nobel prize without any shadow of doubt."

As Vincent returned and I congratulated him, Ronald Dela Rosa, the controversial Director-General of Police, on whose watch nearly 6,000 suspected drug dealers and criminals had been shot in extrajudicial killings, advanced to the microphone. He had arrived mid-meal and had been sitting on Ambassador Gusi's table in a black outfit. He was a smallish, brawny man with a completely bald head.

He began his talk: "People have asked me why I have been given a Gusi Peace Prize. I have the answer: 'I make it safe so the good guys can live in peace and the bad guys rest in peace.'" There was a gale of laughter from the audience. Although *The Guardian* had identified him as the organiser of the death squads, a claim he had denied, he was clearly popular. He said, "I have cut crime by 48 per cent." Someone told me that 3,500 drug deal-ers had handed themselves in to avoid being shot by the death squads, preferring prison to death after dark.

Now Issam came and stood by me. I rose and he said, "I need to talk with you further."

There was a musical entertainment, a singer was singing very loudly. So I said, "Let's talk in the Lobby away from this music."

He nodded. I set off and threaded my way through the tables to the Lobby and sat at the nearest table. I looked up at the huge sun that dominated the ceiling. The orchestra was playing softly. Issam joined me, having made his own way across the ballroom.

I explained my Peace Plan in some detail (see pp.202–206) and how I saw a coming World State. I explained the Supreme Council of Humanity's peace initiative. I mentioned Igor Kon-drashin.

He said, "I know Igor." And the thought crossed my mind that Igor was behind his approach. I immediately dismissed the thought. He said, "I'll take you to Assad but you must write about the situation so Assad knows about it, and bring two advisers who Assad will take seriously."

I said, "Trump hasn't yet appointed anyone to specialise in Syria."

He said, "Perhaps a Congressman. You will fly to Beirut and we will get you in safely by land."

I thought aloud. "Perhaps one of the advisers should be a British expert, perhaps even the new Foreign Secretary Boris Johnson."

He said, "You can't bring Johnson. He reflects the EC's view of Syria, the European Commission's. There are six enemies of Syria. Not America. They are Qatar, Turkey, Jordan, Saudi Ara-bia, France and the UK." Then he said, "It may be a good idea to go to Russia first, to meet Putin first. He controls Syria. Get Igor to get you to Putin." As I expressed doubt about going to President Putin first, he asked me, "Have you got a book here that you can send to Assad with a message in the front?"

I said, "I've got a copy of *The World Government*."

"Good, in your room? Get it now. You can give it to me at our table. Sign it for Assad."

So I went up in the lift to my room, found the book, composed my thoughts and wrote: "For President Assad, these thoughts on a World State abolishing war after the solution to the Syrian war, hoping to discuss my Peace Plan with you." I signed it, dated it "22 November 2016, Manila" and added "Gusi Peace Laureate 2016". I put the book in an envelope so it would not be seen by the diners.

I returned to the ballroom. A male singer was singing on the stage. I walked between tables and sat on the side of the stage, and Issam joined me. I showed him what I had written.

He nodded and said, "Can you add at the end, 'Through Issam Eldebs, your Consul in Manila'?"

So I added that and gave him the book.

He said, "This will be on Assad's desk on Monday. Send me an email on Monday when you return. Get it to me by 8pm Manila time. I am friendly with the Prime Minister who is like this (he put two forefingers side by side, suggesting 'close') with Assad. He will put this on Assad's desk. See you tomorrow."

The singer was still singing and I returned to my seat.

Now Ann told me that while I was out of the room the architect of the Gusi Museum, an American from Los Angeles, spoke and film had been shown of his conception of the Gusi Museum, which would include my picture of a stag.

"It has not been built yet," Ann said. "He showed us the architect's conception of what it will look like. He said he hoped there will be donations towards it. He did not say where the donations will come from. He said there is to be a coffee-table book with all the past Laureates in it, and they will all want to buy it and the proceeds will go towards the Museum. It's a serious project but it hasn't been built yet."

I nodded. What she said fitted in with my view of the saintly Gusi as recognising great achievers and simultaneously advancing his public standing. Ann also said that the Prime Minister of Saint Kitts and Nevis had spoken, and had been garlanded.

Now the formal part of the evening was over. There would soon be dancing for those who wanted to dance. Issam asked if his daughter could take a picture of me handing *The World Government* to him. I duly obliged.

Nicholas Hagger (left) presenting Issam Eldebs, Syrian Consul General, with *The World Government* signed to President Assad, and in discussion with him (centre and right)

Ambassador Gusi requested all Laureates to stand on the stage for final photos. I saw Issam's daughter taking a photograph of me, standing beside Issam. There was a battery of cameras. I looked at each without blinking. On the way out I shook Ambassador Gusi's hand and he cupped his hands and whispered in my ear like the Devil, "I love the painting."

As I left a beautiful young Philippine girl came to me and said, "Would you like to dance?"

I said, "I would love to but I have to go with them," indicating my family and the other Laureates. As we returned Tony said six girls had approached him and asked for their photo to be taken with him. I jested, "They probably wanted to get to know you so you could introduce them to your Laureate father."

I stayed up writing my diary and pondering the events of the day, and did not get to bed until 1.45am. I reflected that I had played a blinder with Issam and had made something happen.

Something dramatic had happened. I had been asked to meet Assad, who looked like winning in Eastern Syria with Russian and Iranian help. I was a Laureate and had been asked to lead a peace negotiation. And a leading member of the Nobel family had been an eyewitness as it happened on his table.

12
Manila: My Stance and a New World Structure

I was aware that a Peace Prize highlights a stance, and that my stance was to be the only Western literary writer to continue the tradition of calling for a democratic World State in the footsteps of Churchill, Truman, Einstein, Eisenhower, Russell, Gandhi, Kennedy and Gorbachev. And I was aware that I was doing this at a time when a wave of populism had turned against globalism and supranationalism in Europe with Brexit and in America with Trump. Little Englandism and American isolationism had won the UK referendum and US Presidential election, and it could be said that I was out of step.

I would disagree. On the contrary, the *'demos'* of the Western countries was out of step with the supranational vision, and I was convinced that the only way of securing a more prosperous, safe and peaceful world for our grandchildren was to stand up for a united world while demagogues stoked up hatred and division and championed their nation-states. And I would make my stand for continuing the tradition of a democratic World State in my two-minute acceptance speech at the awarding ceremony on 23 November.

Gusi Peace Prize awarding ceremony: my speech
The next morning I woke after 9am, showered, washed my hair and, leaving the other two asleep, got into breakfast shortly before it closed at 10.30am. Then I sat in the sun by the swimming-pool for a few minutes.

The Fidlers' three children were standing talking by the pool and their younger boy pushed their older boy into the water. The three children had looked very presentable the previous evening in evening dress, and Fidler had told me, "I've had a problem getting them all looking smart."

I returned to my room and while Ann and Tony spent the day by the pool and Tony worked out in the gym I focused on the awarding ceremony, had a coffee and a bar of dark chocolate for lunch and rested in the afternoon.

We all assembled in the Lobby at 4.30pm, I in my dinner jacket. The Laureates and their families left on two coaches after 5pm and arrived at the huge Philippine International Convention Center before 6pm. Many uniformed police stood outside.

Armed police, security for the Awarding Ceremony

We passed through security and were escorted by a young lady across an enormous foyer to a doorway that led to a narrow passage. Through openings on the left I glimpsed rows of seats in the auditorium, many already filled. We came to the Laureates' room.

The young lady then took Ann back to her seat in the auditorium. Tony was filming and eventually set up his tripod among the seatless photographers and did not worry that he had not been allocated a seat.

The Laureates' room had chairs round the walls and some of the Laureates sat, others stood. Two plates of bridge rolls with scrambled egg and lumps of salmon were placed on a ledge, and someone said, "I'd have something to eat now, there won't be another opportunity until midnight."

The Australian Laureate, Dr Kingsley Faulkner, came and asked me to explain Universalism, which I did. I said: "I start with the unity of the universe and humankind, and that fundamental approach has consequences in several disciplines. Philosophy is no longer about words and logic but about man in the universe, as it was to the early Greeks. History is no longer about slices of history in different countries but is about the history of humankind, *all* the 25 civilizations seen as a whole. Literature is about all world literature, which has one fundamental theme. Religion is about the fundamental experience in all religions, the perception of the divine Light. And politics is about the political unity of all humankind."

He was very interested in what I said and told me that some of the Laureates had been discussing my idea of the fundamental unity of the universe and humankind and its consequences, and all had said that in their view I was "100-per-cent right".

I also talked with Michael Nobel, who was speaking at the event. He said he had read my publisher's leaflet and found my books very interesting. I had announced in my speech the previous evening that I had been a Professor in Japan, where he was now a Professor, and I told him about my meeting with Junzaburo Nishiwaki (see p.xvii), and how he had written out the wisdom of the East for me: "+A + –A = 0". I told him that Universalism reconciles all opposites.

Ambassador Gusi had been sitting in front of a mirror in an adjoining room, having make-up applied to his face as if he were an actor. He stood up and called all Laureates to follow him, and we returned down the passage and walked through a 'gladiatorial' tunnel and emerged into the tiered and now-crowded auditorium. There were 6,000–7,000 in three tiers as in a huge theatre, and the whole event was theatre.

In two aisles with descending flights of steps there were flags, held by armed uniformed marines from the Philippine Marine Corps, and we had to find our flag and stand on the step next to it. My flag was in the nearest set of steps and towards the back, between the flag for Sudan and the flag for the United States. Alongside the descending steps on both sides were crowded rows of seats, all plush and armchair-like with wide arm rests. Seven Laureates (or their representatives) stood on seven steps in my aisle and eight stood on eight steps in the other aisle.

Aware that I was in a jihadist country and that the Union Jack might be associated with the current operation to capture Mosul, I glanced at those sitting next to my aisle and was reassured. They seemed to be smiling students, a few of whom asked if they could take a selfie with me on their phone.

On the step below me there were two Sudanese clad in white robes and 'turbans' and two Sudanese women, and I could see a block of white-clad Sudanese lower down near the stage. Suddenly Tony was among the Sudanese holding up his phone.

"You're on WhatsApp to the family," he said. "You can tell them what you're doing."

So I found myself saying I was waiting to collect my award and that I would be walking alongside my armed marine under the Union Jack.

The Gusi Peace Prize International Committee filed onto the stage and sat in the front row of two rows of chairs, facing the audience. Tony descended to his tripod near the front as the auditorium darkened.

The program started with a doxology (praise to God) conducted by first a Christian and then a Muslim cleric.

Then came the "Parade of Colors". One by one each Laureate was announced individually over a loudspeaker and walked to loud music with his marine and under his flag down the many steps in the half-light through long applause to sit in the second row of seats at the back of the stage before his flag, which his marine had transferred to a flag-holder.

When I was announced my marine hoisted the Union Jack to a holder on his belt and I marched down alongside him. The steps were just short of two paces long, and I had to concentrate not to lose my footing in the half-light while keeping step with the marine, every step required care. We turned left and walked straight and then turned right. On both sides were people standing, clapping and taking photographs in the half-dark, and there were photographers. There was a television desk, for the proceedings were being televised live across the Philippines and carried by CNN via satellite to unknown countries. I was watchful in case one of the applauding young men was an Islamic-State terrorist about to launch a symbolic attack on the British flag, but there seemed to be no sign of any hostility. On the platform an organiser pointed to my seat, on which was stuck my typed name.

Nicholas Hagger walking with his marine under the British flag at the Awarding Ceremony on 23 November 2016

The last Laureate to appear was the Philippine Laureate, the Director-General of Police, who was in olive-green uniform. He was greeted by a roar and he waved presidentially on his way down.

We all stood for the Philippine national anthem and were entertained by a Philippine dance group. Then there were speeches, by Dr Evelyn Gusi and Ambassador Gusi of Gusi Peace Prize International, and, after another entertainment by a Japanese Soka-Gakkai dance group, by Manson Fok. Then, when introduced by one of the three compères (an Australian man, Patrick Crowe, and two young ladies, a Miss-Universe contestant Jewel Lobaton and an Indian lady Venus Raj), the Australian Laureate left his chair and stood next to Ambassador Gusi in the line. Up to half a dozen 'presenters' were called to the stage, and his award, a metallic scroll signed by President Duterte, Ambassador Gusi and Manson Fok, was passed along by the standing presenters to be handed over to him. He stood and held it to be photographed. Then he went to a glass lectern and made a short speech. This procedure was repeated for each subsequent Laureate.

The first Laureate, the Australian, mentioned me in his speech, saying he had been privileged to hear my new thinking.

The Bosnian, Chinese, Egyptian, Indian, Iranian and Japanese recipients followed. The Japanese Laureate, leader of the religious-political movement Soka Gakkai when I was in Japan, was now eighty-nine and too infirm to attend, and was represented by his son.

There was a song by Mikko Gusi, Ambassador Gusi's eldest son. He had signed a recording deal despite having been diagnosed as having a brain tumour, for which he was awaiting an operation. Ambassador Gusi's wife was at the time herself undergoing chemotherapy and could not have been feeling well during the event.

The presentations continued with the Romanian Laureate, the Romanian Minister of Health. The audience had a program but we Laureates did not know in what order we would be called. I worked out that it would be in alphabetical order of our countries with the Philippines at the end. I was only half-paying attention and heard one of the compères announce "Hagger" and came to with a start. Had I been called?

But no, it was "Mrs. Hagger." Ann left her seat near the front and came on stage. What was going on, was Ann collecting my prize? But no, she was a presenter for the Romanian and helped pass on the metallic scroll.

The Laureate for Saint Kitts and Nevis and the Sudanese Laureate's son were the next recipients. Then there was a crash and the Syrian Laureate sitting next to me was on the floor. What was going on? Had he been shot? I bent and helped him to his feet.

In fact, we now discovered, our chairs were three inches from the back of a raised part of the stage and there was an unguarded drop behind us. He had moved his chair back and a leg had tipped over the edge. The chair had tilted and deposited him at my feet. He seemed unhurt and was immediately afterwards called. Issam, the Consul, came up and stood in line to make the presentation. Mousallam spoke without any ill effects. Issam shook my hand as he left the stage. I was next.

The compères introduced me in turn and said how honoured

they all were that I was present. The Australian compère, Patrick Crowe, who I had spoken with the previous evening, gave me a short build-up and the contender for Miss Universe took over. To jazzy music I found my place in the line next to Ambassador Gusi. The Indian compère then read out a list of presenters. She said my presenters were: Abdul Patel Ataweel, the Minister of Plenipotentiary of Libya, actually Abubaker Wanis Ataweel, Libyan Minister Plenipotentiary (named on his seat as Abobaker I.W. Ataweel);[1] Niv Patil, Clinical Professor at Hong Kong University; a Filipino actress, recording artist and film producer, Nora Aunor; a Filipino actor, Lloyd Samartino; and the Gusi coordinator, Rose Gonzales.

Nicholas Hagger (standing at back) being announced at the Awarding Ceremony on 23 November 2016

As I took my place next to Ambassador Gusi I did not have time to reflect that on 7 November Ambassador Gusi and Rose Gonzales of the Gusi Peace Prize International Committee had invited the British Ambassador to present my prize, and somehow a Libyan Minister was making the presentation despite my intelligence work against the Gaddafi regime in 1969–70 as dis-

Nicholas Hagger receiving his Gusi Peace Prize for Literature from the
Libyan Minister Plenipotentiary (right) with Ambassador Gusi looking on
(left), 23 November 2016

closed in *My Double Life 1*. I did not have time to think that the
Libyan Laureate, Director of the Libya Africa Investment Portfolio, who was too ill to attend as he was having treatment for
cancer, was not among the recipients, having had his prize with-

Nicholas Hagger holding his Gusi Peace Prize for Literature (left) and
showing it next to Ambassador Gusi with Michael Nobel second
from left (right)

Nicholas Hagger making his acceptance speech at the Awarding Ceremony
on 23 November 2016

held, and that this Libyan Minister Plenipotentiary had probably expected to present a Libyan award. As the metallic scroll
was passed along by the presenters to the Libyan, a bespectacled
man with receding hair in a suit and tie, I instinctively smiled
and shook his hand and held the award for the photographers
to see.

Then I went to the glass lectern and, aware that I was on a large
screen behind me and seeing myself on a small tilted screen
standing on the floor below me, made my speech, which went
out live on television throughout the Philippines and was carried by CNN. I had two minutes to make my stand on a global
platform and convey a message on universal peace. I said:

> Ambassador and Dr Gusi, fellow Laureates, ladies and gentle-
> men, I'm honoured to have been awarded the Gusi Peace Prize
> for Literature and I'm grateful to the Gusi Foundation for this
> recognition. I understand that I'm only the third UK citizen to
> receive a Gusi award since 2002, and I'm humbled.
>
> In a long literary career of nearly 60 years I've written more
> than 40 books. My literary works include many poems and short
> stories, and poetic epics and verse plays, diaries and autobiog-
> raphies, travelogues and a study of the fundamental theme of
> world literature, and I've written works of history, philosophy,
> and international politics.

In my lifetime I've seen the world go through a miserable period and we could be heading for a *Third* World War. Since 1945 the UN has failed to prevent 162 wars – *162 wars* – and the world has accumulated 15,375 nuclear weapons: *15,375 nuclear weapons*. There were none when I was born. In my books I've tried to analyse what's gone wrong, and find solutions. I've concluded that ideally we need a *democratic* World State with the nation-states staying as they are and a partly-federal government that's *strong* enough to prevent wars and control nuclear weapons. The present United Nations lacks overall authority, and nation-states go to war too readily.

The first two atomic bombs left many international figures in shock and calling for such a democratic peace-bringing World State. These included Churchill, Truman, Einstein and Eisenhower. I have the same vision, and so I'm carrying on this call in *my* works.

As I see it, the UN General Assembly could eventually be turned into a lower house of democratically-elected Representatives in a partly-federal government that includes a World Senate, as set out in my work *The World Government*. I see the UN eventually becoming a UF, a United Federation. A *UF*.

Such new thinking could create a world government with enough authority to abolish war, enforce disarmament and alleviate famine, disease and poverty. This vision of universal peace underlies my two poetic epics on war. Virgil in *The Aeneid* [book 1] foresaw a Roman '*Empire* without limit' which didn't happen until after *his* lifetime, and I've foreseen a *World State* that won't happen until after *my* lifetime. But an Age of universal peace and prosperity is a goal worth striving for, a dream worth dreaming.

In my literary works I've held up universal peace within a new world structure as a vision of hope that can inspire the younger generation to bring in a better world for our grandchildren. I'm grateful to the Gusi Foundation for recognising my body of work, and hope that my philanthropic vision will one day improve the lives of *all* humankind.

Thank you.

To deafening applause I then went along the front row, shaking hands with each member of the Gusi Peace Prize International Committee and my presenters, and then went along the back row shaking hands with each seated Laureate. I then walked back to resume my seat while my presenters left the stage.

The two American Laureates followed me and then came the Director-General of Police, who repeated the statement he had made the previous evening: "Someone asked me, 'Why are you getting a Peace Prize?' I can now answer: 'I make it safe so the good guys can live in peace and the bad guys rest in peace.'" It was casual and sinister, and I instinctively felt he was behind the extrajudicial killings. Again there was laughter.

Nicholas Hagger calling for a democratic World State during his speech on 23 November 2016

There was a speech from a Turkish ex-Laureate and a speech from Michael Nobel, an ex-Laureate and nominator who said the Committee had accepted his two nominations, of the Japanese Soka Gakkai Laureate and Vincent Giampapa. There was more singing, in the course of which there was another crash at the other end of the Laureates, where the Australian, Bosnian and Chinese Laureates were sitting.

This time a chair had disappeared backwards. Despite craning forward, I could not see which Laureate had fallen and whether he had fallen backwards off the stage, but several of the Laureates stood to help him up. It was now clear there was a serious health-and-safety issue regarding the lack of a safety guard behind the Laureates' chairs.

Now all the Laureates were garlanded with silk green flowers and had to stand at the front of the stage with their metallic awards and be photographed. Ambassador Gusi and Dr Gusi then released two white doves. They had blue ribbons attached to their feet. One of the doves flew up to the first tier of the auditorium. The other dove somehow wound its ribbon round Dr Gusi's wrist so it could not fly away until it was unwound. There were closing remarks.

Then the audience came up onto the stage and intermingled with us Laureates. The Director-General of Police was surround-

Nicholas Hagger garlanded with his Peace Prize and a magazine showing Ronald Dela Rosa, who is standing second from left

ed by autograph-hunters and, beside his shoulder, I spoke to him as he signed his nickname, 'Bato' ('The Rock'). I told him, "I can see you as the next President."

He stopped his signing and looked into my eyes, and his look, as I looked into his eyes close up, agreed with what I had said.

I told him that my World State would include the Russian-Chinese-Philippine New World Order that President Duterte claimed to have fixed up in Peru, and said that if we had visited President Duterte as was on the original schedule of activities, that is what I would have told him. Ronald said I could email him.

It was well after midnight and we were now escorted to a large first-floor landing that looked down on the main entrance. A buffet had been laid out with wine and there were waist-high tables at which we could stand and eat. The three of us ate with Vincent and Michael Nobel.

Vincent said of his name, "My grandfather was Sicilian, he emigrated to the United States. I'm descended from a Sicilian family." He said of arresting ageing, "People will soon live to 200 and look 50." I thought again that the biological age of a 200-year-old's brain would be 200. "I'm sixty-seven but my biological age is thirty-seven. No surgery, it's all stem-cell."

Leaning forward, Tony said again, "I'd like to make a film on that possibility."

Vincent said, "I've got a presentation on my laptop. I'll show you tomorrow."

Ronald Dela Rosa, Director-General of Police, (left) being photographed by Chris Cottrell of the *South China Sea Magazine* (on right), see p.151

Back on the coach Niv Patil, the Malaysian Clinical Professor at Hong Kong University who was one of my presenters, sat across the aisle from me. He told me he had encountered the Director-General of Police in the Gents and had told him, "You shouldn't kill the good guys." He said to me, "The police kill those they don't like, not just drug dealers." (Vincent had told me he passed the Director-General saying to a television camera, "Drug pushers are cannibals.")

I thought how brave Niv had been to challenge the alleged architect of the death squads on a one-to-one basis, and how his comment

Michael Nobel (left) and Vincent Giampapa at the end of the Awarding Ceremony

reflected exactly where one should begin with Dela Rosa. Ronald Dela Rosa and President Duterte were Cromwellians who believed with Oliver Cromwell in imposing virtue by tyranny. I resolved to do the same, and after I returned I emailed Ronald and expressed the hope that "you will be able, as you progress, to constitutionalise your methods and efforts as time goes on". He did not reply.

The killings were later described in a letter read out in all

Catholic churches in the Philippines as "a Reign of Terror". By then (early February 2017) they had exceeded 7,000, and the police were heavily involved in delivering Wild-West-style bounty killings. Mayors and politicians were paying police and professional hitmen from $300 to $1,000 per body for dead drug dealers.

In March 2017, after human rights organisations had condemned the killings as a crime against humanity that could be prosecuted in the International Criminal Court, Ronald Dela Rosa (according to the London *Times*) promised a less bloody campaign. Representatives of the Church would accompany police officers on drug raids and there would be "full accountability" and "internal discipline": "I hope this will be less bloody, if not bloodless." Ronald Dela Rosa was trying to constitutionalise his methods.

Back in the hotel Lobby we sat at a table for a while. We had not seen any mosquitoes since our arrival in Manila, although the mosquito-borne Zika virus was present in the Philippines. Now a mosquito flew past us and Tony and I exchanged glances. In our room I wrote my diary and did not get to bed until 2.10am.

Lyceum of the Philippines University
The next morning, Thursday 24 November, I was up at 6.45am to assemble at 8am for the 'Peace Forum at the Armed Forces of the Philippines', which was supposed to begin at 9am.

When I returned from breakfast I found a note Tony had left on the floor in front of our connecting door, that the assembly time was now 11am. He had been telephoned with this message in the small hours. (Over breakfast Fidler had reported that he had had a message in the small hours saying we were assembling at 11am "tomorrow", and he was seeing if there was still an assembly at 8am in case "tomorrow" meant the next day. He told me, "The Syrian Laureate said, 'In the Sudan Monday at 3pm can mean Wednesday at 10am, at least the day is always right here in Manila.' I'm not sure about that.")

The local paper, which was in a bag hung on the room's

outside door handle, had headlines about 'Bato' (the Director-General of Police). He had broken down and wept when told at the previous day's Senate hearings that more than a dozen police had accepted bribes. The organiser of the death squads into whose eyes I had looked the previous evening had a ruthless Cromwellian pursuit of virtue but could be reduced to tears.

The coach left at 11am. We were eventually invited to dismount in a narrow street, and I said to Ann, "I can't see this being an armed forces base." By the entrance steps I read on a board, "Lyceum of the Philippines University". I said, "We're visiting students, not armed forces."

Later Tony overheard that there had been an assassination attempt and the armed forces had to keep order on the streets, so we were diverted at short notice to the Lyceum, an institute of higher education, which could not provide an audience for us before 11.30am.

We climbed four flights of stairs and walked into a large hall where 300 students leapt to their feet and applauded enthusiastically. Many had watched the televised awarding ceremony the previous evening, we were told. We sat at a long table at the front and were each garlanded with a blue ribbon holding a blue rosette. Then we were greeted by the Director.

We were introduced by Ambassador Gusi. Each of us stood and nodded. There was dancing addressed to our long table, and then Dr Fidler, who happened to be sitting at the end of our row, was called to give his talk.

He had prepared a presentation with slides, the presentation he gave at the Sino-Asia Pacific Medical Forum. Believing he would be addressing the army, he had included especially graphic pictures of burns that soldiers might have the misfortune to experience, and he was confronted with students pulling queasy faces and covering their eyes. He apologised for showing horrific material, and suggested they looked away.

Two or three more Laureates were called and gave short speeches at the microphone on the stage. Small baguettes were placed on our table, which would have been hard to eat and

Nicholas Hagger standing after being introduced by Ambassador Gusi at the Lyceum on 24 November 2016

were therefore ignored. Then I was called.

I stood before the microphone and looked down at the sea of faces and free-wheeled. I said how nice their dancing had been and how smart they all looked. I said they were all studying within a discipline and that I saw all the disciplines as being interconnected like the seven bands of one rainbow, and all disciplines reflected the unity of humankind. I covered the unity of philosophy, history and literature.

I said that the fundamental theme of literature was a quest for the One that alternated with condemnation of social follies and vices. I said, "Literature teaches you to be a good person by showing you the opposites." I spoke of wars and nuclear weapons, and the unity of a political World State. I told them they should work for peace and be good people. I left the stage to strong applause.

I was followed by the Prime Minister of Saint Kitts and Nevis, Timothy Harris. He talked about how they must choose their future careers, and he quoted my statistics from my acceptance speech: that there had been 162 wars since 1945 and there are 15,375 nuclear weapons. Sitting next to me while the other Laureates spoke he told me he had 60,000 voters in Saint Kitts and Nevis, and I saw him as a Mayor or Chairman of a Council. He said to me, "You must come. It's sunny all the year round with villages and mountains, everything you need. Come and see me if you come."

Afterwards the Laureates were mobbed. I in particular seemed to be very popular. Everyone had a mobile and everyone wanted

Nicholas Hagger speaking at the Lyceum on 24 November 2016

a photo with me, singly and in a group. Then I was surrounded by autograph-hunters. Tony had so many girls round him taking photos that he had to hoist himself up onto the stage to escape.

Farewell dinner
We arrived back at the hotel, lunchless, through heavy traffic at 5pm, the assembly time for the farewell dinner. The assembly time was put back to 5.30 and then 6. I changed into dinner jacket (having established the dress code from Ambassador Gusi himself at the buffet after the awarding ceremony) and by arrangement went down to the Lobby at 5.30 to meet Issam.

He was sitting with the Syrian Mousallam and Ambassador Gusi. He was talking about a past incident. Ambassador Gusi said, "No, I didn't forget it."

Then I heard Issam say in English in the presence of Mousallam, to Ambassador Gusi, "Your website is rubbish. You haven't changed it since 2013. You're running an International Peace Prize and you haven't changed your website since 2013."

Suddenly Ambassador Gusi stood up and seemed to be upset. I overheard him lament to Issam, who had stood up with him, "Nobody gives me money."

I heard Issam say, "You will get round this."

For months I had assumed that Ambassador Gusi was running the Gusi Peace Prize on a shoestring, using only donated Foundation money. I wondered what else Issam had said.

Eventually Issam sat with me and I was able to discuss some obstacles to the peace process. I agreed to send him my Peace Plan the following Monday for forwarding to Assad. We discussed the merits of my visiting Assad before going to Putin.

Ambassador Gusi kept interrupting, "Go to the coach now." But no other Laureates had gone to the coach. Again, "Where is your wife and son? Tell them to come down, the coach is going."

It was before the revised assembly time. I broke off talking to Issam to ring my room and relay this message.

Ann and Tony duly appeared but the coach did not go for another half hour. During this time I was approached by a photographer who showed me photos he had taken of the week's events featuring me, and I bought them with some of my Philippine pesos.

On the coach as we waited I talked with Vincent. We arranged to see his presentation on our return. We drove to the O.B. Montessori Center at Eisenhower Street, Greenhills, San Juan City. We were escorted through to a large room with a very high ceiling lit with ceiling lights, and were shown to tables.

We sat with Vincent near Billy Chan and Chris, and the conversation was about China's future – Chris talked about living in China – and Russia's fear of US aggression via NATO. Hence the air-raid shelter drills for 40 million Russians living in major cities.

Once again I was approached to be photographed. The bodyguard to the Prime Minister of Saint Kitts and Nevis also came to be photographed. He said in an American drawl, "Nicholas Hagger's changing the world, I'm putting that online."

I had assumed the Laureates would all speak and had scribbled down some points before going down to Issam. We were never called, though item 4 on the program said: "Message, Gusi Peace Prize Laureates." Ambassador Gusi seemed distracted. He was sitting at the table next to mine. He was lost in his thoughts and when the wine waiter came to our table he tapped him on his arm and held out his glass for a refill.

The Iranian Laureate, whose prize was for philanthropy, was next to him and when he left to go to the Gents I left my table and sat on the Iranian's chair and said to Ambassador Gusi: "It's been a very successful week. You must be tired, you've worked very hard. It's almost over, you'll soon be able to rest."

He nodded. His wife beamed at me from across the table. I said to her, "I hope you are feeling... better."

She smiled sadly for she knew I knew she was not clear of cancer – Tony had told me he had heard that she was in stage 3 of her cancer and had a 75-per-cent chance of survival – and she said, "Feeling better. Please pray for me." The Iranian returned and I went back to my table.

There had been chamber music on the stage, and two dozen white-clad Sudanese who monopolised three tables now went up and did a dance, raising sticks and crowding menacingly and seemingly beating someone to death. This went on for some time, and somehow the Laureates escaped making a speech. Then all Laureates were asked to go on stage for a final photo shoot and at last we were intermingling on the floor.

I found myself speaking with Gasim Elledrissi, Director of the Libya Africa Investment Portfolio, who had come to collect the Libyan Laureate's award as he was being treated for cancer. However, Ambassador Gusi seemed to have withheld the award due to his non-attendance. Gasim asked me about my experience of the Gaddafi revolution.

I told him how I had driven to work on the morning of the Gaddafi revolution on 1 September 1969 and how I had driven back through the revolution. I said, "I wanted to ask Gaddafi, 'Where did you go after seizing the radio station?' Because he had a blue Volkswagen Beetle and I was driving a green Volkswagen Beetle."

Gasim said, "He wouldn't have answered you, he was only in the radio station."

I had been taken to the radio station shortly after the revolution,[2] and was interested in his unrevolutionary truthfulness.

I said I knew Shukri Ghanem.

He said, "I knew him well, and his son. Shukri was murdered in Vienna, you know his body was found in the river. I know because a file was marked 'Not to be touched' and a note said to his son, 'If you touch this, the same will happen to you that happened to Shukri.'" Of the current situation in Libya he said, "Many are booted out, hundreds of thousands. Gaddafi kept them in, this lot throw them out." He had strong views on the extrajudicial killings in the Philippines. He told me, "There must be a rule of law."

I asked him if he controlled the $5billion fund in the Libya Africa Investment Portfolio.

He said, "Yes."

Thinking of my Peace Plan I asked if he would be able to lend me $1billion if I asked for it.

He looked at me and said he would have to ask the Libyan Laureate, his boss. "But I will say 'Yes' as you are my father," he told me, "and I will say 'Yes' to your son as he is my brother."

I walked to the coach with Tony and looked for Vincent. He was not on the coach. I realised he had taken a taxi home as he always went to sleep at 10.30pm, part of his program to arrest his own ageing, and so the laptop presentation would have to happen early the next morning. He had said that he would be in breakfast at 6.30am and he could show us before he left.

Tony said, "I can see the TV program. It asks the question, 'Will we really be able to live to 200 while looking 50 in a few years' time?'"

On the way home the coach stopped by two more billboards

of the Laureates, side by side. Ambassador Gusi had been driving his car and telephoned the coach to stop there. The door opened and he came on board.

He seemed quite agitated. From the stairwell near the door he spoke over the microphone: "Look, this is a sacred site to do with Aquino and Marcos." I realised it was by the airport where Aquino, leader of the Opposition, was murdered in 1983, some said on President Marcos's orders. "Only the Gusi Foundation is allowed to put posters here. So this is a sign of the Gusi Foundation's power." There was applause.

He had climbed the steps and now stood on the floor, and we saw that he had bare feet. Someone at the front pointed to his feet. He said, "So I can run."

Ambassador Gusi got off the coach and we resumed our journey, wondering at the significance of his intervention. It was too dark to photograph the two billboards, and we should have been taken to see them during daylight hours on one of our coach trips, perhaps after wreath-laying in Rizal Park.

Then the coach stopped again, and once again Ambassador Gusi came on board barefoot. He said, "You see this poster." We peered into the dark and could just make out its outline. "This is the Police HQ. It has pictures of Dela Rosa – and me. They don't allow anyone else to have a picture next to the Director-General of Police but they have me. So the Police respect the Gusi Foundation. It is a sign of how powerful the Gusi Foundation is though some say it isn't."

The Indian Laureate asked, "Who says it isn't?"

"Jealous people."

Again there was bewildered applause from the coach.

Ann said to me, "He protests too much."

I mused. Gusi had twice climbed onboard our coach to say his organisation was powerful because some were saying it wasn't.

Back in our room I wrote my diary. It was after 1.10am before I got into bed.

Draft of Peace Plan

The next morning, on Friday 25 November, the day *Life Cycle and Other New Poems 2006–2016* and my latest volume of short stories *The First Dazzling Chill of Winter* were published, Tony and I were down for breakfast at 6.30am. There was no sign of Vincent and we found out that he had left the hotel without having breakfast at 6.49. So we did not see his laptop presentation. (Later we discovered that his centre in Costa Rica had not yet been built, it existed only as an architect's impression on video.)

We sat on in the Lobby and reviewed the week. We then went upstairs and I dictated an email to Issam on the procedure of our visit to Assad. Then Ann rang from the Lobby to say that the photographer had some more photos, and I bought them and added them to the previous days' photos.

I sat on with Ann while Tony went up and slept. She said, "I feel that along with his philanthropy Gusi is looking for donations to his Foundation. He is also hoping to increase the esteem in which his family is held and its political influence, and he may be uptight because someone has disparaged the Gusi awards."

Emotionally that made sense of his protestations on the coach, and also of the presence of Dela Rosa among the Laureates. Unlike some of the Laureates who might be in a position to donate, Dr Fidler lived to cure burns and I had foreseen a new world structure that would benefit all humankind. We practised different forms of philanthropy that did not equip us to make huge donations.

Ann and I had caramel sundaes and mango drinks by the pool for lunch, and again I wondered if the philanthropic and saintly Ambassador Gusi quietly subsidised his Foundation out of his own pocket.

Then it began to drizzle and we returned to our room and rested and then packed. Just after 6 I began to draft an email to Issam. Inspiration took over and I wrote a 15-point Peace Plan (see pp.202–206). I broke off before I finished to eat at Spices, one of the hotel's restaurants, and then returned and finished the rest of my draft. We went to bed at 11pm.

Hong Kong: Taoist temple

The next morning, Saturday 26 November, we were up at 6 and after breakfast and settling up were driven to the airport for our 11am flight to Hong Kong. There was no traffic and, being early and having asked, we were given a free upgrade to business class.

We had lunch on the plane – chicken, rice and cheesecake – and landed at Hong Kong in drizzle about 1.30pm. As there was a very long walk to collect our luggage Ann, who was waiting for a knee operation in early January, was pushed in a wheel-chair from the plane to our carousel.

We were driven to the Peninsula, Hong Kong, in a hotel lim-ousine by a strapping Chinese girl who said she preferred it when the British were in Hong Kong as there was more free-dom of speech. We passed some beautiful unspoilt scenery, and I could feel the impact the islands must have made on early-twentieth-century visitors.

The Peninsula in Kowloon was opened in 1928. It was billed as the finest hotel east of Suez. George Bernard Shaw stayed there. In 1967 I had seen a bomb blown up in the street outside the Peninsula and two other bombs were exploded in controlled explosions. Because of its dominance and colonial associations it was a natural target for protesters in the 1960s.

We were met inside the entrance in another spectacular Lob-by. There were masks and faces of classical gods at the tops of marble pillars. We presented our passports at Reception and were taken upstairs to be checked in within our room, 912, which had a breathtaking view of the harbour. The three of us were in this one room as we were only staying one night. We ate spicy duck in the Cantonese restaurant and (having booked) were met at 8pm by a chauffeur-driven limousine and taken for a drive round Kowloon.

We stopped and took a look at the Temple Street Night Mar-ket and then went up the 100-floor ICC (International Commerce Center) building ('Sky-100'). We were at 393 metres on the 100th floor and had a good view of Hong Kong and other islands at night as we walked round, describing a circle. We went on to the harbour and walked by the Ferry Terminal, which I remembered using in 1967. We returned and slept.

Next morning, Sunday 27 November, I finished packing and had breakfast alone. Ann and Tony arrived for breakfast as I left. At 8.35 our three suitcases were collected and put into store near Reception. I then went downstairs and paid. We had booked the limousine for a tour of Hong Kong, and also a guide, Stella, who was waiting for us. We had the same driver as the previous night.

I asked Stella if she was happy with the way things had gone in Hong Kong. She wasn't. She said that in 1997 Hong Kong was promised 50 years of complete freedom as a transition, but that after 10 years China was eroding freedom of speech and undermining the independence of the court system. There were now weekly protests. These had to be booked and no protests were allowed outside the booked times. She said the UK was given Hong Kong "in perpetuity" but was leased the New Territories, Lamma and Lantau until 1997. "There's no airport on Hong Kong island, so there was no point in hanging on to Hong Kong. But Hong Kong is between the West and China."

We had driven to Victoria Park, and on a clear morning saw the setting of Hong Kong and other islands from all angles. There were stunning views. We drove on and stopped at Stanley (named after Lord Stanley, a 19th-century Secretary of State for the Colonies) and saw the market, and then went on to Repulse Bay (named after the battleship *HMS Repulse* which thwarted plundering pirates there in the mid-19th century).

We went on to Aberdeen (named after the Earl of Aberdeen, Secretary of State for the Colonies in 1848), a fishing village, and hired a *sampan*. We passed houseboats and saw fish-eating white egrets and brown sea-eagles and drying yellowfish, catfish, garment fish, greenspot fish, red snapper, shark fish and cod.

We drove on to Central to see the Governor's House near the ferry, where the old Hong Kong began and took shape after 1842. We found the site of the old Hong Kong Hotel, c.1900, in

Pradder Street. It was the old colonial meeting-place until it was replaced by the Peninsula in 1928.

We went on to Wong Tai Sin Temple, a Taoist temple where people can seek the blessing of Lao-Tze, the 6th-century-BC author of the *Tao Te Ching*. Lao-Tze was a poet, not a god, and the temple is a place where his books can be studied and his image can be honoured. The Taoist Wong Tai Sin is said to have discovered the secret of transforming cinnabar (a red mercuric sulphide) into an elixir of immortality and became a Taoist god of healing and good fortune. (I thought of Vincent, who is said to have found the elixir of living to 200 by arresting ageing. Perhaps one day there would be a Giampapa temple.)

On the way in were sculptures of the Taoist animals who give their name to birth years, which are also associated with one of the four elements and either *yin* or *yang*. I was born in 1939 under the rabbit, earth and *yin*, and the sculpture showed a seven-foot tall rabbit holding a book (as those born in a rabbit year tend to become writers). Tony was born under the snake, fire and *yin*, and Ann was born under the tiger, metal (a Taoist element) and *yang*.

We then approached the large main temple, which had a Chinese roof and curly tiles. In a cordoned-off space before the front of the temple people were praying and shaking *chim* sticks to tell their fortunes, and turning up *yin* or *yang* cards. One man was offering a newly-born baby to Lao-Tze along with fruit laid out round his feet. A fire burned in a black iron log-holder, and sculptures of a crane on a turtle before the temple symbolised longevity. Stella said, "People are seeking the blessing of Lao-Tze for their enterprises."

I wondered if one day there would be a shrine to my poems on the Light, the metaphysical Reality or One behind the universe and the common experience of all religions, a modern statement of the *Tao*, and whether newly-born babies would be offered to me. My thoughts on Vincent's work on ageing and on my literary works demonstrated the relevance of this Taoist temple to our own modern concerns.

On the way out we passed a small tiled shrine to Confucius, which promoted the study of Confucian texts and honoured his image. We also passed different bamboos – there were 200 different species – and two peepul- or bo-trees (Indian fig-trees) like the one under which the Buddha achieved enlightenment.

We went on to the jade market, where many stalls were selling inferior jade. Ann found and bought some genuine fluorite. We were then taken to Amigo, a shop that sold beautiful and expensive samples of white, black, green, grey, purple, brown, red and yellow jade, and Ann bought a bracelet of eleven pieces of jade in four colours.

Back at the hotel, having vacated our room we sat in sunshine by the huge windows of the indoor swimming-pool on the seventh floor with a view over Hong Kong harbour, and for lunch we had apple and coconut ice-cream. I wrote my diary in the warm sunshine and then lay on a sun couch and dozed while Tony swam.

Just before 5.30 we went down to the Lobby, where we had booked afternoon tea, and in colonial splendour under the masks and classical gods we drank champagne and ate sandwiches, scones and cakes served on a three-tiered silver cake-stand.

Tony spoke of Ambassador Gusi's impressive network of contacts and nominators, which one of the volunteer co-ordinators had explained to him. She had told him that an American senator had paid for her to have a holiday in the US. The contacts and nominators were systematised, and I heard that only designated, highly competent co-ordinators were allowed to speak to the Laureates. (In February 2017 one of the volunteer co-ordinators became consultant/speaker on implementing federalism in the Philippines in the Department of Interior and Local Government and had to report personally to President Duterte each month.)

We sat on over tea and shortly before 9pm our suitcases were brought out to the hotel's limousine and we were driven to the airport, where we were met and escorted to the check-in.

We boarded our Cathay Pacific plane at 11.20pm and travelled premium economy. Much of the long twelve-and-a-half-hour flight passed in twilit darkness: we were served a meal, then for ten hours the lights were out while we tried to doze, and then we were served breakfast. We put our watches back eight hours and landed at 4.30am. Our car was waiting for us, and we were home by 6.30am.

Everything had gone according to plan. I had been professional: I had gone in, done the business and got out without getting entangled and without our lives being endangered. I had reason to be satisfied, but I still had unfinished business over my Peace Plan.

Epilogue

Peace for our Time: My 15-Point Peace Plan and a Third World War

And so it was that I found myself submitting my 15-point Peace Plan for the Middle East and Eastern Europe. It was inconceivable at the beginning of this story that I would be doing this, but somehow, as a result of a step-by-step sequence of events, this was what was happening.

I had looked back at Chamberlain's predicament with the objectivity afforded by the distance of 78 years, and I had found his aim noble and his reliance on his trust of Hitler naïve. He had been pilloried by history for appeasement, but his initiative had bought time for the West to rearm, and had he succeeded his way would have been infinitely superior to the havoc and wreckage of the Second World War, when over 60 million were killed.

Now I was trying to avert a Third World War, not by appeasement but by organising the rational disengagement from Syria of more than a dozen warring countries and many militant groups. My aim too was noble, and in hoping to influence President Putin perhaps a little naïve, and I knew this all too clearly. I too, like Chamberlain, was calling for 'peace for our time', and was all too aware that, as in Chamberlain's case, it might turn out to be an illusion. But I was clear that had I had an opportunity to meet Hitler in 1939 and head off the Second World War I should have jumped at the chance, for even if the outcome had been a failure, to attempt to avert the Second World War would have been a noble undertaking. And now I was in a position, as a Peace Laureate, to meet President Putin and attempt to avert a Third World War I should jump at the chance for the same reasons. I was clear that attempting to avert a Third World War, even if the attempt failed, was a noble and not an ignoble thing to do.

My 15-point Peace Plan
I had arranged to send my 15-point Peace Plan to Issam so he received it by 8pm in Manila. Ingrid, my PA, came at 9am and, fighting off sleep, I dictated my Peace Plan and sent it at 11.50am (7.50pm Manila time). Issam replied that he was in Malaysia and would send it on Friday.

The next few days I busied myself uploading some photos on my website, reporting my safe return and generally catching up. On that Friday morning there were three emails from Issam asking me to send my "proposal and letter of intent" on my headed notepaper as soon as possible, so he could send it to Assad. I sent it within the hour, and I also sent him a 'visiting-card' Igor had sent me giving the website details of the Supreme Council of Humanity, which was open to hosting further talks.

My email to Issam contained my 15-point Peace Plan which came to me in the Manila hotel room and was designed to bring 'peace for our time'. It was dated 2 December, and was as follows:

Issam Eldebs, Consul of the Syrian Arab Republic

Dear Issam

I thank you for our discussions when we met at the Gusi Peace Prize welcome dinner in Manila on 22 November 2016, on the following day when I received my Peace Prize, and on 24 November before I left for the farewell dinner.

As you know I am working actively for peace in Syria and as I said in my acceptance speech at the Award Ceremony I would like to bring new thinking to the world structure, which has failed to prevent 162 wars since 1945. I hope President Assad has received the copy of *The World Government* which I signed for him (and the message on the same page).

I have a proposal to make. As a Peace Laureate I have drawn up a Peace Plan for Syria and I would like to put it to President Assad and President Putin, and, when they are happy with my Peace Plan, to Donald Trump before his inauguration. As I see it, I would visit President Assad first with an American Syria expert who meets with his approval (if the appropriate expert can be found without holding up the visit) and, if he is happy with the Peace Plan, fly from Damascus to Moscow to put it to President Putin (meeting to be arranged by Igor Kondrashin's contact). If necessary I would fly back to Damascus with a Russian Syria expert (if President Putin so wishes and the appropriate expert is available) before going to President-elect Trump. If I were to receive a direct invitation to visit President Putin first, then I would visit President Putin *before* President Assad.

My Peace Plan seeks to satisfy each of the main participants with regard to something, on the basis of 'something for everyone'. I am flexible and the terms may be modified during my meetings with the two Presidents and the President-elect. However, the italicised theme of each of the 15 points should survive in the final document. The Peace Plan is as follows:

1. President *Assad* will remain in power at least until 2021, to the end of his third seven-year term. He is the symbol of Syrian unity and (as we learned from the falls of Saddam and Gaddafi) his departure would leave Syria in greater chaos than at present. He is needed to provide stability during the transition.

2. Under President Assad's supervision there will be immediate *elections* so all the Syrian combatants can be represented in a new assembly.

3. President Assad will now allow the *pipeline* to carry natural gas from Qatar to Turkey, satisfying those two countries and the US.

4. Russia will be fully compensated for any *undercutting* of Russian natural-gas supplies to Europe. The costing and means of payment of this compensation will be part of the

negotiations, but the principle will be that Russia will not suffer financially in any way.

5. Russia will retain a *base* in Western Syria with access to the Mediterranean.

6. Russia will not attack *Aleppo* while peace talks are held. There will be a no-fly zone and a cease-fire, and as negotiations progress a rolling demilitarised zone, details to be worked out by the experts.

7. The US and Russia will *demilitarise Syria*. Jordan will be compensated for demilitarising the training camps for fighters and will seal its borders. The UK and France will withdraw their hostility to Syria as the US will have achieved its main aim. Turkey, Qatar, Jordan, Saudi Arabia, the UK and France will all cease to train and support Syrian fighters. All Syrian refugees will be free to return to Syria to rebuild their country, and the US, Russia, the UK, France, the EU and China will all benefit from contracts to rebuild.

8. The *Shiite* population of Syria will be guaranteed protection, thus reassuring Iran.

9. *Iraq's unity* will be guaranteed, so Iraq will still be composed of Kurds, Sunnis and Shiites.

10. Before *IS* (Islamic State) can be included in the negotiations it must return the 40 kgs of nuclear material which it seized from Mosul University and which it is hoping to turn into a 'dirty' bomb to release in a Western city. Once this nuclear material is returned IS will be disbanded in Iraq and Western Syria and its fighters will be returned to be integrated in their countries of origin. There will be rehabilitation programs and pacification safeguards to ensure a smooth and safe repatriation process.

11. *Saudi Arabia* will not be allowed to impose a Wahhabist government on Syria, which will be holding elections, but Wahhabists will be allowed to stand in the elections and will face the Syrian electorate.

12. *Israel and Lebanon* will retain their existing borders.

13. The Peace Plan will include talks between NATO and Russia

on the Baltic states. Both NATO and Russia will initially take a symbolic step back. NATO will make clear that it has no aggressive intentions towards Russia and Russia will make clear it has no aggressive intentions towards Estonia, Lithuania and Latvia. NATO and Russia will consider signing a *new peace treaty* that covers their activities in Eastern Europe. Air-raid-shelter drills in Moscow to prepare for the threat of nuclear war will no longer be necessary. There will be reduced tension.

14. At present there is one theatre of war (the Middle East). If war breaks out in the Baltic states there will be two theatres of war and that will by definition be the beginning of a *Third World War*. This must be averted at all costs. Both NATO and Russia will consider signing a clause in the new peace treaty covering Eastern Europe (see 13) guaranteeing the safety of all territories under their protection, including the Russian-speaking peoples in the Baltic states.

15. The US, Russia, the EU and China, along with all participants already mentioned, will look seriously at the possibility of creating a *new world structure* to replace the UN: a democratically-elected World State under which all nation-states would stay as they are and the UN General Assembly would be turned into a lower house of elected Representatives. There would be an upper house, a World Senate, and a partly-federal world government that would be strong enough to prevent war, control the 15,375 nuclear weapons and prevent nuclear material from falling into the hands of terrorists, and work to alleviate poverty, famine, disease and climate change, including future droughts in Africa which seem certain to increase the number of migrating refugees. Such a new world structure, a United Federation of the World (UFW), would aim to bring in an Age of universal peace and prosperity in place of the present prospect of a ruinous and destructive nation-state-led Third World War. Nicholas Hagger will be invited to address the UN General Assembly on the merits of such a new world structure at the

appropriate time.

There will be many details to flesh out and negotiations on disputed points. I will take an American Syria expert to President Assad (if the appropriate expert can be found without holding up the visit, name subject to his approval) and will visit President Putin with the American Syria expert and a translator. President Putin will recommend a Russian Syria expert he trusts who will attend the meeting (if President Putin so wishes and the appropriate expert is available), and I will return to President Assad with the American and Russian Syria experts. I emphasise that, as I said in paragraph 3 of this email, if I receive a direct invitation to meet President Putin I will visit him *before* going to President Assad. I will take my son Tony Hagger to all meetings so he can make a historical film record.

As to the timing, the visits to President Assad and President Putin should be as soon as possible subject to their busy schedules. I will aim to visit President-elect Trump early in the new year and to have an agreement in principle between President Assad, President Putin and President-elect Trump before the inauguration on Friday 20 January 2017. President-elect Trump will then have a clear plan to implement in the first week of his Presidency. Detailed peace talks and negotiations involving the other countries mentioned will follow after that.

Please forward this email to President Assad and to President Putin via the Syrian Consulate/Embassy. Please let me know when I can fly to Beirut to visit President Assad, and an estimated date when I could fly on from Damascus to Moscow if my Peace Plan meets with President Assad's satisfaction in principle. If there is an invitation from President Putin, as I have stressed I will visit him first.

With my thanks and best wishes

Nicholas Hagger
Gusi Peace Prize 2016 Laureate

With hindsight in clauses 4 and 8 I could have mentioned the natural-gas pipeline from Iran to Syria, which Russia supported, and I could have said that that pipeline too should go ahead. But I chose not to mention this as the battle for Eastern Syria was going Russia's and Iran's way, and I saw the Iran–Northern Iraq–Syria pipeline as a consequence of a Russian-Iranian victory that could be sorted out along with the Qatar–Saudi Arabia–Jordan–Syria–Turkey pipeline during the peace discussions.[1]

Issam had also said that I should ask Igor to book my appointment with Putin. I emailed Igor and told him that I had been approached as a Peace Laureate to visit Assad, and that I should keep this confidential until it happened as had been requested. But I said I was then looking to visit Putin and after that Trump. Igor's reply on 8 December included the following paragraphs:

> Svetlana and me have checked all possibilities for your visit to Moscow according to your Peace Plan.
>
> There are possibilities to arrange your meetings in the Public Chamber of Russia, in the Russian Parliament (Gosduma), and maybe, even with the President Putin.

I was not sure whether "meetings in" would involve meetings with one individual in a room or corridor within the Public Chamber of Russia and the Russian Parliament, or whether I would be addressing the Public Chamber of Russia and the Russian Parliament before (if what I said was satisfactory) meeting President Putin.

The fall of Aleppo

Three weeks slid by without my hearing anything from Issam or Assad. I went down to Cornwall and sat again above a calm and later choppy sea and wrote chapters 9 and 10 in two-and-a-half long days (15–17 December). In the course of sitting in my window and writing in longhand above the reconciliation of storm and calm in the sparkling waves I mused on war and peace.

During those three weeks Assad's Syrian army took Aleppo with support from Russia, Iran and Hezbollah – and allowed Palmyra, exposed by the focus on Aleppo, to be retaken by IS. Some 50,000 had been besieged in east Aleppo in an ever-shrinking pocket and after many air-strikes by the Russians and Syrians and the final fall of Aleppo an evacuation was agreed. Buses took pro-rebel families to the countryside round Idlib, where pro-Assad forces were besieged by rebels. A massacre on a huge scale was averted, although Iranian forces delayed the evacuation by burning buses.

During this time the Supreme Council of Humanity's deadline was ignored. Quite simply, Assad along with Russia, Iran and Hezbollah had been bent on capturing Aleppo before talks, and the Obama Administration and its European allies were bent on supporting the rebels in eastern Aleppo, although some of these (for example the Fateh al-Sham Front, formerly al-Nusra) included fighters from al-Qaeda who the US and the UK had opposed in Afghanistan.

Assad and Putin were denounced in the Western press for war crimes in using chemical weapons, bombing hospitals and not providing an earlier humanitarian escape for 50,000 innocent civilians in Aleppo. It was not clear how true these accusations were. Assad hailed his victory as changing history and Obama said he could not slaughter his way to legitimacy.

Recognising realities: my Peace Plan
Three former British Ambassadors to Syria had publicly stated that British policy towards Syria had been a huge mistake and had made matters a lot worse. The ex-British Ambassador to Syria from 1999 to 2003, Peter Ford, claimed on 23 December 2016 that the British Foreign Office had misread and misrepresented the situation in Syria since the start of the conflict, and had got Syria wrong at every step. "They told us at the beginning that Assad's demise was imminent. They told us he'd be gone by Christmas." He said the Foreign Office had falsely claimed that Assad could not control the country when he was "well on the

way to doing so" – he now controlled 80 per cent of the Syrian people – and accused the British Foreign Office of lying. He said that British policy in Syria had "made the situation worse".

Several articles in the British press reckoned that British MPs voted wrongly in 2013 to stay out of the Syrian conflict, thus abandoning the country to Russia, and that the UK government had chosen to support the rebels without knowing enough about them, for the UK was now in alliance with factions of al-Qaeda. The articles suggested it would have been better to support Assad. It was said that, influenced by the Arab Spring in other countries, the UK made a wrong decision to help depose Assad in favour of the "so-called moderate opposition". Despite the Brzezinski Plan of 1997 and its Arab Spring, many began to draw the conclusion that for the last four years the West had been on the wrong side in Syria and had let Russia back into the Middle East.

Now Russia was demonised by the US for hacking into the US Democratic Party's emails and influencing the American election, and peace looked further away than ever. The dream of 'peace for our time' looked a hopeless illusion.

I was clear that regardless of who the UK government was supporting – and it had supported the rebels and had worked along with the US to overthrow Assad – Assad was winning and it was unreasonable to expect a winner to resign immediately. As I had seen from the overthrow of Saddam, Gaddafi and Mubarak, a Middle-Eastern country without its dictator is more chaotic than with its dictator, and I wanted stability to continue and not to disintegrate into rule by militias as in Libya. Yes, there should be democracy, and my Peace Plan aimed to secure this. It was unreasonable to expect Russia to pack up and go home without retaining its main base in Syria.

My Peace Plan sought to recognise the realities in Syria, which Western diplomats seemed not to be doing, and to bring an effective peace that could set Syria back on a path of future growth and prosperity. To get the foreign interventionists out (Jordan, Qatar, Turkey, Saudi Arabia, America, UK, France, Iran,

Lebanese Hezbollah and Russia), they all needed the pipelines they supported to be permitted by Assad: the Qatar–Saudi Arabia–Jordan–Turkey pipeline supported by the US and the Iran–Northern Iraq–Syria pipeline supported by Russia. I sought to bring stability, democracy and prosperity to Syria by my Peace Plan, and at the same time to bring about a reduction of tension in Eastern Europe.

Not in my Peace Plan, but kept back for the negotiations, was my proposal that Syria and the Crimea should now be in a Russian sphere of influence and Afghanistan in an American and Western sphere of influence.

If my Peace Plan was approached from the perspective of nation-state self-interest, it would not be taken up. But if all could see that from a supranationalistic perspective there was a

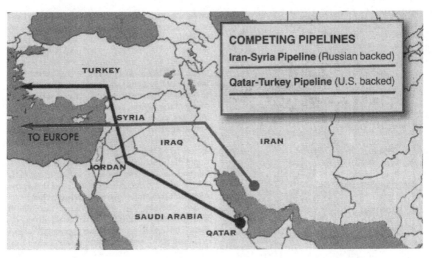

Map of two pipelines traversing Syria, one from Iran (supported by Russia) and one from Qatar (supported by the US)

greater good that could lead to universal peace and prosperity rather than ruinous war and a legacy of rubble, then my Peace Plan provided a basis for a new world structure and 'peace for our time'.

Peace and goodwill

I returned to my Forest home in Essex overlooking oak-trees, and dictated chapters 9 and 10 and then amended the print-out.

It was now the time of Christmas cards. Eleanor Laing MP, the Deputy Speaker in the House of Commons, in response to my card of a stag in a blizzard, out in the cold, sent me a Christmas card of a child's drawing of Father Christmas riding a sleigh drawn by a stag-like reindeer through the night sky above Big Ben, bringing the gift of universal peace and goodwill from a supranational order above the Houses of Parliament.

I had emailed Issam asking if there was any news of a reply to my 15-point Peace Plan. On Christmas Eve he reported that "head office" had asked for a specific reason for my interviewing Assad and that he had replied on my behalf. In Manila he had told me that my Peace Plan would go straight to his friend the Prime Minister to be laid before Assad, and now "head office" – of the Syrian consulate? of Assad's administration? – was asking why I needed to meet him. It looked as if Assad's view had changed now that he had recaptured Aleppo, and that he was more interested in recapturing the rest of his lost territory than in reaching a peace agreement.

A new Cold War

Suddenly there was a new Cold-War atmosphere. On 29 December, soon after news that Donald Trump would deploy Henry Kissinger, aged 93, to reset the US's relations with Russia and with only three weeks of his presidency to run, Obama announced the expulsion of 35 Russian diplomats as spies for the Kremlin-backed hacking of the Democratic Party's computers and releasing of emails that showed Hillary Clinton in a poor light to help Trump win the Presidential election. This was in response to a report in a joint document compiled by the CIA and FBI confirming Russian hacking.

In addition, two Russian government compounds suspected of being used for intelligence purposes were shut down, and there were new sanctions against nine Russian entities and individuals. There were apparently other retaliatory actions, presumably of a cyber nature, that would not be made public. Russia refused to retaliate until after Trump's inauguration, and would wait to see what policies Trump pursued. Russia would judge Trump by his actions.

Trump now had to decide whether to follow the Republican-supported intelligence experts who had found the Russians guilty of cyber offences, or whether to revoke the expulsions and sanctions. He disparaged claims that the hacking had affected the election and said he found Julian Assange, the editor-in-chief and founder of WikiLeaks, more credible than the CIA. The Republican Senator John McCain branded the hacking "an act of war" and demanded a harsher response. With this sort of pressure from Republicans within his own Party could Trump ignore Obama's expulsions, let alone revoke them?

It then emerged that US intelligence had allegedly warned Trump that Russian "operatives" were in possession of information that could be used to blackmail him following his stay in Moscow to host a Miss Universe pageant in 2013. US intelligence had allegedly drawn his attention to a 35-page dossier compiled by an ex-MI6 intelligence agent now in private business as a consultant, which suggested that Trump had been cultivated by the Kremlin for over five years and that the Kremlin had collected information to blackmail him. This dossier had not been corroborated by news agencies and was unverified, and had been leaked into the public domain on the internet and carried by CNN. In a swashbuckling press conference Trump denounced the leak as "fake news" and blamed the intelligence services for a "disgraceful" leak, which the intelligence services strongly denied. In a feud with the CIA leadership he described the alleged CIA leak as reminiscent of Nazi Germany. (He followed this up with a feud against the press for "lying" in showing photographs proving that the crowd at his inauguration was much smaller than the crowd at Obama's two inaugurations.) I decided that until the story of the leak was verified I would discount it.

But it looked as if, from a Tillerson-led and Kissinger-led resetting of the US relationship with Russia on a more friendly basis, the US and NATO-led Europe were plunging back into the hostile atmosphere of the Cold War. It looked as if a new Cold War had begun. Whereas I had been happy to visit Russia and have a meeting in the Russian Parliament and meet President Putin although my past intelligence links were openly on the internet, I was now uneasy and had to think twice about the wisdom of going to Moscow even though I had a supranational-istic perspective. For Russia still had a nation-state outlook and if there was about to be another Cold War, there was now a pos-sibility that I might not come out.

Russian cease-fire

Now it was announced that Russia, acting as a superpower without US involvement, had reached a deal with Turkey (the seat of the former Ottoman Empire that historically included the Middle East) in which President Putin and President Erdogan (the Turkish leader) would "guarantee" a cease-fire between the Syrian government and the rebel opposition forces excluding: IS; the Fateh al-Sham Front (formerly known as al-Nusra Front, which had just allied with an IS Front group) and groups af-filiated with them; and the Kurdish PKK (which was based in Turkey and Iraq).

There were talks between the two sides and towards the end of January there was a Russian-led meeting of Russia and its allies Turkey and Iran in Astana, the capital of Kazakhstan. Re-bels sat with their opponents in the Syrian army. There was no American representative at Iran's wish, but the US Ambassador to Kazakhstan attended as an observer. It was hoped that these talks would lead to a full conference with the US and its allies in Geneva.

Despite the cease-fire and taking advantage of the exclusion of the Idlib-based Fateh al-Sham Front from the deal, Assad's forces were bombing the 44,000 displaced evacuees from east Aleppo who were now sheltering in towns around Idlib, and were about to begin a ground operation against Idlib and western Aleppo, where 750,000 Sunni refugees were sheltering. The war looked set to continue outside the zones covered by the cease-fire.

Things had changed. Following the fall of Aleppo Assad was now in command of 80 per cent of the people in Syria. The realities were being recognised, and there was now no need for me to broker a peace between the warring sides, they could do it for themselves in Astana and Geneva. Would there be a new Yalta there, a new division of the world between the US and Russia, with both sides having new spheres of influence? Would the peace include Eastern Europe and head off a Third World War? Time would tell.

Commitments in the UK

The new year was with us. Ann had a knee operation on 9 January. On 13 January I had sclerotherapy on my right leg, and had bandages from toe to groin for 14 days. As a Christmas present my son Matthew had given me tickets for 16 January to hear Stephen Hawking look back on *A Brief History of Time*, which was relevant to my Universalism. I could not be away from the UK for a while.

Now that Assad was in control of 80 per cent of Syria and was bombing Idlib despite a Russian-backed cease-fire, would I get to explain my Peace Plan to him face to face? Should I be flying into dangerous Beirut, where British hostages had been kidnapped and held in the 1980s, and should I be crossing dangerous terrain into Syria? In the new Cold-War atmosphere following Obama's expulsion of 35 Russian diplomats, would I get to address the Russian Parliament and meet Putin and tell him face to face that there must not be a Third World War? And should I be doing this?

I did not know. All I could say was that when I was asked I stood up and agreed to undertake these risky journeys and hold these meetings. Perhaps my voice – in Athens, in Manila and in my email containing my 15-point Peace Plan which had apparently been circulated to Assad and Putin on 2 December

2016 – had already contributed to influencing the Syrians and the Russians into sparing and evacuating the besieged, who knows. Perhaps the 15 points of my Peace Plan had already been digested by Assad and Putin and had already influenced their talks, and it was not necessary for me to see them? Perhaps I had already got my points across, who knows.

I was clear it was the wrong time for me to press for meetings with Assad and Putin, but I had stated my Peace Plan and as a Peace Laureate I remained ready to go if the call came. But I had obligations in the UK and a new writing program – I had to write *World State* and bring out *Selected Letters* – and I would have to resume normality and fulfil my domestic and literary commitments while I awaited an opening to carry forward world peace.

The world changes

Suddenly the world changed. The advent of Trump and his new assertive policies took the public's attention away from Syria and made the prospect of such a peace opening appear more remote.

I had posted my latest book *The Secret American Destiny* to Trump on 6 January 2017. It had the Statue of Liberty, guardian of refugees, on its front cover, and it was dedicated: "To the incoming American President in November 2016, who has the power to urge the UN General Assembly to establish a democratic, bicameral world government, a partly federal World State with limited supranational authority to enforce peace and disarmament." I signed the book to him on that page. In my book the American destiny was to set up a democratic World State. I was intrigued that Trump included the word 'destiny' twice in his inauguration speech on 20 January 2017, but did not say what the destiny was: "We share one nation, one home and one glorious destiny" and "Your voice, your hopes and dreams will define your American destiny."

In his inauguration speech Trump announced that he would put "America first" in trade, and on the same day he pulled out of the Trans-Pacific Partnership (TPP) trade agreement (whose

12 nations included Mexico). He had announced that he would build a \$12 billion 1,954-mile-long wall to keep Mexicans out of the US, particularly Mexican drug dealers – a throwback to the Berlin Wall and nation-states' obsession with borders – and this was now to be paid for by a 20-per-cent tax on imports from Mexico, which would have catastrophic consequences for many Mexicans. He announced that his main goal in foreign policy would be to "eradicate IS completely from the face of the Earth". He declared that there would be a missile defence shield against Iran and North Korea.

The UK's Prime Minister Theresa May was the first foreign leader to visit Trump. She spoke of the US and UK leading the world as internationalists and halting the eclipse of the West by China and Russia, and she asked for a trade deal that might replace some of the 44 per cent of UK exports to the EU's single market. Trump handled the meeting personally but although the US President can cancel trade agreements with the TPP, Canada and Mexico (for example) he cannot create new agreements, which have to involve Congress. Trump's book *The Art of the Deal* (ghost-written by Tony Schwartz) states that he must be the winner in every deal. As his policy was now "America First" and the UK already exported 17 per cent of its total exports to the US in 2016 as opposed to 44 per cent to the EU (from which it would be walking away or on which it would be paying tariffs of up to 51 per cent as required by World Trade Organisation rules, thereby reducing British exports), it was hard to see what material gain there would be for the UK in such a deal.

(According to a study of Britain's post-exit prospects by the British National Institute of Economic and Social Research,[2] if the UK left the single market and signed agreements with the EU, the US and growth economies including China, Russia, Canada, New Zealand and Australia, the income from the UK's goods and services would be reduced by £197 billion. The UK's exports and imports to and from the EU would fall by 22 per cent, or 30 per cent with a "hard Brexit". A free trade agreement with the Brics nations – Brazil, Russia, India, China and South

Africa – would only add 2.2 per cent to the UK's trade, and a deal with the 'Anglo-American' economies – the US, Canada, New Zealand and South Africa – would only add 2.6 per cent.)

Walking down a slope on camera, Trump held May's hand. It was said that Trump has a fear of slopes, bathmophobia, and that he had clutched May's hand for support. Whatever the truth, for a few seconds it seemed that the two leaders were holding hands, and this image of the special relationship went round the world. Despite their apparent closeness, on the same day Trump announced the banning of all new refugees, and of new travellers to the US from seven Muslim countries. He had already announced that he would ban all Muslims from entering the US (except for the Mayor of London). Now, in defiance of the symbolism of the Statue of Liberty, who had long welcomed refugees (including his own German grandfather Friedrich Drumpf in 1885), and in a clash of civilizations with echoes of the Nazis' racist treatment of the Jews that seemed in breach of human rights and was later suspended by the courts as uncon-stitutional, all refugees were banned for four months and US borders were required to turn away all travellers from Iraq, Iran, Sudan, Libya, Somalia and Yemen during the following three months, and from Syria indefinitely.

Theresa May had invited Trump to London on a State visit, and there were now outraged calls across the political spectrum in the UK for Trump's visit to be cancelled, or at least postponed. US state officials considered bringing legal challenges, and the British Government announced that it did not support Trump's bans (which might increase home-grown support for IS) but that the State visit would go ahead. May's "global Britain" (which may have been a spin for "the Commonwealth") now seemed at odds with Trump's "buy American" and "hire American". The UK's pursuit of free-trade deals, which had already resulted in working groups exploring trade deals with 13 countries, seemed to be in conflict with its support for human rights and the prin-ciples of tolerance and openness. The British Prime Minister ap-peared to be begging for trade deals because she had turned her back on the single market and had to find alternatives at all costs from a position of weakness.

Trump's chief trade adviser now accused Germany of "abusing the euro" by grossly undervaluing it to boost exports at the expense of America. He was signalling a trade war between the dollar and euro zones. Donald Tusk, President of the European Council, retaliated in an open letter to the leaders of the EU's 27 member states. Presumably taking account of Trump's support for Brexit and his defiance of European supranationalism, he wrote that Washington was now an external threat to the EU along with an assertive China, an aggressive Russia and radical Islam, and that Trump's "worrying declarations" were among challenges faced by the EU that "put into question the last 70 years of American foreign policy".

It was now clear that there was a new world grouping. No longer were the US and EU allies. Now the US, the UK and perhaps Russia would be in alliance, with Germany and the EU on their own. And, Tusk said, from now on the UK would be tied to a superpower: the US, Russia or China.

Trump's America-First policy had much to do with reducing the out-of-control American deficit that had derailed America's project to spread democracy and liberal values throughout the world. George W. Bush had intervened in the Middle East to spread democracy, and America had become unpopular. Barack Obama had calmed things down by not intervening in the Middle East, a course indicated by his receipt of a Nobel Peace Prize at the outset of his presidency. However, Obamacare and other policies had caused the deficit to rise. The American deficit for 2016 alone was around $590 billion, and the accumulated American deficit since the deficits began in 1970 had reached about $14 trillion by the end of 2016. The American project had stalled because of America's huge indebtedness, and it could not restart until the deficit was sorted out. America would be great again when the deficit was under control. Trump, a billionaire who understood finance, sought to control the deficit by protectionism, and the American project would then be able to resume spreading democracy throughout the world.

Was Trump, whose mother was Scottish, implementing his own agenda as an alleged opponent of the Establishment élite, as was presented in the press? Or was he acting on behalf of the Establishment élite's New World Order while seeming to oppose it? His net wealth in September 2016 was $3.7 billion (down $800 million from the previous year),[3] and many websites linked him to the Establishment's New World Order. David Rockefeller and Edmond de Rothschild were among those who invested in Resorts International, which Trump controlled as chairman from 1987 to 1988, and Rothschilds saved him from bankruptcy at this time through Wilbur L. Ross Jr, Senior Managing Director of Rothschild Inc.[4] (Churchill, whose bust was returned to the Oval Office in the White House, was also saved from bankruptcy by Rothschilds through Sir Henry Strakosch in 1938 after putting Chartwell on the market[5] and in return agreed to support a new homeland for the Jews in what would become Israel in 1948.) When Trump paid off a debt to a Rothschilds bank he banned Jacob Rothschild[6] from his Mar-a-Lago Club at his $200-million Versailles-like 'palace' in Palm Beach, Florida, which on 18 January 2017 he officially named his Winter White House. (The Club membership fee was doubled to $200,000 after the 2016 American election.) I have commented on his links to the Rockefellerites Tillerson and Kissinger (see p.141). However, his executive order that the Keystone XL and Dakota pipelines should go ahead seemed to oppose Rockefellers' support for action to combat global warming. There was talk of his being a creation of the Council on Foreign Relations (CFR), which was set up by Rockefellers, but the CFR's statements urging him not to proceed hastily in implementing his policies suggested otherwise, and there were reports that the Bilderberg Group were hostile to Trump.

He was, then, officially an anti-Establishment candidate, but as the Establishment depended on international banking interests he could be regarded as the Establishment's candidate whose American nationalism, isolationism and protectionism would lead to global governance. It was still possible that he would reduce the American deficit in his first term and then take steps to bring the world together through a democratic World State under American leadership in his second term, but only time would tell. He had a clear agenda on the day of his inauguration and began to put it into effect immediately, and at this early stage of his presidency whether the agenda was his own or an élite's could only be a matter of speculation.

All Trump's changes made a peace agreement in the Middle East seem more distant.

Dream of comprehensive 'peace for our time'

On 27 January reports surfaced that Assad had suffered a stroke and was bedridden with a limp left hand. A Saudi newspaper claimed he was suffering from a brain tumour and was being treated by a Russian-Syrian medical team on a weekly basis, and had undergone medical tests in Moscow in October 2016 (before I met Issam). Several other reports claimed that he had been shot by one of his bodyguards and had died. It was also said that his brother was running the country until he recovered.

Were problems connected with Assad's health the reason why Issam had asked me to wait? I did not know, and in the absence of conclusive evidence I discounted the reports, which persisted into March.

At the end of January there were new reports that the Syrian regime had ethnically cleansed large swathes of the country, and were concentrating on the rebels around Idlib, with the support of 15,000 Iranian militia fighters. The fighting had continued. It was clear to me that I had not been asked to go to Syria as Assad wanted the war to continue and did not want a peace agreement yet.

In early February a report by Amnesty International accused the Assad regime of secretly killing 13,000 civilians in mass hangings carried out in the basement of Saydnaya military prison in Damascus between 2011 and 2015. The hangings took place between midnight and dawn on Tuesday mornings. The prisoners were blindfolded and told they would be executed only minutes before being hanged. They all left their slippers outside the execution room. Inmates could calculate how many had been hanged each night by dividing the number of slippers by two. The UK Foreign Secretary Boris Johnson said he was "sickened" by the news, and that Assad had no future.

I had seen that only a strong man would have the power to hold elections in Syria, and that realistically the West had to deal with Assad. But I viewed the prospect with mounting distaste. Somehow peace had to be brought to Syria, but now I did not relish the prospect of visiting Assad, for whose self-interested principles I now had nothing but contempt. Peace in Syria seemed more elusive as each day passed.

Until there was peace throughout the Middle East, including in the Yemen, my dream of 'peace for our time' would remain just that, a dream, and would only turn out to be an illusion if Russia re-invaded the Baltic states and Eastern Europe.

As a Peace Laureate I had called for a peace agreement to bring a settled way of life to the Middle East and to Eastern Europe, and I was hopeful that, even if I was not able to explain it to them, Assad and Putin would rise to the supranational vision of the 15-point Peace Plan I had circulated to them. I hoped that without my mediating they would soon deliver a comprehensive 'peace for our time' that would avoid a Third World War.

If not, I would be waiting to step in to reason with them. My dream was still intact, I was still filled with hope and longed for a time beyond my 15-point Peace Plan when all humankind would belong to a democratic World State – a United Federation that embodied a new world structure – and would benefit from a universal peace.

31 May 2016 – 17 February 2017[7]

Appendices

Towards a World State

Appendix 1

My Universalism and World State

A paper presented by Nicholas Hagger to the World Philosophical Forum at their Symposium in Athens (4–9 October 2015) throws light on the emergence of his Universalism, on his vision of unity, on his dialectical method and on the influence of Plato's *Republic* on his statecraft and view of a World State. At the end Nicholas Hagger appeals to the UN and the US President to urge the UN General Assembly to consider the benefits of inaugurating a partly-federal supranational World State.

> 'I never stopped thinking how things might be improved and the constitution reformed.... Finally I came to the conclusion that all existing states were badly governed, and that their constitutions were incapable of reform without drastic treatment and a great deal of good luck. I was forced, in fact, to the belief that the only hope of finding justice for society or for the individual lay in true philosophy, and that mankind will have no respite from trouble until either real philosophers gain political power or politicians become by some miracle true philosophers.'
>
> Plato, letter VII, stating the theme of *The Republic*,
> c.353/2BC

It's a pleasure to be addressing fellow Universalists in the cradle of Greek democracy, which was founded during the reforms of Solon in c.594/3BC and established by Cleisthenes in c.508/7BC. We are in the heart of the Athenian political empire of Themistocles and Pericles, and near the prison where Socrates was put to death in 399BC and near Plato's Academy, the school for statesmen Plato founded in 386BC. Plato's philosophical dialogues established Socrates' dialectical thinking, and his *Republic* associated philosophers with an ideal political state and the practice of statecraft. Plato's pupil Aristotle set out the constitution of the Athenians, the political system of ancient Athens, in *Athenaion Politeia*, c.329/8BC, a further example of a philosopher practicing statecraft.

Ancient Greek political philosophy and statecraft devised a new system of universal government by free citizens for Athens, and now we modern political philosophers and practisers of statecraft are following in the footsteps of Plato and Aristotle as we devise a new system of universal government by free citizens for the world, which I call Universalism.

How I Came to Universalism

I'd like to tell you how I came to Universalism. In the early 1960s I was a British-Council-sponsored lecturer at the University of Baghdad in Iraq and I then spent four years as Visiting Professor at three universities in Tokyo, Japan, where I also wrote speeches on world banking for the Governor of the Bank of Japan and tutored Emperor Hirohito's second son in world history. I was asked to teach a postgraduate course at one of my universities on 'The decline of the West', which I based on Gibbon, Spengler and Toynbee, and while doing this I saw a fourth way of understanding history, which led to my study of 25 rising and falling civilizations, *The Fire and the Stones* (1991). In that work of historical Universalism, which sees all world history as an indivisible unity, I saw civilizations as rising following a mystic's vision of metaphysical Fire or Light that passed into their religions.

I titled the Preface 'Introduction to the New Universalism' and in January 1991, nearly 25 years ago, wrote that 'an Age of Universalism is ahead'. I developed the philosophical implications of Universalism in *The Universe and the Light* (1993), which contained three essays. In the middle one, titled 'What is Universalism?', I pointed out that the word 'Universalism' incorporates the words 'universe', 'universal' and 'universality'. Universalism sees each discipline from the perspective of the whole of humankind. A Universalist sees the universe as a unity – sees the oneness of the universe, of humankind and of all world history.

I led a group of a dozen British Universalist philosophers in London from 1993 to 1994. Like the Existentialists who had different shades of Existentialism we all had different shades of Universalism but were able to call ourselves Universalists. I went on to have 43 books published in seven disciplines, all from a Universalist perspective. I reflected the oneness of the universe in my philosophical work, *The One and the Many* (1999). I set out philosophical Universalism in *The New Philosophy of Universalism* (2009), which sees the philosophical universe as an indivisible unity and the traditions of philosophy within a whole; and literary Universalism in *A New Philosophy of Literature* (2012), which presents the fundamental theme of world literature. I've described all this in two autobiographical works published earlier in 2015, *My Double Life 1: This Dark Wood* and *My Double Life 2: A Rainbow over the Hills*, which was subtitled 'The Vision of Unity'.

My Vision of Unity

I arrived at my vision of unity in Japan. I visited Zen Buddhist temples and meditated, and found myself on a Mystic Way outside denominational religion: I underwent an awakening, then purgation, then illumination (which I experienced in Japan and more profoundly in London) and eventually, after ordeals, a centre-shift that left me permanently perceiving unity. I came to see the world and the universe as a unity *instinctively*. I reflected the vision of unity in my literary work: in over 1,500 poems, more than 300 classical odes, two epic poems, five verse plays, a masque and over 1,000 short stories.

I don't exclude the rational approach but I'm aware that the reason, the rational faculty I used in my university teaching, analyses and makes distinctions and seeks differences within separate disciplines, and fragments. I discovered from my experience that there is also an intuitive faculty that perceives unity, that pieces together the fragmented disciplines and restores their wholeness and unity. My Universalist approach to the world's problems combines these two faculties. The vision of unity draws strength from science's rational recognition of the order in the universe and from the intuitive perception of the oneness of the universe and of humankind.

Philosophical Universalism and the Metaphysical Perspective
My philosophical Universalism sees the universe and humankind as a whole. It reflects the oneness of the universe and includes the metaphysical view of manifestation: the universe manifests from Nothingness to Non-Being, to Being and (with the Big Bang) Existence – through four levels or tiers of metaphysical Reality. My philosophical Universalism restores the metaphysical perspective of the universe which in the 1920s and 1930s was stripped aside by the sceptical, secular Vienna Circle who were more interested in logic and language than in the universe.

I have set out the metaphysical philosophical tradition in my books, for example in chapters 1 and 2 of *The New Philosophy of Universalism* ('The Origins of Western Philosophy' and 'The Decline of Western Philosophy and the Way Forward'). I have also set out the scientific, more empirical tradition which co-existed with it. The two traditions arguably began with Plato and Aristotle and co-existed at the Academy not far from here.

My philosophical Universalism reconciles the two traditions. The universe manifested before the Big Bang from the infinite, which the Presocratic Anaximander of Miletus called 'the boundless' (*to apeiron*), an eternally moving Reality, c.570BC. The universe has been expanding since the first whoosh of inflation in the first second, and is now shaped like a shuttlecock (the 'ball' with a ring of feathers batted in badminton) and surrounded by the infinite from which it manifested. I have a picture of a surfer on the front cover of *The New Philosophy of Universalism*. His feet are in space-time on the edge of the expanding universe, but his head, arms and body are in the infinite, the 'boundless'. The surfer is a symbol of Universalism's reconciliation of the metaphysical and scientific/social perspectives and traditions.

My Dialectical Thinking: +A + −A = 0
Dialectical thinking can be found in all my books. Junzaburo Nishiwaki, Japan's T.S. Eliot, introduced me to it in 1964, 51 years ago. In a restaurant with sawdust on the floor, just him and me drinking *saké*, I asked him, 'What is the wisdom of the East?' He wrote down: '+A + −A = 0.' Above 0 he wrote 'Great Nothing'. I immediately grasped what he meant. All the opposites – day and night, life and death, time and eternity, finite and infinite, every thesis and antithesis – are reconciled within a synthesis, an underlying unity. This synthesis is the Universalist reconciliation. He said, 'The Absolute is where there is no difference.' Metaphysics + the scientific, social perspective = underlying order within the universe on which the philosophy of Universalism is based.

This dialectical thinking goes back to the symposia ('drinkings together') in the elegies of the Greek lyric poet Theognis of Megara (6th century BC) and in the Socratic dialogues of Plato's *The Symposium* (c.385–370BC) and Xenophon's *The Symposium* (late 360s BC). 'Dialectic' was explained by Plato in *The Republic*, book 7 (c.380BC) as a method which challenges its own assumptions, and dialectical thinking may look back beyond Plato's Socratic dialogues to Heracleitus. The dialectic of Marxism, taken from Hegel, is well-known: +A (thesis, workers) + −A (antithesis, employers) = 0 (synthesis, the Communist State which allegedly kept them in balance). I arrived at my dialectic not through social thinking but, as I have said, through the ultimate vision of unity of mysticism and metaphysics. My dialectic now includes social thinking: +A (the metaphysical perspective) + −A (the secular, social perspective) = 0, the Universalist vision of unity and its expression in statecraft.

My Universalism – and Seven Disciplines
My Universalism, which is similar to secular Transuniversalism in some respects, has applications in a number of disciplines. In *My Double Life 2: A Rainbow over the Hills* I set out seven disciplines and describe them as bands in a rainbow. Universal-

ism has applications in mysticism, literature, philosophy and science, history, comparative religion, international politics and statecraft, and world culture. (It also has applications on the environment, but we'll leave that aside as environmental Universalism is an aspect of scientific Universalism.) My works reflect all these disciplines and have Universalism at their core. It can be said that there are seven Universalisms like bands of a rainbow: mystical Universalism; literary Universalism; philosophical and scientific Universalism – I treat them as one as I see the two as enmeshed and scientists such as Hawking have claimed (wrongly) that science has replaced philosophy; historical Universalism; religious Universalism; political Universalism; and cultural Universalism. But there is in actual fact just one Universalism which, like an overarching rainbow, includes these seven bands.

My Universalism sees each discipline as a unified whole – thus my work on literary Universalism, *A New Philosophy of Literature*, sees all world literature as a whole and presents the fundamental theme of world literature – and sees all disciplines as a unified whole. In my works Universalism reconciles all opposites, including classical and Romantic styles in literature, rational and intuitional approaches in philosophy, metaphysical and secular perspectives in the seven disciplines – and nation-states and federalism in international politics.

Historical Universalism and my World State
I now want to dwell on historical Universalism, which sees world history as a whole. I have said that according to my study of civilizations in *The Fire and the Stones* (revised and brought up to date in *The Light of Civilization* and *The Rise and Fall of Civilizations*), each of 25 civilizations rose following a metaphysical vision which passed into its religion, and declined when it turned secular and lost contact with its original metaphysical vision. After passing through 61 similar stages each civilization passes into another civilization (just as the Egyptian and Mesopotamian civilizations passed into the Arab civilization in 642 and their

own gods were abandoned for Allah).

The goal of historical Universalism is to create a partial World State within this pattern, a partly-federal supranational state that would abolish war, nuclear weapons, famine, disease and poverty and run the world for humanity on the principle of universality. If such a World State comes into being within the rising-and-falling pattern, it will last for a while like the Roman Empire, not forever. Eventually the rising-and-falling pattern of civilizations will resume, but the world will have benefited from the abolition of war, nuclear weapons, famine, disease and poverty while the World State lasts.

This World State would be formed within a civilization, and of the 25 civilizations in my study the North-American civilization is the youngest and most energetic living civilization, in stage 15 of its 61 stages (an expanding stage), whereas the European civilization is in stage 43 (a stage in which a civilization passes into a conglomerate, in Europe's case the European Union) and the Byzantine-Russian civilization has just left stage 43 (the USSR) and entered stage 46 (federalism, the Russian Federation). In historical terms as the only superpower the North-American civilization is well placed to set up a World State as it is in the same stage the Roman Empire was in before 218BC when it expanded its Republican Empire in Carthage, Macedonia, Greece and Spain as a result of the two Punic Wars; and the UN's headquarters is within its borders.

I have set out details of a democratic World State in *The World Government* (2010) and in the second volume of my American trilogy (written for the American market), *The Secret American Dream* (2011). The third volume, out in 2016, *The Secret American Destiny*, repeats my calls for the US to encourage the UN, which is inter-nationalist and between nation-states, to begin discussions on creating a supranational partly-federal World State within the stages of the 14 living civilizations. The 14 living civilizations are the North-American, European, Byzantine-Russian, Andean, Meso-American, Arab, African, Indian, South-East-Asian, Japanese, Oceanian, Chinese, Tibetan and Central-Asian civilizations. I have set out 850 global constituencies and the structure of the World State in these books.

Initially the nation-states would empower a partly-federal supranational authority (a World Commission, World Parliamentary Assembly and World Senate) to deliver seven goals:

1. bringing peace between nation-states, and disarmament;
2. sharing natural resources and energy so that all humankind can have a raised standard of living;
3. solving environmental problems such as global warming, which seem to be beyond self-interested nation-states;
4. ending disease;
5. ending famine;
6. solving the world's financial crisis; and
7. redistributing wealth to eliminate poverty.

The partial supranational authority would make progress on the world's most critical problems covered by these seven goals. Otherwise civilizations and nation-states would continue as they are. Nation-states would be giving up some power in these seven areas to improve the world but would retain internal power. A more absolute World State may emerge at a later stage after everyone has got used to a limited supranational authority.

The practical way my World State would be set up is as follows. Discussing a partial supranational authority at the UN General Assembly would come under the UN's global education policy. Encouraged by the US, the UN General Assembly of nation-states would discuss the implications of approving a World Constitutional Convention after agreeing all the safeguards in all the world's regions. It would eventually act to join the new supranational World State. The 14 living civilizations' rise-and-fall pattern within their separate civilizations would be suspended in the areas of the seven goals (but would continue at the local regional level), and they would enter a form of federalism for a while. Five living civilizations – the European, Japanese, Oceanian, Chinese and Tibetan civilizations – are in stage 43, the union stage, and their unions would pass into the new federation. Eight living civilizations – the Byzantine-Russian, Andean, Meso-American, Arab, African, Indian, South-East-Asian and Central-Asian civilizations – are in stage 46, a federalism stage, and their federalism would pass into the new World Federation.

The only superpower, the expanding North-American civilization, would preside over the World Federation in its stage 15 just as the Roman civilization presided over the states in the Republican Roman Empire's Mediterranean states before 218BC. My World State is akin to the 'Universal State of the Earth' (USE) and the WPF's vision of the self-government of humanity as a whole. Calls for such a World State have been made by President Truman, Einstein, Churchill, Gandhi, Bertrand Russell, Eisenhower, John F. Kennedy and Gorbachev.

I emphasise that the World State or World Federation would be *partly* federal in limiting itself to the seven goals: bringing peace and disarmament between nation-states; sharing resources and energy; solving environmental problems such as global warming; ending famine; solving the world's financial crisis; and redistributing wealth to eliminate poverty. Nation-states and civilizations would continue at local regional level outside these seven areas.

A World State will only last as long as the expansionist phase of the North-American civilization, which began with stage 15. The Roman civilization's expansionist phase after the beginning of stage 15 lasted from 341BC until Rome was sacked in 410, then in 455 and again in 476, between 700 and 800 years. The European civilization's expansionist phase after the beginning of stage 15 (which included the Crusades) lasted from 951 to 1914, nearly a thousand years. When the North-American expansionist phase ends the World State will break up and all 14 living civilizations will leave the World Federation and return to their rise-and-fall pattern. Apart from the seven federal areas they will have continued in this pattern at local regional level, and their return from the World State through the pattern of stages will therefore be seamless. The rise-and-fall pattern of the dead civilizations can be found in *The Fire and the Stones* (revised as *The Light of Civilization* and *The Rise and Fall of Civilizations*).

Reunification of World Culture

To achieve the formation of a World State there must be a re-unification of our fractured world culture. The seven disciplines of world culture are divided between metaphysical and secular approaches, and Universalism can reconcile these and reconcile world culture, as I show in my next book, *The Secret American Destiny*, which is out in November 2016. It must not be forgotten that of the world population of 7.33 billion in July 2015, 4.6 billion – 63 per cent – regard themselves as religious believers, i.e. as having some sort of metaphysical outlook and perspective. The WPF's Transuniversalism is secular, and although it does not reject the traditional religion of the 4.6 billion, the WPF focuses on the universal and scientific principles followed by 37 per cent of humankind.

My Universalism seeks to combine within the seven disciplines of world culture the secular outlook the WPF has and the metaphysical outlook, to prepare the ground for a Universalism in which *everyone* – *all* world citizens, including the 63 per cent who are religious – can have a stake, and therefore for a coming World State.

My Appeal to the UN

I've told you about my Universalism and World State. We have been working in the same area for several years, and it would be good to join forces. Ultimately I would like to see a debate between the nation-states on the benefits of setting up a World Constitutional Convention in New York to found a World State, the 'Universal State of the Earth' (USE) whose constitution we are inaugurating this week. Igor Kondrashin has kindly suggested that I might become a special envoy of the WPF to lobby the UN.

To carry the momentum forward I now want to make an appeal to the UN, under whose umbrella – through UNESCO – we are now meeting. And so I appeal to the UN and to Ban Ki-moon, please take on board what I have said. Please timetable a presentation within the General Assembly to the assembled nation-states about the benefits of forming a partially-federal supranational World State that can declare war, nuclear weapons, famine, disease and poverty illegal and bring in universal order for all humankind. I am prepared to address the UN General Assembly and give this presentation, if invited. I also appeal to the incumbent American President Obama, recipient of the Nobel Peace Prize in 2009 and believer in a World State, and to the next American President to lend their support for such a debate.

Not far from here Plato, practicing statecraft for his school for statesmen, devised his ideal republic in *The Republic*, in book 6 of which he showed Socrates associating the philosopher with practical government through his conception of the 'philosopher-king' or 'philosopher-ruler'. We modern practisers of philosophical statecraft who are creating a World State look back to Plato's ideal society in which it is essential (Plato says in letter VII) that "real philosophers gain political power or politicians become by some miracle true philosophers", and to Socrates' association of philosophers with practical government.

I appeal to the UN and to the US President of the day, please continue the spirit of this long tradition of statecraft. Please consider the merits of an ideal democratic, partly-federal World State – a new supranational 'republic' – that can solve the world's problems (war, refugees, nuclear weapons, famine, disease and poverty) on the basis of Universalist reconciliation.

Appendix 2

The Rainbow-like Parabola: 61 Stages in a Civilization's Life Cycle

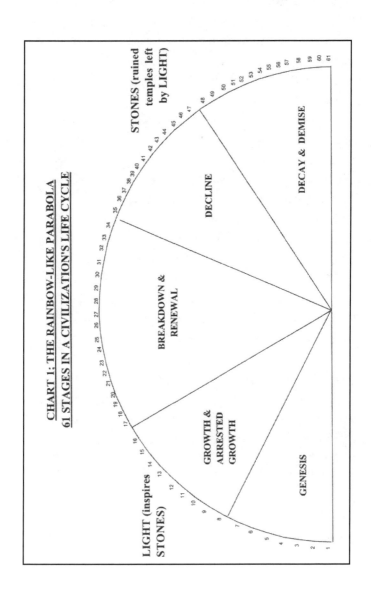

CHART 1: THE RAINBOW-LIKE PARABOLA
61 STAGES IN A CIVILIZATION'S LIFE CYCLE

LIGHT (inspires STONES)

STONES (ruined temples left by LIGHT)

GENESIS

GROWTH & ARRESTED GROWTH

BREAKDOWN & RENEWAL

DECLINE

DECAY & DEMISE

1 Light originates in earlier civilization
2 Light migrates to new culture
3 Light absorbs new culture
4 Light creates new religion through religious unification
5 Light precedes genesis
6 Light creates Central Idea amid 16 alternatives
7 Light attracts, converts & unifies peoples around Central Idea
8 Light strong during growth
9 Light inspires stones
10 Doctrinal controversy round Light
11 Political unification
12 Schism between supporters of rival gods
13 Foreign military blow
14 Arrest in growth of secularized civilization (50 years)
15 Counter-thrust: expansion into Empire. Light-led renewal of growth
16 Heroic epic literature with god of Light-led growth
17 Creation of Light-based heretical sect
18 Persecution of heretical sect
19 Decline of religion as a result of heretical sect & foreign influence
20 Mystics resist decline
21 Foreign military blow
22 Breakdown of civilization (100 years)
23 Secularization in response to foreign threat
24 Revival of past culture of another civilization
25 Civil War: Rulers vs heretical New People
26 New People in limelight
27 Heresy grafted on to Central Idea as new religious focus
28 New people's heretical renewal of Light and Central Idea
29 Geographical expansion of New People
30 Secession from New People's God
31 New People persecute seceders and become New Orthodoxy

32 Scientific materialism weakens religion
33 Artistic reaction
34 Further expansion into Empire over-extends civilization
35 Light weakens as energy is dispersed abroad
36 Light disappears from official religion
37 Breakdown of certainties after military event
38 Central Idea/Religion weaken, Arts become secular
39 Rationalism & scepticism weaken religion
40 Industrial decline as civilization over-extends itself
41 Colonial conflict ending in decolonization & occupation
42 Proletarianization & egalitarianism
43 Loss of national sovereignty to secularizing conglomerate
44 Syncretism & Universalism around Light
45 Revival of lost past of civilization
46 Counter-thrust under foreign federal influence
47 Economic decline & inflation, class conflict
48 Light ceases to be publicly recognized by religion
49 Invaders undermine Lightless religion
50 Foreign invaders destroy Stones
51 Loss of Central Idea as peoples secede to foreign invaders' culture
52 Final independent phase
53 Further occupation by foreign power
54 Contemplative mystics turn from decaying religion to foreign cults
55 Civilization resists occupier
56 Occupier persecutes defectors from its cults
57 Coteries continue Light & Central Idea in mysteries
58 Further occupation
59 Occupier's religion suppresses & kills Lightless religion
60 Sudden final conquest or religionless civilization
61 Demise of civilization which now passes into a successor civilization

Appendix 3

Founding a World State: Step-by-Step Approach, Seven Goals, Structure and Funding

Objective:
To found a democratic, bicameral world government that is partly inter-national and partly supranational with a World Commission, World Senate of 92 and World Parliamentary Assembly of 850 based in the UN General Assembly as set out in *The World Government* and *The Secret American Dream*. For its agenda see the 7 federal goals (below). (These are taken from *The Secret American Dream*, p.191 and can be found in theletter to Ban Ki-moon, see http://wpf-unesco.org/eng/use/letban. htm.)

Step-by-step implementation:
1. Meetings with the US President and UN Secretary-General after their staffs have studied the structure (see below).
2. The US President proposes the 16-point inter-national/ supranational structure (see below) to the UN General Assembly and requests the delegates to support its supranational approach that can declare war illegal, enforce it with a peace-keeping force and begin disarmament.
3. The UN General Assembly establishes a World Constitutional Convention to draw up a world constitution that would establish the new institutions in the scheme.
4. All nation-states vote to grant federal powers in the areas of the seven goals to a new World Commission. Nation-states thus voluntarily opt to create the institutions and structure of the world government set out in the attachment/enclosure.
5. A World Commission is created with legal basis in the UN's authorisation.

6. The World Commission declares war illegal and the declaration is enforced by a world peace-keeping force, the World Armed Force, co-ordinated by the US.
7. The process of multilateral disarmament begins.
8. The UN General Assembly turns itself for part of its time into an elected World Parliamentary Assembly with 850 representatives.
9. Global governance proceeds as institutions are created, and points 2–7 on the agenda are tackled.

Seven Federal Goals of a World State

A World State, a supranational authority with legal power to declare war illegal, President Truman's dream, could pursue an agenda of seven federal goals:

-   bringing peace between nation-states, and disarmament;
-   sharing natural resources and energy so that all humankind can have a raised standard of living;
-   solving environmental problems such as global warming, which seem to be beyond self-interested nation-states;
-   ending disease;
-   ending famine;
-   solving the world's financial crisis; and
-   redistributing wealth to eliminate poverty.

Structure of World State or World Federation

A World Federation would exist at partly inter-national (between nation-states) and partly supranational (federal) levels. At the inter-national level (between nations):

1. The UN General Assembly could be converted into an elected World Parliamentary Assembly of 850 seats. This would be a lower house at the inter-national level. It would legislate supranationally in conjunction with the World Senate, acting as a global legislature in some sessions, as well as representing individual nation-states'

parliaments.

2. All the offshoots of the UN General Assembly would continue to operate: the Economic and Social Council, the International Criminal Court, the International Court of Justice, and the UN organs (UNDP, UNHCR, UNICEF and UNEP) and specialised agencies (FAO, UNESCO, WHO, and WTO).

3. All members of the new Assembly would belong to one of the world political parties: a World Center/Left or Social Democratic Party, a World Center/Right Party, a World Socialist Party, a Liberal-Centrist Party, a World Green Party, a Far-Left Party, a Far-Right Party, and a Party for World Skeptics.

4. The UN Security Council would be converted into a veto-less UN Executive Council of five Permanent and 12 Non-Permanent Members.

At the supranational level:

1. A World Commission of 27 Members drawn from all regions of the world could be established.

2. A World Senate of 92 Senators could be set up. This would be an elected upper house like the US Senate. Senators would belong to World Parties. The Senate would work with the World Parliamentary Assembly in the same way that the upper and lower houses work together in the US Congress. The World President would have a power of veto similar to that of the US president.

3. There would be World Senatorial Committees to monitor the implementation of the seven federal goals.

4. A World Openness Committee, a World Senate committee, would control the agencies of the *élites*. The Committee would scrutinise all candidates for world officialdom in terms of their possible links to the Syndicate. The Committee would receive advance copies of all agendas of meetings of Syndicate agencies such as the Bilderberg

Group and Trilateral Commission, and would receive all minutes of their meetings. Two members of the Committee would attend all meetings of these agencies and report back to the Commission. Thus, the Syndicate would be allowed to go on functioning but their activities would be controlled and they would be excluded from secret decision-making and subject to investigation by the civil police and to law enforcement.

5. A World Council of Ministers could represent 29 World Departments, each of which would work closely with Senatorial committees covering its field: World Finance; World Treasury; World Peace; World Disarmament; World Resources; World Environment; World Climate Change; World Health (ending disease); World Food (ending famine; crop-growing programs); World Regions, Communities, and Families; World Labour (or World Work and Pensions); World Housing; World Economic Development; World Regional Aid and International Development (ending financial crises); World Poverty (eliminating poverty by introducing a minimum entitlement of $10 per day for all world citizens); World Population Containment (as opposed to reduction); World Energy Regulation; World Transportation (world aviation, roads, shipping, and rail); World Law; World Oceans; World Space; World Education; World Citizenship (law and order); World Culture and History; World Sport; World Unity in Diversity; World Dependent Territories; World Foreign Policies (liaising with nation-states' Foreign Ministers); and World Human Rights and Freedom (guaranteeing individual freedoms, including freedom from population reduction under the new system).

6. A World President would be elected every four years like the President of the United States.

7. Candidates for World President would each be nominated by one of the world political parties. There would be several candidates and each would be vetted by the

World Commission and the Senatorial World Openness Committee. The President would lead the World Cabinet of the World Council of Ministers and be responsible for achieving the seven federal goals.

8. There could be a World Guidance Council of elder statesmen and distinguished world figures. They would meet every three months to advise the World Commission, World Senators, and World Council of Ministers.

9. There would be World Leaders' Meetings for heads of nation-states or their foreign ministers. There would be a Regional Leaders' Meeting for the leaders of the 13 main regions, which are based on the 14 living civilizations: North America; Europe; Japan; Oceania; China; Tibet; the Russian Federation; South America; Islam (representing Muslims in West, Central, South and South-East Asia and North and North-East Africa, and focusing on Indonesia and India which have the world's largest Muslim populations); Africa; India; South-East Asia; and Central Asia.

10. The World Bank and World Investment Bank would be overhauled to operate at a supranational level. The World Bank would continue to make loans to poorer countries for capital programs to reduce poverty.

11. An executive of international lawyers would help the World Commission, World Senate, and World Parliamentary Assembly (the world lower house based on an elected UN General Assembly) turn the World Commission's proposals into international laws. It would liaise with the World Peace Enforcement Committee and the World Court of Justice.

12. The World Court of Justice would have 25 judges and would hear acts brought by the World Commission against nation-states for breaking a directive. It would rule on legal disputes between nation-states. A World Court of First Instance would exist alongside it to hear actions against the World Commission for deeds or failure to act. World Judicial Tribunals would hear cases in

which world law needed to be enforced, and would enforce international laws.

13. The World Armed Force or World Rapid Reaction Force
of 200,000–400,000 troops would serve the World Commission, the World President, the World Senate, and the
World Court of Justice. There would be a reserve force of
300,000–600,000.

Funding and Peace Dividend

The funding would be afforded out of the existing budget of the
UN. Funding of the UN General Assembly would be switched to
the World Parliamentary Assembly. There would be a peace div-
idend, a phasing out of the global military spending by nation-
states which totaled $1,472.7 billion ($1.4727 trillion) in 2008 and
$1,745 billion ($1.745 trillion) in 2012, of which $1,049.8 billion
($1.049 trillion) was spent by NATO alone in 2008 and $1.02 billion ($1.02 trillion) in 2013.

Nearly $1.5 trillion per annum minus the cost of financing the
World Armed Force plus the saving from not having to replace
nuclear weapons, could be diverted to benefit humankind.

Appendix 4

Diagram: The Structure of the World State

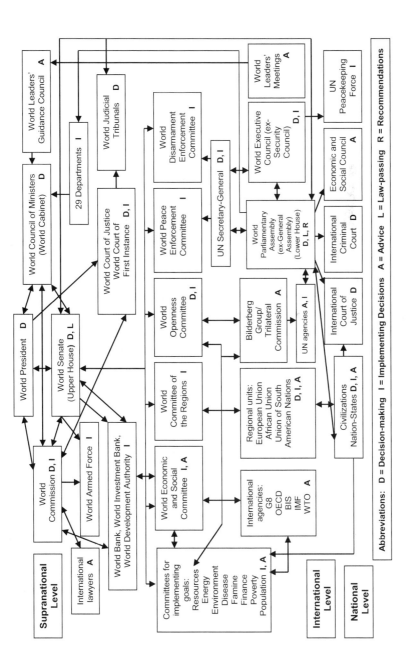

Diagram/Flow Chart of the Supranational Authority: The Structure of the World State

Abbreviations: D = Decision-making   I = Implementing Decisions   A = Advice   L = Law-passing   R = Recommendations

Appendix 5

On the Illegality of War

At present we have an international law that is based on the relations between nation-states. A country, or nation-state, is permitted to defend itself when attacked. In international law self-defence is a legal basis for war. In the 21st century questions have arisen as to whether the US invasion of Afghanistan was a self-defensive act in response to 9/11; whether the invasion of Iraq was a self-defensive act in response to the threat of weapons of mass destruction (which were never found); and whether the use of drones is a self-defensive act against terrorists. Apart from self-defence, war is illegal under the current system of international law. Attacking civilians is a war crime.

The law of war is a branch of the international law that governs relations between nation-states. It concerns acceptable justifications to engage in war and the limits to acceptable wartime conduct. It deals with declarations of war, surrender, the treatment of prisoners of war and the prohibition of certain weapons; also with non-participants and the wounded. International humanitarian war includes the Geneva Conventions and Hague Conventions.

Nation-states can group themselves together to form a supranational union. A supranational union is a multi-national political union in which power is delegated to a supranational authority by the governments of nation-states. The EU is such a multi-national political union and has features of supranational government. The coming World State will be a grouping of nation-states into a supranational union. It will declare that all war is illegal and enforce disarmament. It will set up a world army to police violations. Under a supranational union all independent countries will be states in a United States of the World. No nation-states will attack other nation-states and so war will no longer be self-defensive and can therefore be declared illegal.

Supranational law has no precedent as there has been no fully supranational law until now (although aspects of EU law have supranational features). When all the nation-states are within a partly-federal, supranational World State war will be abolished and declared illegal. In global terms war will then be illegal under any circumstance.

So, fellow poets, please support the concept of a World State that can abolish war and declare it illegal.

Appendix 6

Urgent Global Problems, Inactive Nation-States and Decisive Supranationalism

The current situation on the earth is not good. For more than five years, longer than both the First and Second World Wars, there has been a war in the Middle East that looks like the beginning of a proxy Third World War, with the US and Russia both involved in bombing different factions on opposite sides. The Arab Spring that toppled regimes in North Africa was resisted by Assad, and different jihadist groups including Islamic State have been fighting each other. Jihadist groups have launched attacks in Europe, America, North Africa, the Philippines and Indonesia as well as in Afghanistan and the Middle East.

Islamic State (IS) has chemical weapons and has recently fired a mustard gas shell at the Qayyarah air base in northern Iraq where US troops were helping Iraqi government forces prepare an assault on Mosul. IS has seized 40 kgs of nuclear material from the University of Mosul and is reported to be attempting to develop a 'dirty bomb' which it can detonate in a Western capital, perhaps via a drone. President Obama was so concerned by the Brussels bombers' attempt to obtain nuclear material by stalking a nuclear scientist that he convened a conference in Washington for 50 Western leaders from 31 March to 1 April 2016 to ask what they would do if a drone-borne 'dirty bomb' exploded in their territory.

That's just in the Middle East and its ramifications. Elsewhere, nine countries have between them 15,350 nuclear warheads (Russia 7,300 and the US 6,970), according to the Federation of American Scientists, 2016. North Korea has getting on for 10 nuclear weapons and allegedly the means to deliver them, and boasts of being able to attack the United States. Satellite photos show that China (which has 260 nuclear warheads) is creating military bases in the South China Sea, to the alarm of much of Asia. And NATO regards Russia as being expansionist in Georgia, Crimea and the Ukraine and there are tensions between Russia and the Baltic states of Estonia, Latvia and Lithuania. There is a stand-off in the Baltic between NATO and Russia, with both sides conducting exercises with in excess of 30,000 troops. There has been unrest in many other parts of the world, including India and Pakistan.

We live in a troubled time in which nation-states compete with nation-states in local and proxy wars. Recently the perspective of nation-states has been strengthened by a wave of nationalist populism – of would-be leaders expressing the so-called wishes of their peoples at the expense of governments – that has swept the West and thrown up Trump in the US, Brexit in the UK and similar nationalist feelings in many other European countries.

One consequence of the disorder has been the refugees. Some 65 million displaced people from war-ravaged and poverty-stricken countries are on the move, and many desperate families have escaped their poor domestic situations and reached Europe, often in leaky boats involving loss of life. The lot of those displaced by war is indeed wretched. Among them are many economic migrants wanting to live and work in freedom on good wages under the protection of European benefit and medical systems. Europe has not room for them all. A poor country like Greece has already had to settle and feed 300,000 migrants who are angry at being cooped up and, as in Lesbos recently, inclined to burn down the fenced camps in which they are compelled to live.

What all these situations have in common is war, the threat of a nuclear explosion (and subsequent nuclear winter of minus 50C), and nation-states guarding their borders and unable to afford a massive influx of unwanted refugees. The world system is based on nation-states. The UN is 'inter-national', 'between nation-states', and has no authority or jurisdiction to put a stop to the wars. There have been 162 wars since 1945 which the UN was unable to prevent.

Quite simply, there needs to be a new system. There needs to be a world government with enough supranationalist authority to declare war illegal, enforce disarmament, dismantle 15,350 nuclear warheads and prevent the need for refugees to flee in the first place by improving their living conditions and guaranteeing peace, a global solution called for in the 20th century by Churchill, Truman, Einstein, Eisenhower and Gorbachev. Where possible the displaced would be encouraged to return to the country they left to rebuild their ruined cities and reinvigorate their local economy. Where the displaced need to be resettled in a new country the supranationalist authority would allocate them to different parts of the world on a fair basis. The key is to make the living conditions in all countries so good that the masses do not want to leave, although there will always be economic migrants seeking to improve their lives.

There are many other serious global problems. Natural resources and energy need to be shared so humankind's standard of living can be raised. There are environmental problems including global warming and climate change which need to be addressed on a supranationalist basis. Disease and famine need to be eradicated throughout the world. The world's financial structures need to be reformed and wealth needs to be redistributed to eliminate poverty. All of these goals are better solved by a supranational authority than by nation-states defending their borders.

All these military and environmental problems need to be addressed by a coming World State for the benefit of all humankind. The WPF's letter to Ban Ki-moon on 9 October 2015 identified seven goals which a supranationalist authority could implement. They are:

- bringing peace between nation-states, and disarmament;
- sharing natural resources and energy so that all humankind can have a raised standard of living;
- solving environmental problems such as global warming,

which seem to be beyond self-interested nation-states;

- ending disease;
- ending famine;
- solving the world's financial crisis; and
- redistributing wealth to eliminate poverty.

People all round the world are crying out for something to be done now, but the governments of nation-states and the UN seem powerless to do anything to end the misery. Because of the disorder in the world a supranationalist authority needs to begin to implement these goals as soon as possible. A supranationalist body therefore has to establish its authority worldwide as soon as possible. A World State must have practical credibility and support from at least one of the great powers while it is getting established and accepted as a supranationalist authority. When a World State is set up by consent as opposed to conquest, the process of getting established and accepted is bound to be slow. But the urgent world situation is crying out for a fast process and speedy results.

In the interests of speeding the process up, in my books since 2010 I have seen the way forward as a fundamental reform of the UN that would turn the UN General Assembly into a lower house of 850 Representatives in a world government that would include an upper house of 92 Senators, as set out in *The World Government* (2010). This would be a World Federation of nation-states that would be partly federal and have enough authority to start implementing the seven goals. Such a United Federation would be an interim federation of nation-states, to advance supranationalism and allow a World State to grow rapidly. During this process the masses would be 'supranationalised' and widespread acceptance of the eventual World State would be accelerated.

Last year, making common cause with the WPF, I chaired the WPF's Constitutional Convention and established the USE as a supranationalist authority to start implementing the seven goals. In a time of nationalist populism when electorates are turning away from partially-supranationalist bodies such as the EU, the USE will need to have credibility and support from one or more of the great powers to become established and widely accepted. It will seek to spread its supranationalism by turning the masses into 'citizens', Aristotle's *politeia*. The Athens of Aristotle's day contained around 250,000 people, and supranationalising 7.33 billion is going to take a lot longer than raising the consciousness of the *demos* in the 4th-century-BC Athenian city-state. If the global population can be supranationalised speedily, everything is fine and there is no problem. But if it can't, what then? The international situation is urgent – the Middle Eastern war, the nuclear threat and the 65 million refugees – and supranationalising the global population has to start making measurable progress now. We can't wait a couple of generations, we can't even wait a couple of years. The Middle Eastern war, the nuclear threat and the 65 million refugees must be tackled now. In a few years' time babies will have been born in refugee camps and spreading war will have created more refugees, and there will then be 100 million refugees and rising.

Our urgent question today is: what is the fastest way to get supranational activity happening, how can a supranationalist body designed to solve all the most serious global problems establish its authority most quickly? Educating the masses so they can be aware 'citizens' in Aristotle's sense of the word is fine, but we cannot wait decades for progress to be made. We cannot even wait a year. Supranationalising an institution such as the UN is a halfway house, an interim stage to get something happening on a worldwide basis that can begin now. One delegation to the UN General Assembly, one presentation and the establishment of a Constitutional Convention to consider turning the UN into an elected world government, and the representatives of 193 countries in the UN General Assembly can exert pressure on their leaders, who will in turn eventually supranationalise the world's masses. Has anyone got a better idea to solve the problem within the next year or two?

The current situation on the earth and the serious global

problems demand a way forward that will establish a decisive supranational authority quickly and urgently, before a colossal war culminates in a nuclear catastrophe that will make it too late for any supranational authority to implement any of the seven goals.

22–23 September 2016

Notes and Sources

Prologue
1. See http://ww2today.com/chamberlain-announces-peace-for-our-time.
2. Richard J. Evans, *The Third Reich in Power*, pp.338–339.
3. See http://www.bbc.co.uk/bitesize/higher/history/roadwar/munich/revision/1/.
4. See http://www.independent.co.uk/news/world/middle-east/isiss-dirty-bomb-jihadists-have-seized-enough-radioactive-material-to-build-their-first-wmd-10309220.html.
5. See http://www.telegraph.co.uk/news/2016/04/01/isil-plotting-to-use-drones-for-nuclear-attack-on-west/.
6. See http://www.war-memorial.net/wars_all.asp.

PART ONE
1. A Russian Writes
1. See http://conscious.tv/nonduality.html?bcpid=45947084001&bckey=AQ~~,AAAAAE7B3aU~,DSQ0D72IolIep00vk9UFiWrrRgGzNWe0&bclid=46629186001&bctid=4151526382001.
2. Nicholas Hagger, *The Secret Founding of America*, p.xiii.
3. *Letters of Ted Hughes*, pp.663–668.
4. See http://www.tandfonline.com/doi/full/10.1080/08850607.2016.1177408.
5. Paul v. Gorka, *Budapest Betrayed*, p.54.
6. Gorka, op. cit., pp.82–83.
7. Karen De Young, in 'Bin Laden Took Part in 1986 Arms Deal, Book Says', http://www.washingtonpost.com/wp-dyn/content/story/2008/03/31/ST2008033102952.html, states that Osama bin Laden flew to London in 1986 to help negotiate the purchase of Russian-made surface-to-air missiles to be used by Arab fighters battling the Soviet military in Afghanistan, according to Steve Coll's *The Bin Ladens: An Arabian Family in the American Century*, Penguin

Press, 2008. The deal for Russian SA-7 missiles was arranged via contacts with the German arms manufacturer Heckler & Koch through an associate of Salem bin Laden. Osama bin Laden and his half-brother Salem bin Laden met the contacts several times at the Dorchester Hotel, London. According to Context of '(Early-Mid 1986): Salem Bin Laden Asks Pentagon to Supply Missiles to Arab Afghans, Receives No Reply', sub-heading 'Mid-1986: Osama and Salem Bin Laden Purchase Anti-Aircraft Missiles in London', http://www.historycommons.org/context.jsp?item=aearlymid86salempentagon, the bin Ladens were in London in mid-1986 buying anti-aircraft missiles, and in late 1986 Osama bin Laden was establishing the first training camp in Afghanistan for Arabs fighting in the Soviet-Afghan war. They apparently flew from London to America. They may have stopped in London in early November during their return to Afghanistan.

8. Nicholas Hagger, *Collected Poems 1958–2005*, pp.93–94.

2. St Petersburg
1. See https://www.theguardian.com/world/2015/may/30/russia-entry-ban-european-politicians-eu-moscow.
2. For images of Kronstadt naval base, see https://www.google.co.uk/search?q=kronstadt+naval+base&espv=2&biw=1280&bih=633&source=lnms&tbm=isch&sa=X&sqi=2&ved=0ahUKEwjbupyGpZHPAhVsLsAKHZqHA5cQ_AUIBygC.

3. Tallinn, Estonia
1. For the image of this tree, see Nicholas Hagger, *The Dream of Europa*, pp.118–119.
2. See http://uk.reuters.com/article/uk-russia-military-exercises-idUKKBN0EN10020140612.
3. See http://www.telegraph.co.uk/news/worldnews/europe/russia/11702328/Russian-forces-practised-invasion-of-Norway-Finland-Denmark-and-Sweden.html.

4. War and Peace

1. See https://www.theguardian.com/world/2015/aug/26/mus
    tard-gas-likely-used-in-suspected-islamic-state-attack-in-
    syria.
2. See https://www.theguardian.com/world/2003/feb/14/iraq.
    unitednations1.
3. See http://www.publications.parliament.uk/pa/cm200203/
    cmselect/cmfaff/uc1025-i/uc102502.htm.
4. See 'Chilcot Report', p.76; see also Peter Oborne, Not the
    Chilcot Report, https://books.google.co.uk/books?id=OCu
    QCwAAQBAJ&pg=PT62&lpg=PT62&dq=550+shells+filled
    +with+mustard+gas&source=bl&ots=irTv6NbECy&sig=GY
    TOMYvHsI-HVOIoNjUH2-zr3Ws&hl=en&sa=X&ved=0ah
    UKEwjJxtepsYnPAhXpJMAKHasFAiMQ6AEIHDAA#v=on
    epage&q=550%20shells%20filled%20with%20mustard%20
    gas&f=false.
5. Nicholas Hagger, *Armageddon*, p.489.

5. Athens and World State

1. See http://glob-use.org/eng/use/pap/constit.htm.
2. See http://wpf-unesco.org/eng/use/letban.htm.
3. See http://glob-use.org/eng/use/decl/declar.htm.
4. See http://wpf-unesco.org/eng/resolf/photo-e-6.htm. Scroll
    down list of photographs to find an image of the signatures.

PART TWO

6. Gusi Peace Prize for Literature

1. See http://libwww.essex.ac.uk/speccol.htm.
2. See http://libwww.essex.ac.uk/Archives/Nicholas_Hagger/
    Hagger.html.

7. The UK Referendum on the EU

1. See http://www.cityam.com/247058/pound-has-not-been-so
    -sterling-after-brexit-currency.
2. See http://www.ifs.org.uk/publications/8296.
3. See http://www.gleichstellung.uni-freiburg.de/dokumente/

treaty-of-rome.

4. See https://www.rt.com/news/338086-isis-chemical-lab-mosul/.
5. See https://www.rt.com/news/210631-isis-uranium-dirty-bomb/.
6. See http://www.telegraph.co.uk/news/2016/04/01/isil-plotting-to-use-drones-for-nuclear-attack-on-west/.
7. See http://bgr.com/2016/03/28/brussels-attack-dirty-bomb/; and see http://www.forbes.com/sites/jamesconca/2016/03/29/terrorism-in-brussels-shadowed-by-dirty-bomb-plans/#61ed36997506.
8. See http://www.nrc.gov/reading-rm/doc-collections/fact-sheets/fs-dirty-bombs.html.
9. See http://www.express.co.uk/news/uk/654158/Islamic-State-ISIS-SAS-London-terror-attack-dirty-bomb-radioactive.
10. See https://www.theguardian.com/uk-news/2016/apr/01/a-terrorist-dirty-bomb-us-summit-asks-world-leaders-to-plot-response.
11. See http://aanirfan.blogspot.co.uk/2014/08/isis-run-by-simon-elliot-mossad-agent.html.
12. Terry Waite, *Taken on Trust*, 25th Anniversary Edition with new chapter, *The Sunday Telegraph*, 4 September 2016, p.23, 'A Third World War has already started'.
13. See http://www.bbc.co.uk/news/world-europe-36575180.
14. See https://www.thesun.co.uk/news/1291950/russia-war-putin-is-building-a-super-army-and-preparing-for-a-large-scale-conflict-as-nato-struggles-to-control-him-intelligence-experts-claim/.
15. See http://www.telegraph.co.uk/news/2016/10/10/gorbachev-warns-world-is-at-dangerous-point-amid-us-russian-face/.
16. Gideon Rachman, *Easternisation: War and Peace in the Asian Century*.
17. Nicholas Hagger, *My Double Life 1: This Dark Wood*, pp.423–424, 436.
18. Nicholas Hagger, *The Rise and Fall of Civilizations*, pp.289–

290, "from c.2020".

19. Nicholas Hagger, *My Double Life 1: This Dark Wood*, Appendix 4, pp.505–516.

8. Athens Again: United Federation of the World and Speedy Action on Syria

1. See https://www.theguardian.com/world/2012/apr/19/greece-military-spending-debt-crisis.

2. See http://jubileedebt.org.uk/reports-briefings/briefing/europe-cancelled-germanys-debt-1953.

3. See https://www.theguardian.com/world/2014/jun/19/us-depleted-uranium-weapons-civilian-areas-iraq.

4. See https://fas.org/issues/nuclear-weapons/status-world-nuclear-forces/, at the time of going to press there are 15,375.

9. Athens Again: World State and Plan for Peace Talks at Delphi

1. See http://glob-use.org/eng/use/sch/index.htm.

2. See http://www.resultados.blogdeconcursos.com/051_02/.

10. Peace Initiative: Urgent Statement

1. Christopher Ricks, 'Bob Dylan is a genius – but reducing his songs to "literature" is dangerous', The Telegraph, 14 October 2016, see http://www.telegraph.co.uk/music/what-to-listen-to/bob-dylan-is-a-genius--but-reducing-his-songs-to-literature-is-d/.

2. See https://www.youtube.com/watch?v=wciGmi1nZHU.

3. See http://glob-use.org/eng/use/decl/statmt-2.htm.

4. See Ronald L. Ray, American Free Press, 21 and 28 November 2016, 'Mideast Wars are for Oil, Gas & Israel'.

5. See https://soundcloud.com/watkins-media/the-secret-american-destiny and https://itunes.apple.com/gb/podcast/watkins-media/id1077360493?mt=2.

6. Emanuel M. Josephson, *Rockefeller: 'Internationalist', The Man who Misrules the World*, pp.204–231, particularly p.212; Josephson, *The Truth about Rockefeller, Public Enemy No.1,*

pp.44, 133.

PART THREE
11. Manila: Peace Laureate and Invitation to Visit Assad
1.   Gusi Peace Prize – Vision and Mission Statement.
2.   The original book, a novella (first edition 1886), was titled *Strange Case of Dr Jekyll and Mr Hyde*. It was subsequently published as *Dr Jekyll and Mr Hyde* and as *The Strange Case of Dr Jekyll and Mr Hyde*, and also as *Jekyll & Hyde*.

12. Manila: My Stance and a New World Structure
1.   The Libyan was introduced wrongly by a lady compère as "Abdul Patel Ataweel, the Minister of Plenipotentiary of Libya" (accurate phonetic transcription from recording on film), but written on his seat in front of Ann, which Tony filmed, was "Abobaker I.W. Ataweel" (accurate visual transcription from film). He can be found online with a correct picture as Abubaker Wanis Ataweel, see https://www.facebook.com/abubaker.wanis.9/about?lst=14594 87189%3A100003152084808%3A1480510112. There is no mention of his position online but he seemed to be Minister Plenipotentiary for Libya. He lived in Tripoli.
2.   See *My Double Life 1: This Dark Wood*, pp.272–273.

Epilogue
Peace for our Time: My 15-Point Peace Plan and a Third World War
1.   See map from Oil-Price.Net, https://www.google.co.uk/search?q=competing+pipelines+iran-syrian+pipeline&espv=2&biw=1236&bih=580&source=lnms&tbm=isch&sa=X&ved=0ahUKEwiP172joabRAhUrI8AKHW_RDuEQ_AUIBygC#imgrc=Pq0LQzy4-UzxGM%3A.
2.   See http://www.thetimes.co.uk/edition/news/trade-deals-wont-make-up-for-eu-single-market-losses-3lrnv7q7h.
3.   See http://www.forbes.com/donald-trump/#28dc59b4790b.
4.   See http://philosophyofmetrics.com/how-rothschild-inc-sa

ved-donald-trump-freepom/.

5. See Nicholas Hagger, *The Syndicate*, pp.54–55 and pp.379–380 for several sources.

6. See http://harddawn.com/trump-banned-rothschilds/.

7. In fact: 31 May, 17, 20, 23–24 June, 5–14, 26–31 August, 1–19 September, 28–31 October, 1, 5–7 November, 15–17, 19–24, 27–31 December 2016; 1–9, 12, 18–19, 23, 26–27, 30 January, 1, 16–17 February 2017.

Bibliography

Briggs, Asa, *Secret Days*, Frontline Books, 2011.

Brzezinski, Zbigniew, *The Grand Chessboard: American Primacy and its Geostrategic Imperatives*, Basic Books, 1998.

Evans, Richard J., *The Third Reich in Power*, Penguin, 2005.

Gorka, Paul v., *Budapest Betrayed*, Oak-Tree Books, 1986.

Hagger, Nicholas, *Armageddon*, O-Books, 2010.

Hagger, Nicholas, *Collected Poems 1958–2005*, O-Books, 2006.

Hagger, Nicholas, *Life Cycle and Other New Poems 2006–2016*, O-Books, 2016.

Hagger, Nicholas, *My Double Life 1: This Dark Wood*, O-Books, 2015.

Hagger, Nicholas, *My Double Life 2: A Rainbow over the Hills*, O-Books, 2015.

Hagger, Nicholas, *Overlord: The Triumph of Light 1944–1945*, O-Books, 2006.

Hagger, Nicholas, *The Dream of Europa*, O-Books, 2015.

Hagger, Nicholas, *The Fire and the Stones*, Element Books Ltd, 1991.

Hagger, Nicholas, *The First Dazzling Chill of Winter*, O-Books, 2016.

Hagger, Nicholas, *The New Philosophy of Universalism*, O-Books, 2009.

Hagger, Nicholas, *The Rise and Fall of Civilizations*, O-Books, 2008.

Hagger, Nicholas, *The Secret American Destiny*, Watkins Publishing, 2016.

Hagger, Nicholas, *The Secret American Dream*, Watkins Publishing, 2011.

Hagger, Nicholas, *The Secret Founding of America*, Watkins Publishing, 2007, 2016.

Hagger, Nicholas, *The Syndicate*, O-Books, 2004.

Hagger, Nicholas, *The Warlords*, Element Books Ltd, 1995.

Hagger, Nicholas, *The World Government*, O-Books, 2010.

Letters of Ted Hughes, selected and edited by Christopher Reid, Faber and Faber, 2007.

Oborne, Peter, *Not the Chilcot Report*, Head of Zeus, 2016.

Rachman, Gideon, *Easternisation: War and Peace in the Asian Century*, The Bodley Head, 2016.

Waite, Terry, *Taken on Trust*, 25th Anniversary Edition with new chapter, Hodder and Stoughton, 2016.

Index

Note: Page numbers for illustrations appear in italics. Titles of books where the author is not indicated are by Nicholas Hagger. Entries are mainly in alphabetical order but in some cases, where they describe a narrative, in chronological or page order.

BOOKS

O-BOOKS

SPIRITUALITY

O is a symbol of the world, of oneness and unity; this eye represents knowledge and insight. We publish titles on general spirituality and living a spiritual life. We aim to inform and help you on your own journey in this life.
If you have enjoyed this book, why not tell other readers by posting a review on your preferred book site?